D0776162

FILM SCHOOL

The True Story of a Midwestern Family
Man Who Went to the World's Most Famous
Film School, Fell Flat on His Face,
Had a Stroke, and Sold a Television
Series to CBS

STEVE BOMAN

BENBELLA

BENBELLA BOOKS, INC.
DALLAS, TEXAS

All of the events described in this book happened as related; some time frames were altered slightly and many names and identifying characteristics have been changed.

BenBella Books, Inc.
10300 N. Central Expressway, Suite 400
Dallas, TX 75231
benbellabooks.com
Send feedback to feedback@benbellabooks.com

Printed in the United States of America
10 9 8 7 6 5 4 3 2 1

Library of Congress Cataloging-in-Publication Data is available for this title.
ISBN 978-1-936661-05-3

Editing by Brian Nicol
Copyediting by Deb Kirkby
Proofreading by Cielo Lutino and Michael Fedison
Cover design by Melody Cadungog
Cover art by J.P. Targete
Text design and composition by Neuwirth & Associates, Inc.
Printed by Bang Printing

Distributed by Perseus Distribution
perseusdistribution.com

To place orders through Perseus Distribution:
Tel: 800-343-4499
Fax: 800-351-5073
E-mail: orderentry@perseusbooks.com

Significant discounts for bulk sales are available.
Please contact Glenn Yeffeth at glenn@benbellabooks.com or (214) 750-3628.

What use is it to speak of inspiration?
To the hesitant it never appears.
If you would be a poet,
Then take command of poetry.
You know what we require,
We want to down strong brew;
So get on with it!

— JOHANN WOLFGANG VON GOETHE, from *Faust*

Contents

Foreword

One of the basic tenets of good storytelling is that an author must make life very difficult for his characters. The closer to the impossible those challenges are made, the stronger the dramatic tension and the deeper the audience's connection with the characters in the story will be. By this—or any—measure, Steve Boman tells a whopping good story in FILM SCHOOL. It's made all the more harrowing and compelling by being fact, not fiction. Steve, his family, friends, and classmates suffered a great deal to give us an exciting and unpredictable story. They did so with moments of both anxiety and grace, plus humor, perseverance, and ever-present doubt on their relentless march through calamity, triumph, epiphany, and more than anyone's share of medical hurdles.

Many of the conflicts and obstacles dramatically depicted in this book had already been faced, for better and worse, by the time I first met Steve. In fact it was his last semester as a graduate student at USC when he enrolled in my advanced scene writing course, a small and intense seminar taken primarily by film students who harbor serious aspirations as screenwriters. When we first met, none of those trials—or their scars—was evident in Steve. He just seemed like a good-natured guy from my home state. We bonded over Minnesota lore: "Ya, you-betcha." We've both had the fabled, and mostly apocryphal, accent surgically removed.

Film schools didn't even exist a century ago, and they only came into their own as a means of entering and excelling in film and television when a handful of film school alumni in the 1970s surged to the top of the entertainment industry. Their names are now universally known, and several of those grace the buildings that form USC's School of Cinematic Arts. As a result of those early successes and an ever-growing stream of talented and ambitious film school graduates, "going to film school" has come to be a crucial step on the trajectory to success behind the camera.

Like many before him and more yet to come, Steve set his sights high and chose the most efficient path available to those of us without connections and easy opportunity: a few years of intense study, trials, errors, failures, disasters, learning, networking, alliance building, goal setting, and endurance testing. He chose film school and was accepted by the oldest and best of the growing array of choices: USC.

What followed would far exceed the typical experience of film school, but at the same time, in the hands of a talented storyteller, Steve's journey focuses the reader's attention and compassion in unexpectedly intimate ways. His approach is reminiscent of the Harvard student who became an able-bodied seaman in the 1830s and sailed in a tall ship around Cape Horn to write the classic of experiential journalism, TWO YEARS BEFORE THE MAST. Richard Henry Dana grants his readers the real experience along with the insights of a trained observer. In FILM SCHOOL, Steve Boman does the same: You will learn what film school really means, how it unfolds, how it impacts the dreamers and drivers who find themselves there, and how it gets the better of everyone at some point. You will become part of a family as it faces incredible challenges, you will discover how some friends rise to some occasions and others fall by the wayside, and you will explore the deadly serious business of learning how to entertain.

Like a good film or a good TV program, FILM SCHOOL will give you an experience well worth having. Enjoy it.

David Howard
Founding Director of the Graduate Screenwriting Program
School of Cinematic Arts
University of Southern California

Introduction

When I was accepted to the film production program at the University of Southern California, I was in my late thirties. One of my brothers was a bit skeptical. He asked me what actually happens in film school.

"I dunno," I told him. "I'll find out when I get there."

I wasn't being snarky. I really didn't know.

Before I applied to USC, I tried to find out as much as I could about film school—any film school. But there wasn't much of any depth either on the web or at bookstores. Going to USC's School of Cinematic Arts as a graduate student in film production meant I was going on a three-year journey, and I wanted to know what I was facing on that journey. Sure, universities put out glossy brochures and feature websites that make the whole enterprise look just wonderful, like the world's most exciting cruise ship adventure, full of smiling students and attentive instructors. But they made *me* skeptical. I wanted to see a photo of, say, a student sitting in the rain, a broken camera at his feet, with another student yelling at him. That would have seemed more realistic.

I also didn't know anyone who had gone to film school, anyone who could give me the inside dope. As an adult, I had worked as a reporter in the Midwest and on the East Coast for both newspapers and radio. I had covered thousands of stories, but the film business wasn't on my beat. I do have a couple of close college chums who are successful actors in Los Angeles, and although they are a great help, they hadn't gone to film school either.

So I was mostly in the dark about what I was facing. When I got to USC, I found many of my classmates were in my same position. We were like travelers without guidebooks or even a decent map. I found the journey was much different than what I expected. From the time I was admitted I planned to write a book about my experiences. What you're holding is the result.

This is a personal book about my time at USC. I graduated from USC in 2009 with a master of fine arts degree in film production. This book explains what happened to me and some of the people I met in film school and in Hollywood. I'm not providing an encyclopedic overview—just one person's story.

There are obvious shortcomings to this method. Like the fable of the blind men describing an elephant, whose descriptions depend on which part they touch (*It's as thick and immovable as a wall! . . . No, it's thin and flexible like a whip! . . . No, it's a sharp spear!*), my observations are incomplete. I went to one specific film school to study film production. Hopefully, others will write of their observations so the entire elephant can be fleshed out.

Now, most retellings of the parable of the blind men and the elephant are high-minded. They don't include a blind guy who yells: *That elephant is nothing but a huge pile of manure! And I stepped in it!* When I went to USC, I stepped in plenty of manure. You'll hear about it in the book. I don't intend to run for office. I just aim to tell a true story.

I wish I had read something like this before I went to USC. I would have been better prepared, quicker to focus on what is important at film school, and quicker to brush off the unimportant stuff.

A key part of going to film school is learning to hustle yourself and your ideas shamelessly—something that doesn't come naturally to me, a somewhat self-deprecating Midwesterner. So I'll merely say this book is *completely and unbelievably awesome*! It's a perfect companion for anyone who wants to know what it's like to have a second chance at a new career, or who dreams of selling a television show to a major network, or who wants to know what it's like to navigate Hollywood as an outsider. Or for those who want to know what it's like to keep moving forward after bad medical news. I write about all of these subjects because I experienced them.

By the time I finished my first semester at USC, I knew I had a pretty good story on my hands. Film school is an inherently interesting subject. In school, we make short films and TV episodes and write scripts, and these activities clearly fascinate lots of people. When I mentioned I was going to film school at USC, it seemed everyone wanted in on the action. Other soccer dads said they wanted to visit me in Los Angeles. Friends wanted to act in my films. I was offered scripts by neighbors. A coworker ruefully told me, "I'd trade my left nut to go to film school."

I knew I was on to something. I was going to an institution that prepped students to work in that big, glamorous world of moving pictures, and that's interesting to plenty of people. Film school is to Hollywood as baseball's minor leagues are to Major League Baseball—but with a lot more smoking.

This book is greatly aided by the fact that students and staff at USC are exceedingly colorful. And I witnessed plenty of conflict. I was sure I had a good story to tell. Little did I know *how* good it would be. By the time I finished at USC, I:

1. Made some very good films.
2. Had a stroke.
3. Sold a television show to CBS.
4. Killed a wild mountain lion with my bare hands.

Scratch #4. That's a lie.

The other three did happen. I really did make some good films, I really did have a stroke, and, not long after that, I dreamed up a TV show, one that aired on Sunday evenings on CBS. It was called THREE RIVERS.

There is one more piece to this story. I went to film school as a middle-aged guy *not* because I was seeking personal enlightenment or having the kind of midlife crisis that is usually treated by getting a divorce or a new sports car. I went because my career had skidded into the ditch and my wife had cancer and I felt I was running out of options.

A ttending film school at USC was a great privilege, and I thank my large extended family and many friends from the bottom of my heart for supporting me. I would never have been able to do any of this without them.

My wife, Julie, first suggested going to film school. She thought it was a perfect place for me. She also raised our three daughters as a de facto single parent for the long months when I was away from home. It was very hard for her, and my heart goes out to anyone trying to raise children as a single parent.

My parents, Tom and Mary Boman, didn't blanch when I told them my desire to go to film school, even with three young kids (one still in diapers). They always gave an encouraging word and a sympathetic ear. My father-in-law, Stan Schwantes, spent hundreds of hours babysitting our kids while I was at school and Julie was at work. My mother-in-law, Jean Schwantes, went so far as to quit her job at a nursing home and move two thousand miles to help take care of our kids for four months so I could start school. Unfortunately, she died of lung cancer before I could graduate from USC. I wish she could have been there to see me get my degree.

And it went beyond family. Carl and Irene Christensen, a retired couple living just outside Los Angeles, allowed me to live in gracious splendor in their house while I attended USC. And what an intriguing couple they are. Carl is a rocket scientist retired from NASA's Jet Propulsion Lab. Irene spent a year of her childhood in a Japanese internment camp and became an elementary school teacher. I first met them when I was eighteen and traveling by motorcycle; I did landscaping for them for a time. I call them my "Los Angeles parents." Irene cooked many meals for me while I was at USC, and both of them served as the first filters for this book.

Finally, I would also like to thank whoever green-lighted my application at USC. Early on, I often felt I was admitted by mistake or because of a clerical error, and that somewhere a talented young guy also named Steve Boman was denied the chance to attend USC.

Oh well. His loss, my gain.

Let me say a few words about the process of researching and writing this book. Everything in this book happened. I only write about what I witnessed.

None of my classmates or instructors or people at CBS knew I was planning to write a book about my experiences. During my time at USC, I took notes and kept a journal. I did it all quietly. I changed the names of some of my classmates and instructors to protect their privacy. I used some people's real names (such as Drew Casper, Ted Gold, Curtis Hanson, Donald Sutherland, Peter Krause, Alex O'Loughlin, and more) because they are well known and there is no reason to disguise their identity or because they are such unique characters they deserve to be recognized. Some of my classmates and instructors may recognize themselves in this book despite the pseudonyms. I know several of them will be famous in the future simply because of their talent and drive. Looking back, what I should have told my brother is this: film school is, quite simply, a great and unpredictable adventure.

Enjoy the adventure; enjoy the book.

TAKE 1

1

Standing Up, Standing Out

January 2004: USC's School of Cinematic Arts

We file into the screening room, forty-eight of us. The room is warm and it smells like nervous sweat and cheap deodorant. We are the incoming class of spring semester graduate students at the University of Southern California's vaunted School of Cinematic Arts' production program. We are going to learn to be directors and writers and producers at the world's oldest and most prestigious film school. It is our orientation day.

Every year, USC admits roughly one hundred students into its graduate production program. Half start in late August, half in January. I'm in the spring semester class. More than two thousand people went through the lengthy application process. I am one of the lucky few admitted to the program.

I catch my reflection in a window. There's no hiding the fact I'm an old man among the group. Most of the other students are in their twenties. Some look like they're straight out of college; a few are in their late twenties. My hair is going gray, and I'm a year away from hitting forty.

The other film students generally look very cool and hip and very . . . L.A. Most wear a similar uniform: a faded T-shirt, ripped jeans, and flip-flops. Sunglasses are the norm. I don't see many guys who've shaved in the past three days. Long hair is in, but a few guys have shaved heads. A lot of students snub out a cigarette before entering the building, and plenty look as if the last physical workout they got was running to beat closing time at Taco Bell.

I look like a middle-age contractor here to fix the air-conditioning system. My graying hair is cut short, and I shaved that morning. In addition to a golf shirt I bought from Sears, I'm wearing crisp new Levis and a pair of Red Wing construction boots. My posture is military straight. I don't smoke. I wonder if I should slouch, just to look cool.

I don't. It just doesn't feel right. I'm not going to try to fake it. I'm not a trendy young *artiste*. I'm a middle-class, middle-of-the-road, middle-aged Midwestern suburban dad with a wife and three kids who's going to the most famous film school in the world for a three-year program that will give him a chance to write and direct and produce films and television episodes. I'm excited as hell, but I feel a weight settle in my stomach. *I knew I would be a fish out of water, but Jiminy Cricket, I didn't think it would be* this *obvious.*

I ignore the window reflection, make my way into the screening room, settle into a seat, and survey the other students. It's clear most of us don't know anyone else. We all keep an empty seat next to us. I nod to a guy in the row behind me. He looks thin, about twenty-five. He's wearing a black T-shirt, flip-flops.

I attempt a conversation. "It feels good finally to get started, doesn't it?"

"I suppose," he admits. "Are you on the faculty here?"

I smile. It's a question I will get used to answering. *Are you faculty? Are you on staff? Are you a coach?*

"No. I'm here as a student," I answer. He forces a smile but has nothing else to say. He looks at his phone and finds something important on it.

Then, in the back of the room, two women see each other and let out a yelp. I hear snippets of their excited conversation.

No way! I didn't know you were even applying here! That's sooo cool! I thought you had another year at Stanford!

The women, both with sunglasses perched on their heads, cell phones clutched in their hands, hug. The other students around me also watch the two women with slight envy. It must be nice to know someone.

The vibe in the auditorium is all first-day nervousness. It's like the first day of fifth-grade summer camp. Even though this is graduate school, and we are supposedly older, wiser, more mature, and much better at new social interactions, we are still nervous. At least I am.

I have a tremendous amount riding on my journey through film school. I'm spending far too much money on tuition and spending long weeks away from my wife and kids in order to attend USC. I wonder how I'll fit in. What little I know of film school is that it is apparently very collaborative. I'll be spending hundreds of hours working with people who could be my own children.

Just before coming to USC, I read a book called *The Lucifer Principle*, by Howard Bloom. The book discusses how scientists have discovered that the way in which animals find their pecking order can differ from group to group. Scientists found that group dynamics are so complicated there is almost no way to predict those dynamics beforehand. The bottom line—as a chimp, sometimes you'd be the chump, sometimes you'd be the champ. Scientists discovered the same was true for humans.

I wonder how I will fit in. I've spent years working since I finished college. I've worked as a reporter for two newspapers, reported for a radio network, spent time as a transplant coordinator at the University of Chicago hospitals. I've been married since before some of my classmates were in grade school, and I have three daughters. I've always loved the buzz and excitement of the newsroom and the operating room. I like talking with people. I get along with nearly everyone. A friend of mine once said I "would have fun at the bottom of a cesspool." How could my time at film school be any different?

We're about to start the orientation when a small man with a mop of wild hair bursts through the doors, the last one in. He's electric with energy and all smiles. He works his way around the auditorium and plops into a chair next to me. We grin at each other. He's sure happy!

A faculty member takes the podium. The orientation is starting.

In the weeks leading up to orientation, I had practiced a speech I would give if we introduced ourselves. I honed my speech while jogging, while in the shower, while driving. I felt it had all the elements of why I was coming to grad school, where I had been, where I wanted to go.

Hey there. I'm a guy a decade and a half out of college with three beautiful daughters, a lovely wife, and a journalism career that was sidetracked as I supported my wife's dream of attending medical school and becoming a doctor. But my wife, not long ago, discovered she had cancer, and during her recovery, I applied to this institution so I could jump-start my career and take some of the load off her shoulders.

It went on. And on. As I huffed and puffed on my jogs, I went over and over my speech. It constantly changed. One thing was certain—in my imagination, my fellow students dabbed tears from their eyes *and* laughed uproariously as I told my life's tale.

STANDING UP, STANDING OUT ■ 13

I'm jolted back to reality inside the screening room when a short, smartly dressed woman is introduced. She's the dean of the film school. She tells us what an honor it is to have us. We hear our program is one of the most selective in all of academia. More selective than Harvard Law School. More selective than all medical schools. We all nod and feel very lucky.

We then hear lots of dos and don'ts from other faculty. Mostly they're don'ts. Don't film on the edge of tall buildings. Don't use real guns. Don't use anything that even looks remotely like a gun without first talking to your instructors. Don't fall asleep behind the wheel and crash into a tree.

One of the instructors tells a story about a former grad student that makes the room go quiet: the student had been a medical doctor prior to applying to USC's film school as a production student. Going to the first year of film school, he reportedly said, was harder than anything he had to do in medical school or residency.

I feel like we're grade school campers gathered around a fire, hearing horror stories from the camp counselors. *There was a kid who tried to sneak away from his cabin one night a few years ago. Nothing was ever found but a piece of his shirt. A bloody piece. He was an orphan, so he didn't have any parents who called the cops, and since the camp wanted to keep the story quiet, you never heard about it. Until now . . .*

Apocryphal or not, the doctor-who-came-to-film school story gets my attention—I witnessed my wife go through medical school. But I'm skeptical. I doubt making films and writing stories can be as hard as dissecting a cadaver or passing biochemistry. Finally, a female instructor takes the podium and asks us to introduce ourselves. I smile. *Perfect.* I've got my speech all ready. Then she says, "Let's keep it short. Just tell us your name, where you went to college, and what your degree was."

I think, *What about my awesome speech?*

She points to a student in the far back corner. "Why don't you start?"

He gets up, nervous. It's hard to hear him from where I'm sitting.

"Ahhh, hi, my name is (mumble) and I went to Yale. I graduated two years ago with a major in (mumble). I was going to go to law school but decided on this instead. I'm really glad I did. I look forward to working with you all."

He sits down. The next person gets ups. She's from UCLA. Then there's a guy from Harvard. A Japanese guy who struggles with English. Then a petite Asian woman introduces herself, coughing. She apologizes, says she's sick, and is from Wisconsin. She majored in film production. It sounds like she said her name was Fee Fee. Did I hear it right? Did she really say *Fee Fee*?

Soon afterward, a thin guy with a beard stands up to introduce himself. He's nervous and very emotional. He's got a heavy New York accent and he's intensely earnest. In a wavering voice, he explains he applied several times to USC but had been rejected each time. Finally, he says, he got in. He says he is so grateful to be here. He clasps his hands together like he is a serf thanking a king for giving him a little extra grain to survive the winter. He seems ready to burst into tears. He's really letting his inner self out for all to see.

The introductions come closer. I'm getting nervous. I wonder if maybe I should do my speech. That would show some *cojones*.

The man next to me with the mop of hair stands up. He looks like a stunt double for Roberto Benigni, the Italian actor/director of LIFE IS BEAUTIFUL. And he sounds like Benigni! He explains that when he flew in from Rome, the airline lost his bags so he hasn't changed his clothes in days and he just retrieved his luggage from LAX. *That* explains the slight wave of body odor that wafted my way when he sat down. He tells some jokes in his lilting Italian accent. Everything he says sounds so comic! The class laughs. He, too, expresses his appreciation for being accepted at USC and says it was his dream to be studying at a place that is so well known. He goes on and on. The class laughs along with him. His speech is great. He's very funny.

I know my goose is cooked. How can I ever say something remotely clever after that?

I make a snap decision. If the happy Italian had wowed them with a funny, meandering, off-the-cuff story, I would impress my classmates with brevity. I would be a man of few words. I would say less than anyone else. After all, less is more, right?

I start talking fast as I rise to my feet. "I'm Steve. I went to Gustavus Adolphus College in St. Peter, Minnesota. I graduated so long ago I don't remember what I studied."

I sit down. I took all of eight seconds. The room is silent. Someone coughs slightly, probably Fee Fee.

I slowly feel my face flushing red. The *less is more* thing didn't go over well. Edit that. It went over badly. My joke bombed. *I graduated so long ago I don't remember what I studied?* Not a tiny chuckle penetrated the dead air of the screening room after that dud.

And Gustavus Adolphus College? Most everyone else comes from boldface names on the list of America's Best Colleges. I went to a small college smack-dab in the middle of Minnesota farm country, a school named after a seventeenth-century Swedish king, Gustavus Adolphus, the Lion of the North, a military leader revered for his strategic skills in the Thirty Years War, but . . . big f'kn' deal. Who knows anything about small Midwestern colleges here among graduates of Yale and Harvard and Stanford? Was that *The Gus Davis Dolphins?*

I think about the chimp studies. First impressions are vitally important and I flubbed mine. I'm already the oldest guy in the class. I don't have a film studies background. I hardly have *any* filmmaking experience, period. Now I feel I've made my first step into becoming something not so great. I feel the other chimps judging me: zero in a golf shirt, oldster in an Oldsmobile, potential poison.

T he campus of the University of Southern California is a beautiful place. It's leafy and quiet, an oasis of calm just a few miles south of downtown Los Angeles, and the tidy square campus is surrounded by a high wrought-iron fence. The film school is located in the heart of this exclusive private university.

The history of film schools is relatively brief. Moving pictures are, all things considered, a very recent invention. The first public projection of a film took place in 1895, in France. For the next thirty years, filmmaking was a fledgling and intensely fast-growing industry/art form. Filmmakers were self-taught or apprenticed to established talent.

In America, filmmakers worked mainly on the East Coast in the early years. And then, in 1910, a director named D.W. Griffith shot a film, OLD CALIFORNIA, in a dusty part of Southern California called *Hollywood*. The sky was almost always sunny, land was plentiful, and production companies discovered they were a long way from the banks out East, giving them a few extra days of float to come up with enough cash to cover their expenses. Within a decade, Hollywood was the place to be.

In 1927, a few dozen Hollywood heavyweights gathered and created an organization called the Academy of Motion Picture Arts and Sciences. The dashing actor Douglas Fairbanks Sr. was elected the Academy's president. The Academy wanted some gravitas. Filmmaking wasn't just an experiment anymore. It was an industry. An art form. And a swell way to make some serious cash.

Fairbanks' first order of business was to create an awards ceremony to honor the industry's own. He wanted to give out "awards of merit for distinctive achievement" in film. In 1929, the first Academy Awards were handed out.

Fairbanks' second order of business was to create a film school. He approached the University of Southern California with his idea. USC said yes, and the USC film school was born the same year as the Academy Awards.

"From early on, the school focused on moviemaking rather than academics," *The New York Times* noted in a 2006 article, "with its very first course named 'Introduction to Photoplay,' only later branching into film theory and critical studies. Hollywood was never far from the campus; Douglas Fairbanks and Mary Pickford were among the early lecturers."

Other instructors were producer/studio honcho Darryl Zanuck, director D.W. Griffith, and fellow director Ernest Lubitsch. All were towering figures in the film world. To this day, Hollywood "players" regularly rotate through USC as instructors or lecturers.

Today, the USC School of Cinematic Arts is the largest film school in the world, with roughly 850 undergrads and 650 graduate students. The program is not only tightly associated with Hollywood, the production program in particular models itself on Hollywood studios, and in fact looks like it. The campus has several large soundstages, rows of editing bays, many screening rooms, and an atmosphere of gossip, competition, envy, and the unmistakable feeling that something exciting is going on—pretty much what I found to be true at a real studio. At USC, students take on all the roles of filmmaking. They're producers, directors, cinematographers, sound editors, picture editors, writers, composers, special effects gurus, gaffers, grips, grunts, and gofers.

Other institutions eventually followed USC's lead and created their own film schools. In 1939, ten years after USC and the Academy of Motion Picture Arts and Sciences conceived their school, the publicly funded University of California Los Angeles created its own film school. On the East Coast, New York University created its Tisch School of the Arts in 1965.

In the last few decades, film school programs have been popping up like mushrooms after a long rain. They now include big institutions and small, and they also include the Zaki Gordon Institute at Yavapai College in Sedona, Arizona, (founded in 2000), the Ringling College of Art and Design in Sarasota, Florida, (founded in 2007), and the New York Film Academy (founded in 1992), whose advertisements seem to find their way onto every other film-related website and a thousand bus-stop benches.

Film schools are a hot ticket now, with more than 110 American institutions offering degrees in film.

The rise of film schools in the last forty years can be traced to four names: Lucas, Spielberg, Coppola, Scorsese. These four men—George Lucas, Steven Spielberg, Francis Ford Coppola, Martin Scorsese—dominated and transformed filmmaking starting in the 1970s. All went to film school. George Lucas went to USC, Spielberg went to Long Beach State (even though his heart was with USC—he was rejected by USC three times), Coppola went to UCLA, Scorsese went to NYU.

These directors created AMERICAN GRAFITTI, STAR WARS, RAIDERS OF THE LOST ARK, JAWS, CLOSE ENCOUNTERS OF THE THIRD KIND, THE GODFATHER, APOCALYPSE NOW, MEAN STREETS, TAXI DRIVER, RAGING BULL, and so many more.

By the 1980s, film schools were suddenly hot. Everyone wanted to be a director, and film schools were seen as a way to become one. The demand for film schools exploded. (That is not to say the demand for film school *graduates* exploded.)

Led by USC, film schools changed the way Hollywood works. For much of the twentieth century, directorial giants in the film world worked their way up through the industry. Alfred Hitchcock,

No. 1 on the *MovieMaker* magazine list of most influential directors of all time, started as a title card designer in his teens; five years later he was directing. Orson Welles started as an actor and radio playwright. John Ford got his start working as a handyman, stuntman, and bit player for his filmmaking older brother. Stanley Kubrick began his career as a magazine photographer a year out of high school before shifting to newsreels. Billy Wilder was a newspaper reporter in Germany before becoming a scriptwriter and then director. Howard Hawks was a race-car driver, aircraft designer, and flyboy before he turned to scriptwriting and then directing. These giants of the film world learned their skills inside the industry, most of them at a young age. Hawks was the only one with a college degree, and his was in mechanical engineering.

The filmmaking world today is a very different place than it was forty years ago. Going to film school is now a common route into film and television production. Thousands of people in the industry have attended film school. USC alone has more than ten thousand graduates with some type of film degree. The following recent Oscar-winners also attended film school (this is an incomplete list, but you get the point):

Kathryn Bigelow, director of THE HURT LOCKER, got her MFA at Columbia University.

Ron Howard, director of A BEAUTIFUL MIND, attended USC.

Joel Coen, director (with brother Ethan) of NO COUNTRY FOR OLD MEN, attended NYU.

Ang Lee, director of BROKEBACK MOUNTAIN, attended NYU.

Roman Polanski, director of THE PIANIST, attended Poland's National Film School.

Dustin Lance Black, writer of MILK, attended UCLA.

Michael Arndt, writer of LITTLE MISS SUNSHINE, attended NYU.

Conrad Hall, cinematographer of ROAD TO PERDITION, attended
USC.

Robert Richardson, cinematographer of THE AVIATOR, attended
the American Film Institute.

And Luke Matheny, a thirty-five-year-old former journalist and
2010 graduate of New York University's film program, won
an Oscar in 2011 for his short film, GOD OF LOVE. The mop-
headed Matheny also charmed the Oscars telecast audience
with his acceptance speech, in which he thanked his mother
for preparing food for his crew.

Film schools are popular because moving pictures are popular.

"The cinema is an invention without a future," famously stated
Louis Lumière, the nineteenth-century Frenchman who invented
the motion picture camera. Lumière was brilliant but awful at pre-
dicting the future.

If you believe the statistics provided by the Motion Picture Association of America, the moving picture business (film, television,
web) today employs more than two million Americans and con-
tributes $140 billion in combined payroll (from studio executives
to the kid sweeping up spilled popcorn at the Cineplex). Whatever the exact numbers are, they're big. And the impact of film and
television on our society far exceeds any measurable dollar totals.
Weekend box office tallies are big news. TV ratings are big news.
The rates charged for Super Bowl commercials are big news. Everything to do with the world of moving pictures is big news. What
would we do without the drug scandals of young film stars? Or
the falls-from-grace of old film stars? Or the returns-to-grace from
the formerly fallen-from-grace stars? It's gotten to the point where
reviewers of films are themselves celebrities.

It's no surprise perhaps that one former movie actor became a
two-term president of the United States after being a two-term

governor of California (Ronald Reagan) and a current actor became another two-term governor of California (Arnold Schwarzenegger).

In little more than a century, the moving picture business has grown from nothing to the colossus it is today. The relative newness of the industry—and the newness of film education—means there is no standardized path for film schools in the same way there is for law schools or medical schools. Whether you're a first-year medical student at the University of North Dakota or at Florida State University, classes are essentially the same. After two years, every medical student takes the same national standards test.

In contrast, film schools can be many different things. Institutions vary, course lengths vary. Even in production film programs, there can be a different emphasis. Some schools do big films with big crews. Other schools send students into the field solo or in groups of two or three. Some programs emphasize experimental films; some emphasize commercial films.

At USC, the graduate production division is set up so that students tackle ever-larger films, semester by semester. It's a three-year program, with six semesters. (USC has fall and spring semesters, each four months long, with a month off from mid-December to mid-January. There is a short summer semester, too, with limited class offerings.)

In my first semester, we'll shoot solo projects. We'll produce, shoot, direct, edit, and mix our own short films. Everything is shot on video.

The second semester at USC, we'll work in partnerships. We'll do two six-minute films. For the first half of a semester, one partner will write and direct and do sound, while the other partner will shoot and edit. During the second half of the semester, the roles will be switched. In contrast with the first semester, when we shoulder a basic video camera, during the second semester, we'll shoot with ancient German Arriflex film cameras, loaded with color film. The cameras are so old the U.S. Army used similar models back in the Eisenhower administration.

By the third semester, we'll move to larger group projects. These are either fiction films (on film) or documentaries (on video). Every semester, USC's graduate production division makes seven group films. Four of the films are fictional, three are documentaries. The fiction films, part of a class called Production 546, are roughly twelve minutes long. The documentaries, done under the aegis of Production 547, are about twenty-six minutes in length. Students do everything on these films, with limited faculty involvement on set. The size of the crews varies from seven to eleven students. USC underwrites the cost of these films.

Here the specialization starts, and the competition begins in earnest, because instructors pick the students who will be the directors and producers for fiction films, and the directors for documentaries. Then, those lucky students will choose which of their fellow students will crew on their projects. It's a competitive, zany time of musical chairs and hurt feelings and intense politicking—with students vying for what they perceive as the best films and the best positions, and directors deciding who to choose and who to reject and begging students to fill empty positions. It's a remarkable event, filled with shifting allegiances and betrayals and high fives and tears. In that sense, USC is a real studio system, with gossip and favoritism and misinformation running fast and furious. This competition is a core principle of the entire USC film school experience.

In the fourth semester (the last half of year two), students who crewed on a film in the third semester can compete to be directors for these 546 and 547 films.

The third year (semesters five and six) is generally when students work on their thesis films—longer self-funded films—and crew on other thesis films. In these semesters, students can also apply to direct or produce one of the 546 or 547 films. The lucky people chosen to direct a USC-funded film don't have to do a thesis film nor do those who write a feature film script.

Every graduate production student will write and direct at least six films, work on several more, and possibly write a feature-length script. Every production student thus takes on every aspect of film-making: writing, producing, directing, lighting, sound recording, editing, sound design, graphics, distribution. A USC production student is in some ways a jack of all trades, master of none.

It's a big honor to direct one of the USC-funded feature films and documentaries, as only about 15 percent of USC production students are chosen to do so. It is, I suppose, a bit like being chosen to be on the Law Review in law school or making honors in medical school. (Full disclosure: I was chosen to direct a USC-funded film.)

USC has a reputation for student films that are very Hollywood-like—that is, high production values, traditional three-act storytelling, and sometimes seriously large budgets. In 2006, USC grad student Ari Sandel won the Academy Award for Best Live Action Short Film for his twenty-minute student film, WEST BANK STORY—an intensely high-gloss comic riff on the classic 1961 musical WEST SIDE STORY. Sandel's film is set in a fictional West Bank neighborhood, complete with competing falafel stands, real camels, and huge dance numbers with actors dressed in Middle Eastern costumes. If there's a film school other than USC where students can top *that* kind of production, I've yet to hear of it.

After orientation, classes start. All first-semester graduate production students carry essentially the same course load. The instructors may be different, but the classes are the same, with minor differences.

In my first semester at USC, I am taking a film history course with a professor named Drew Casper. I have a screenwriting course taught by Ross Brown. And I have a massive class called Production 507. Under the umbrella of this class, I have an acting course, a sound engineering class, a cinematography course, and a directing class. These specialties are taught by a variety of instructors, but there's always one head-honcho instructor in charge of each 507 group. Five-oh-seven—that's what it's called. Not five-hundred-and-seven. Just 5-OH-7. USC's film school has used the same class identifying numeric system for decades. Students don't use the title of classes; they use the numbers. New students quickly get used to the notion. Soon, we all sound like mechanics discussing V-8 engines when we refer to our classes: *I didn't get a lot out of my 507, but my 546 was awesome. How'd ja like your 508? Pretty rough?*

The forty-eight of us in our semester are divided into three 507 subgroups. The only place we intersect is in our sound course, taught by a genius named Tomlinson Holman, the creator of THX surround sound. In all the other 507 classes—cinematography, acting, directing—I will spend almost all my time during the semester with fifteen other graduate production students in my 507 section. The only time I'll interact with students from the other two 507 sections is in large group lectures (sound, film history) and in my one small screenwriting class.

At USC, a film student taking a full load typically takes eight to ten credits per semester. It takes a minimum of fifty-two credits to graduate with a master of fine arts degree in film production.

The program is not cheap. At the time of publication of this book, USC charges about $1,500 per credit, so a degree costs about $80,000 just for tuition. Add to that all the other costs of schooling, including class fees, insurance, books, transportation, and that all-important food and shelter. Some of my classmates run up tabs of $150,000 or more. Thesis films are self-funded, which means students foot the bill, and many USC thesis films run up serious mid-five-figure production costs. It's not unheard of for students to rack up $150,000 or even $200,000 of debt.

It's an expensive place, and I'm acutely aware I'm spending my kids' college funds to go to USC. I don't want to dwell on it too much, but I'm spending close to $200 a day just for tuition.

According to what little I have heard, the time commitment for 507 is pretty intense. I like hearing that because I want to get every last dime's worth from the class. The rumor mill is already buzzing from the first day of classes. I hear gossip about students from previous semesters who dropped out because they couldn't take the stress, about students who started eating too much or stopped eating, or started drinking like hard-living writer Charles Bukowski. I think this is a bit silly. It's only a class, after all.

Still, 507 is a big deal. The lead instructor of every 507 group is also a big deal because this one instructor establishes the ground rules for the semester. This instructor sets the tone for how we will critique our films. This one instructor will determine the grade we get for the class. We students know a bad grade in 507 can seal our doom because we will be shown the door if we don't maintain at least a B average.

I have a problem. My lead 507 instructor seems to hate my guts from the first time he meets me.

The instructor is tall—about six foot two—and thin and muscular. He's not much older than I am and has an almost-shaved head, a four-day stubble, a frayed trucker's cap pulled low over his eyes, a pair of torn bell-bottom jeans, and a faded gray T-shirt. In my mind, I give him a nickname: Frayed Trucker's Cap or FTC.

FTC introduces himself to our class by sitting in a chair, head down, inside the classroom. He appears to be sleeping or meditating or just plain ignoring us. We students file past and quietly take a seat. We hardly know each other, much less who this guy is. We *think* he's the lead instructor, but maybe he's a wayward parent or a homeless guy. A couple of my classmates look at me questioningly, wondering if I have a clue what's going on. I shrug. I know as little as they do.

We're in the Robert Zemeckis Center for Digital Arts, an outpost of sorts for lowly first-year production students. The Zemeckis building is located several blocks from the main campus, outside the iron fence that surrounds USC. To get to Zemeckis, we have to walk across the hot Shrine Auditorium parking lot every day, which guarantees most of us are sweaty by the time class starts. So now, on this first day of class with FTC, we're sweaty *and* confused.

Finally, the mysterious FTC lifts his head. He introduces himself. He talks slowly. He has a nasal, languorous accent no one in class can put a finger on. It sounds like a Deep South–Southern California–Mainline Philadelphia mix. He talks about what will happen in the class, how we each make five short films. His favorite word seems to be *dour*, as in, "I find this film very dour," or, "The mood in the scene was very dour." He pronounces it *dooooooooer*. He stares at the ceiling for long seconds while he formulates a thought. The energy in the room slowly drops while he stares.

Aware that I had muffed my first introduction, I want to be a bit more expansive among this smaller group of classmates, a group I will be in close contact with for the entire semester. So I'm dropping the *less is more* thing. I look around at my fifteen classmates. Five are women, ten are men. We're a collage of colors and accents. There's a guy from Japan, another from India, and a woman who was born in Ecuador. There are plenty of children of recent immigrants, and we're from the four corners of the United States. I'm by far the oldest—by almost a decade—but a fair number of my classmates worked after graduating from college prior to applying to USC. One is a novelist, another worked for a film studio in marketing, another worked as a young executive for a major corporation, another worked in television.

I'm not the only married person: two of the women are also bringing spouses along for this ride through film school.

As we go around the room, sharing a bit more of ourselves, a thin student with a Deep South twang captures our attention. J. says he grew up in a small town and that his grandfather ran the local movie theater. He says he watched films constantly, and that one day, when he was a teenager working at the theater, his grandfather had a massive heart attack in the projection booth. J. says that as his grandfather lay on the floor, barely breathing, he uttered a wish that someday J. would become a filmmaker.

J. pauses, looks up. We are all holding our breath.

Then he breaks into a huge grin. "Naw, that's not true! You kidding?" he drawls. I laugh. I was hoping for a few jokesters on campus. J.'s comedy is funny and concealing because J. never says a word about his real background, whatever it is. He's cleverly done his own version of *less is more*.

Then it's my turn. I'm completely straight. With just sixteen of us, we can each spend a few minutes introducing ourselves. I tell people I had been a reporter, I am married, I have three kids, and I've hardly done any filmmaking. I add that my total filmmaking experience is making two safety videos for a large agribusiness—a job I stumbled into because I was writing speeches for some executives of the company at the time. I feel more comfortable with the smaller group. I'm still smiling about J.'s shaggy-dog story and compliment him on his great tale.

The students nod approvingly at my story. There's a sense of warmth from them.

But not from FTC. From the first time we meet, he projects an icy chill. Whenever I speak, he stares at me, a frown on his face, his arms folded. By chance, I'm sitting directly across the room from him in our half-circle of chairs. I can hardly see his eyes under his baseball cap as we face each other. As class goes on, I notice that every time I say something or add a comment, FTC rolls his eyes slightly or sighs with what seems to be thinly disguised disdain. I'm wondering what I'm doing wrong. Did FTC read my application essays and find something distasteful? Is he mistaking me for someone else? Did I unwittingly steal his parking spot? Does he hate me because I've privately nicknamed him Frayed Trucker's Cap? He's not giving the icy vibe to everyone in the class—with some of the women in particular he's loose and friendly. But with me, he's like ice.

As I walk from class, I wonder what set him against me.

2

A Class Act

The term *film school* can mean different things at different schools. Some schools offer classes in film production only. Other institutions emphasize film theory or critical studies. Saying "I'm in film school" is therefore about as descriptive as saying "I'm studying the humanities."

For example, USC students can get graduate and/or undergraduate degrees in the following categories. All these categories are under the umbrella of the School of Cinematic Arts—USC's formal name for its film school.

1: Writing about films and television shows and interactive media. Called Critical Studies. Students learn to dissect films and write critical commentary. They watch films, listen to lectures, write papers. Hundreds of undergrads at USC take this route. A much smaller number of MA and PhD students get their degrees in this field.

2: Producing. Students study how to produce a film or television show. Budgeting, staffing, selling, industry techniques, and, I would hope, learning which large black automobile to buy should they hit it big.

3: Animating films and television shows, and game development. Officially called Animation and Digital Arts. Students learn all of the cutting-edge stuff that will make them exceedingly marketable to places like Pixar. A faculty member told me the school has trouble holding students until they complete their degrees because of hiring pressure.

4: Writing films and television shows. Students learn (and write) what goes on between Fade In on the first page and Fade Out on the last page.

5: USC now offers something called an Interdivisional Media Arts and Practice degree. It's a PhD program in which students design their own course of study.

6: Making films and television shows. This is the production division. Students do everything in the process: write, shoot, record, edit, produce, animate, cast, direct. Here, students can choose to specialize. But everyone has to do every part of making modern moving pictures. Students are also required to take courses from the critical studies program and the screenwriting program. Undergraduates focus on the core classes for two years. Graduate students are in a three-year program.

The production division is the one that allows students to follow in the footsteps of Lucas and Spielberg and Scorsese and Coppola, and it's the program that trains people to do everything that goes into making a film or television show. This is the program I'm in.

C hastened by my time with Frayed Trucker's Cap, I look forward to my first day of American Sound Film, Post-World War II. Based on the description in the USC course catalogue, it may be my cushiest course. Every week we watch a film or two in class and listen to a lecture by Dr. Drew Casper. We have to write only one paper. That's it!

The course is held in the cavernous Eileen Norris Cinema Hall, a 341-seat movie theater in the heart of campus. The darkness, the air-conditioning, the padded movie theater seats, the enormousness of the hall, and the knowledge that I've got a little break from the intensity of 507 relaxes me. I grab a seat five rows from the front. I'm early, and Casper, a slight fellow with close-cropped blond hair and a chiseled face, is quietly walking between the aisles and introducing himself to some of us students. This is an open course—anyone enrolled in USC can take it—so there are undergraduate film students, graduate film students, engineering students, sorority girls, freshmen, and me. Most of my fellow 507 students are enrolled as well, but we're spread out in the auditorium. I like having a little time to be by myself.

Dr. Casper works his way toward me. He offers his hand. His handshake is polite and soft. He asks my name, then follows up with, "Do you prefer Steve or Stephen?" I tell him Steve. We talk for a few moments, and he gently asks about my background. He's so quiet I have to lean forward to catch his words.

Casper thanks me for taking his class and moves on to some other students. I sit down in my padded seat, pleased and a little bit smug that I am already on a first-name basis with this professor.

A few minutes later, the lights dim and Casper walks to his podium atop a stage in front of the large curtained movie screen. He talks softly. His assistants hand out syllabi to the 120 of us in the auditorium.

I know Casper is a critical studies professor, and I'm leery of what I might hear. I'm steeling myself for terms like deconstructionism and Marxist–feminist theory. I was an English major in college in the 1980s and the little I heard of that mumbo-jumbo was enough.

I'm also on guard because I had recently read an article in the *Los Angeles Times Magazine* by David Weddle titled "Lights, Camera, Action. Marxism, Semiotics, Narratology. Film studies isn't what it used to be, one father discovers." Weddle's article opened with the following scene:

"How did you do on your final exam?" I asked my daughter.

Her shoulders slumped. "I got a C."

Alexis was a film studies major completing her last undergraduate year at UC Santa Barbara. I had paid more than $73,000 for her college education, and the most she could muster on her film theory class final was a C?

"It's not my fault," she protested. "You should have seen the questions. I couldn't understand them, and nobody else in the class could either. All of the kids around me got Cs and Ds."

She insisted that she had studied hard, then offered: "Here, read the test yourself and tell me if it makes any sense."

I took it from her, confidently. After all, I had graduated 25 years ago from USC with a bachelor's degree in cinema. I'd written a biography of movie director Sam Peckinpah, articles for Variety, Film Comment, Sight & Sound, *and written and produced episodic television.*

On the exam, I found the following, from an essay by film theorist Kristin Thompson:

"Neoformalism posits that viewers are active that they perform operations. Contrary to psychoanalytic criticism, I assume that film viewing is composed mostly of nonconscious, preconscious, and conscious activities. Indeed, we may define the viewer as a hypothetical entity who responds actively to cues within the film on the basis of automatic perceptual processes and on the basis of experience. Since historical contexts make the protocols of these responses inter-subjective, we may analyze films without resorting to subjectivity . . . According to Bordwell, 'The organism constructs a perceptual judgment on the basis of nonconscious inferences.'"

Then came the question itself:

"What kind of pressure would Metz's description of 'the imaginary signifier' or Baudry's account of the subject in the apparatus put on the ontology and epistemology of film implicit in the above two statements?"

I looked up at my daughter. She smiled triumphantly. "Welcome to film theory," she chirped.

This is what I want to avoid by going to USC's production division, and I dearly hope Casper, a critical studies professor, won't veer too much into this gobbledygook. It is bad enough I am spending nearly $3,000 to hear a film history course. If I have to listen to references to Jacques Derrida, I'll want to put a gun in my mouth.

As his lecture starts, Casper begins talking about the post–World War II political scene and the state of the filmmaking industry at that time. His language is clear, to the point. He puts films in a political and social context without referring to *imaginary signifiers* and the like.

I am pleased. I settle in for a nice listen, my notepad and pen ready. Casper is giving an overview of 1950s American history to start the class. He's talking quietly. He then jots down HUAC on a blackboard and without missing a beat looks at me and says, "Steve, what is this?"

Is he really asking me a question? I thought this would be an easy class—sit and listen and watch and maybe eat popcorn. The whole class seems to tense up. *Oh crap! Casper is going to demand answers from us?*

Casper stands on the stage, staring at me. He's waiting. I know the answer. "The House Un-American Activities Committee," I say. He nods, then adds a slight embellishment: "Yes," he says. "The House of *Representatives* Un-American Activities Committee."

And with this, Casper is off. His voice gets louder, he starts pacing the stage. Without missing a beat, he starts popping more questions to us students. Casper is revealing his true self. The lamb is becoming the lion. His initial quiet and slow delivery is now machine-gun rapid. He talks about the studio system and in the middle of a sentence turns to a woman who, like me, had engaged in some preclass handshakes with him.

"Why is this, Susan?" Casper demands. Susan sits with her mouth moving like a fish tossed into the bottom of a boat. She doesn't know the answer. I feel bad for Susan, as I didn't fully understand what Casper was talking about either.

We all quickly understand what's going on. Everyone the oh-so-polite Casper has introduced himself to before class is now getting grilled in front of 120 other students. He has half a dozen names in his quiver, and he keeps coming back to us. If we don't know an answer, he will ask another student on his list until someone answers it correctly. In this case, Casper moves on to another of his targets.

"Michael? Michael? Yoo-hoo! Wake up, Michael!"

I sit rigid in my seat, laughing inwardly, and waiting for Casper's next question. He comes to me with two other questions—easy ones. But so much for relaxing. This is supposed to be my pop-corn-eating class, but instead I'm on Casper's pimp list. There is no assigned reading for this first class, and his questions focus on political and historical events. The lecture ends after ninety intense minutes. I feel exhilarated and relieved.

When we take a short break before watching the first film, a few other graduate students approach me. I don't know them well. They give me lukewarm congratulations for being in the spotlight and getting my answers right, but I smell the competitive spirit in the air. The vibe seems to be: *Good for you, but we really wouldn't mind if you failed.* I give them lukewarm thanks in return. I don't tell them I've been an avid reader of history. I'm still figuring out the game here at USC. I don't want to show the cards in my hand too soon. Less is more.

My other non-507 course is Introduction to Screenwriting, officially known as CTWR 528. The class has only a dozen students, all production students. Some are from the other two 507 subgroups, and I don't know most of them. I do recognize Paulo, the happy Italian from orientation. We share a smile. The instructor is a pleasant bear of a fellow named Ross Brown who introduces himself as a semi retired TV guy.

Brown's résumé is impressive. He wrote for the superhit THE COSBY SHOW, spent more than a half-dozen years as head writer on the ABC comedy STEP BY STEP, and, in total, was executive producer of more than one hundred episodes of broadcast televi-sion. What makes me want to hug his feet is the fact that Brown was an assistant director on National Lampoon's VACATION, a classic film based on an even more classic short story.

Brown introduces himself, and he laughs a lot. He listens hard to us, nodding emphatically. He's very encouraging, and he works hard to make us feel comfortable. After the surprise of Casper's metamorphosis, I'm a little wary. I wait for Brown to drop his cheerful enthusiasm and go on the attack. I'm waiting for some kind of transformation.

It never comes. Brown remains upbeat and positive through the entire first class. This class has a unique feel: it's smaller in size than all my other courses. Casper's lecture has 120 students; my 507 has sixteen. This class feels tiny, intimate. We meet in a simple little classroom. No projector. No sound system. Just a handful of people sitting around a table.

In class is a wild-haired redhead, S., from my 507 group. S. is a comic guy, very self-deprecating. Next to him is a Goth girl in a black motorcycle jacket and black nail polish and intensely pale skin. She puts out a tough *don't mess with me* vibe, but her toughness seems an act. There's a pleasant, short-haired, freckled woman who looks about thirty. Fee Fee, still coughing, is in this class, as is Paulo, the happy Italian, and a couple other students.

We are all production students. I feel comfortable with the keyboard, far more than with a camera, so I'm looking forward to this class a great deal.

The first class is a disappointment, however. Brown keeps up an encouraging chatter, but there's not much discussion. S. makes a few comic asides but otherwise is quiet. No one wants to speak out. I find this distressing as I want the writing classes to be as intense as the production coursework. I'm here to direct, but I also plan to write scripts—and sell scripts.

Eventually, Brown assigns us a group reading. We go around the class, each of us reading a few paragraphs. A couple of the students in the class stumble over some pretty easy words. They're nervous—that may explain some of it—but I'm learning that the students have widely different backgrounds. So far in school, I've met a business major, an engineer, a novelist, a former teacher, and a

French major, along with a large number of people who studied film production or critical studies as undergraduates. The least articulate students appear to be those who studied film production as undergraduates. Maybe it's just a fluke or maybe it means they simply feel more comfortable letting a camera speak for them. A little voice calls out in my head: *Or maybe they're not that smart after all.*

After class ends—we are meeting in an upper floor of an education building near the film school—we stand quietly in front of an elevator door, waiting. The elevator takes an absurdly long time to arrive. The silence is awkward. We're still in the first week of film school and it's clear no one is feeling at ease. My guess is that if we were simply participating in a conference a few days long, we'd all be chatting and sharing information. But spending three years together seems to up the ante and creates a resistance to small talk and jokes. No one seems to want to stick his or her neck out. Everyone is reticent at first.

As I mentioned earlier, USC is surrounded by a high wrought-iron fence. It's a stately fence, the kind you might find outside a Beverly Hills mansion. The fence isn't just for show, and the difference between being inside the fence and outside the fence is dramatic. Many of the neighborhoods near USC are dirty and potentially dangerous. The broken sidewalks are littered with broken bottles, dried barf, and a thousand flattened pieces of gum. Because it doesn't rain for six months at a time, the streets and sidewalks get dusty in an Old West way. Many of the side streets are potholed and lined with beater cars (the locals) and new autos (the students). Directly to the north of campus is fraternity and sorority housing—and lots of off-campus student housing. To the south is the L.A. Coliseum, where the USC Trojans football team plays. To the west are low-income housing and more student rentals. To the east are the Harbor freeway and more low-rent neighborhoods. The campus is on the edge of the sprawling area known by Los Angelenos as South Central. The area has been renamed by city officials as South Los Angeles, but whatever the name, the reality hasn't changed a whole lot over the decades. Shootings, muggings, rapes, and property crime are common. The area is home to more gangs than there are NFL teams. I talked to a glum-faced USC student one day who was filing a police report because he'd had all four wheels stripped off his old, nondescript Mazda two blocks west of campus the night before. The thieves did it the old-fashioned way, using cement blocks and the cover of night.

A darker story occurred when twenty-three-year-old Bryan Frost, a USC film student from Boise, Idaho, was stabbed to death two blocks north of campus. Frost, who was walking with friends early one morning in 2008, apparently banged on the gate of an apartment complex. That upset twenty-five-year-old Travion T. Ford of Los Angeles, whose mother lived in the complex. The two men got into an argument, and eventually started fistfighting. Frost, a West Point cadet who transferred to USC, apparently got the best of Ford in the brawl, and Ford ran into his mother's apartment. Moments later, Ford came back out with a knife and stabbed the film student in the chest. Ford was convicted of second-degree murder and sentenced to sixteen years to life in prison.

That's outside the fence. Whenever I'm outside the fence at night, I pay close attention to my surroundings. I don't walk outside the campus much after dark. I'm lucky to have a car that I park near campus.

Inside the USC campus, inside the fence, it's a different story. The sidewalks are clean and the grass is impeccable. The security is excellent. And given that there's very little auto traffic allowed on campus, it's very quiet. *Stately* and *relaxed* come to mind. The greatest danger facing students inside the fence is getting hit by a miniskirted coed pedaling a beach cruiser with a cell phone pressed to her ear. Once inside campus, it's really like being on the inside of a nice country club. The buildings are gorgeous, and fans of architecture rightly enjoy strolling around the campus. Even people who've never been to USC have seen glimpses of it. Dozens of films and television shows have been shot on campus, including FOREST GUMP, THE GRADUATE, GHOSTBUSTERS, LEGALLY BLONDE, CSI: NY, ENTOURAGE, COLD CASE, and 24.

Compared to sprawling public universities, USC feels positively tiny. It's possible to walk from one end of the campus to the other in ten brisk minutes, and jogging around the perimeter is a popular thing to do, taking barely fifteen minutes to circle the campus fence at a slow trot. Despite the small size of the campus, more than thirty thousand students attend USC.

The campus is also very much in Los Angeles. The high-rises of downtown are just a few miles away. On a clear day, it's possible to see the Hollywood sign far to the north if you stand on the upper floors of a campus building. The rejuvenated Staples Center (home of the Lakers) is a short bike ride away.

The USC School of Cinematic Arts is located on the north side of campus, very close to the dental school, the music school, and the athletic offices. It's a sweet and funny mix: football players and dental students and music students and film students share the sidewalks of the north side of campus. The athletic dining hall—the Jocketeria—is just a few hundred feet from the film school. Ditto with the athletic hall of fame, a glass lobby where you can see the treasures of USC football history. The USC football program and the USC film school are the two highest profile programs on campus; they are located cheek by jowl, and there is absolutely no mistaking who belongs to which program. The muscular mastodons chowing down on tall stacks of pork chops in the Jocketeria are not film students. The thin guys smoking and drinking coffee while sitting on boxes of camera and lighting equipment are not football players.

N or are there many graying students sitting on those camera boxes. Very few people over forty have gone to film school at USC. It seems understandable.

- It's expensive. Every year I'm at USC, for the same amount of money, I could buy a nice new automobile and drive it off a cliff.
- There's a little rumor floating around that Hollywood is not welcoming to *older* people. In 2010, many of the major networks, studios, and talent agencies agreed to a $70 million payout to settle an age discrimination lawsuit filed by Hollywood writers. Those awarded monies in the class-action suit were writers *forty and older.*
- There's no guarantee of work when a student graduates with a degree in film production, no matter what the age. None. Before I applied to USC, I spoke with an admissions director and asked if they had data on what happens to students after they graduate. He said the school did not track that information other than anecdotally. It seemed a polite way of admitting that many students don't work in the industry after completing their degrees. Comparing film school to law school or medical school is like comparing apples and oranges to beef liver.
- The entertainment industry is heavily based on relationships. Starting in the field with a ten- or twenty-year disadvantage in cultivating relationships is hard to overcome.
- Film and television are not family-friendly fields. The days are long. Work can be sporadic; travel is often required. It is a

game for those with energy and perseverance. While at USC, I hear many stories from successful graduates who said the years immediately after leaving film school are ones of poverty and constant struggle.

- Film schools are hard places to fit in socially as an older student. I'm married. I'd like to stay that way. Clubbing/barhopping/going to the strip club is not on my schedule, which makes it hard to socialize with some of the younger students.

Perhaps someday, older film school students won't stick out like sore thumbs. At one time, law schools were mainly places for fresh-faced college grads. But now no one bats an eye when a cop or a housewife goes to law school. A neighbor of mine, a woman with five kids, went to law school in her forties. It's the new normal.

As to being married—in case you missed it, people in the moving picture industry seem as attracted to marriage as Superman is attracted to Kryptonite. Just a scattering of my classmates are married. Less than 5 percent by my count—a far smaller percentage than in my wife's medical school class at the University of Chicago. There, more than a quarter of the med students in her class were married by the time they graduated.

And kids? Forget it. During my years at USC, I knew of only two other production grad students who had children. One was a Korean who was going to return to Seoul; the other was married to an NFL player. They each had one child.

Then there was me, who had three.

At my next 507 production class, there is a break in the ice. FTC seems a little more cheerful this time around. Maybe he had a cup of coffee with the upbeat Ross Brown. Whatever the reason, the frown is missing. I'm fully aware, more than I was in college, that instructors are regular humans, prone to having—gasp!—bad days. In college as a nineteen-year-old, I was once surprised when an English professor, his eyes lined with tiredness, said we might someday understand what it was like to sleep on a couch after a marital spat. I didn't understand him at the time.

FTC gives us our first assignment. We are to make a two-minute silent film, edited in the camera (which means we have to shoot every scene in order—no rearranging scenes). We each have one day to shoot it over the weekend.

We are limited to one day because every camera will be shared by three students. We will air the films on Tuesday. It is now Thursday. We are assigned our class equipment: a well-used Sony PD150, a basic digital camera that we are told to operate in manual mode. No auto-focus, no auto-white balance is allowed. My camera partners are Fee Fee and an exchange student from India who is pursuing his PhD in critical studies.

In the hallway during a class break, a few of my classmates express their fears. They hadn't expected to have to do a film so quickly, with such short notice and with such limitations (no dialogue, no real editing, and having to shoot in sequence). They are worried about finding locations, actors, writing a story. They worry about having just one day to shoot.

I look forward to the shoot. I figure the shorter and more elemental the project, the less chance there is for me to screw up. I've never done this before.

My classmates' main worry seems to be finding actors. Yes, there are thousands of actors in Los Angeles, but actors are loath to spend their time on tiny, low-quality student exercises because they want to stack their demo reel (and résumé) with good material. An in-camera exercise by a new grad student isn't likely to look very good—or make them look very good.

Thus, if someone agrees to be an actor in a class exercise, it is a labor of love. As film students, we'll often be too busy to act in each other's class projects. Because of that, friends, roommates, and relatives get pressed into service. My classmates who grew up in Los Angeles—like red-haired S.—have an advantage because they have so many friends and family to lean on. Newcomers to L.A. are at a disadvantage.

I smile because I have an ace up my sleeve. I will use my own children as actors! For such a simple and short exercise, they will be perfect. And because I don't live in a cramped student apartment but rather in a nice sunny rental house in the far suburbs of Ventura County, I have plenty of places where I can shoot.

A story immediately pops into my mind, one remarkably true to life. In my story, my four-year-old will covet her big sister's training-wheel-equipped bicycle while she sits on her tiny tricycle. Then, during a nap, my four-year-old will dream about the bike and ride it through a grassy suburban park. I know my four-year-old will light up the screen with her big grin.

Every camera partnership has to decide how to split up the camera for the three-day weekend: My partners agree I will take the camera first, shoot my film Saturday morning, then drive the camera back to USC for a handoff Saturday afternoon to Shorav, the PhD student from India. He will shoot Sunday, and then Fee Fee will have the camera all day Monday. The school-owned Sony is in a protective plastic case the size of an airline carry-on bag. We are also sharing a heavy-duty tripod, which also comes in a rather large carrying bag. Together, they weigh about twenty pounds. I carry a bicycle messenger bag with my laptop and class books and legal pads. It weighs another fifteen pounds, at least.

After class, I carry all of it to my car, parked on the fifth floor of the Shrine Auditorium ramp. It's another hot day. I walk up the parking lot steps, carrying some forty pounds of gear. My clothes are too warm. The Shrine has a big ramp—the place used to be home to the Academy Awards and still gets used for events like the Screen Actors Guild Awards. I finally get to my car. I'm sweaty.

As I stand next to my car, taking in the view of campus from the parking deck, I realize I'm a real film student, finally. I am one of those people who walk the sidewalks of USC towing heavy cases of film equipment behind them.

I am a film student. Suddenly, I feel a wave of excitement pass through me. It's taken nearly two years of planning and applications to get to this point, and here I am, putting film equipment into the trunk of my Oldsmobile.

I admire how professional my equipment looks. It's all stamped with U-S-C, and both camera and tripod look as if they've been on a hundred shoots. I actually dance a little jig in the quiet parking ramp, I'm so dang happy.

I'm also exceedingly thirsty! All day I've been walking, walking, walking, and sometimes racing to get to classes on time. In the trunk of my car, I have a quart of apple juice and a few bottles of water. It's been a long day and a long week. I love apple juice. I drink the whole bottle. I load the equipment in and take a breather. My legs are tired, and it seems I've walked a hundred miles during the first week around campus.

I inspect the camera one more time: it's heftier than a standard consumer video camera, and I've got an extra lens and a charger in the eggshell-foam-lined case. I get in my car and slowly circle down to the ground floor.

Then my stomach takes a jump. I realize the quart of apple juice is not settling well. Not well at all. I realize I have a problem.

I park illegally outside the Zemeckis building and waddle past the front desk attendant. I cross my fingers that a bathroom is available—one is!—and close the door as fast as I can. I have a massive attack of diarrhea. As my guts contract and my forehead sweats, I worry if I'll get a parking ticket and I worry if I'll be able to navigate the freeways without soiling my pants and I wonder how my kids are and how Julie is and I realize on this day I paid another $200 of money I don't have to go to class with a bunch of people half my age.

I calculate between cramps that it's costing me five dollars of tuition money just to sit in this lonely bathroom stall.

Trying to measure the importance of moving pictures on our society objectively is impossible. Their influence on pop culture dwarfs their economic value. For example, I once wrote speeches for executives at Cargill, the largest privately held corporation in the United States. Cargill's yearly revenues now hover in the $120 billion range. By comparison, total yearly revenue for CBS, the most successful broadcast network, is in the $13–14 billion range. By revenue, Cargill absolutely dwarfs CBS. It's almost ten times bigger! But when was the last time you heard anyone talking about Cargill? Most people have no idea the company exists. Yes, it exports a quarter of the country's grain and supplies a fifth of the country's meat supply and shapes every single egg in every single Egg McMuffin. But Americans ignore it. They have food in their stomachs, so they can concentrate on more important matters, like Brad and Angelina.

The biggest entertainment companies are Walt Disney, News Corp., and Time Warner. The ranks of these companies according to the *Fortune 500* list in 2010 are fifty-seven, seventy-six, and eighty-two, respectively.

Film and television punch far beyond their weight class. They are like professional sports. Millions of kids dream of being pro athletes, yet a nearly infinitesimal slice of them actually become pro athletes. And millions of people dream of being in the moving picture business. A few actually make a living at it. I know the odds when I start. They suck, almost as bad as the odds of making a living as a newspaper reporter.

Saturday morning comes and my kids are thrilled. I've been away from home all week. I arrived home late Friday night, my stomach fully settled after my encounter with the apple juice. Julie and I live only fifty-five miles to the northwest of USC, in the suburb of Camarillo, which is in Ventura County, but it's too far for me to commute in L.A. traffic. If I drive in rush hour, it can be a four-hour round-trip. So Monday night through Thursday night I sleep in a house in La Cañada, an upscale suburb located next to Pasadena that's about seventeen miles from campus. When Carl and Irene Christensen heard I was accepted to USC, they called me and told me I could stay at their home. For free.

It was a stunningly generous offer. I worried I'd be intruding on their lives and making too much of a ruckus, but my worries were overruled by the simple math of it: I saved serious time and lots of money. I soon realized their house offered much more than merely a place to sleep. Their neighborhood is an oasis of peace and quiet—so different from USC. Horse trails wind through the neighborhood. At night, I sometimes hear the plop of oranges falling off a nearby tree. And in the evenings and early mornings, I chat with Carl and Irene.

Weekends, I'm home in Camarillo with Julie and the kids—and her mom, Jean, who is living with us while I go to school and taking care of the kids while Julie is at work. So I live a life in triplicate. There's my USC life, my life in La Cañada, and my life in Camarillo.

On Saturday morning, I explain that Maria, my four-year-old, will be the lead character. Lara, who is eight, thinks that is a great idea because she really isn't interested in acting. I do warn Maria (with all my vast wisdom of film shoots) that acting for film can be pretty boring. She brushes off my warning. She wants to get going.

Sophia, who is two, doesn't understand what we're doing. She just grins and races around the house.

My first film shoot is a playful lark. The day is sunny and warm. My kids and Julie are excited to see my official USC camera and tripod. Julie is amused by the crudely drawn storyboards (all stick figures) I created in preparation for the shoot. I spend the morning in the house, carefully setting up shots. Then I call for Maria, the star. She looks wistfully at her big sister's bike, right on command, and glumly pedals her tricycle in our suburban garage. It takes only an hour or so to shoot a minute of tape.

When it comes time for the dream sequence, I direct Maria to act as if she's asleep. She does a great job of not giggling. Then I pull out the special effects: I smear a little Vaseline on the edges of the screw-off lens dust cap. Our whole crew—me, Julie, and all three kids—heads to the local park just down the street. When we get there, Lara climbs on the monkey bars while Sophia toddles around. I stand nearby, my camera and tripod ready. Maria rides Lara's bike on the sidewalk, past the monkey bars, grinning widely. I stand next to other dads with my camera. No one has any idea what I am doing. I look like any other suburban dad videotaping his kid learning how to ride a bike. Yes, I've got a tripod, but no one gives me even a sideways glance. One hundred feet away a woman is videotaping a birthday party. To the unpracticed eye, my boxy Sony looks like any other out-of-date camera.

An hour later, we're home again. I check what I've shot on playback. It's far from perfect, but it's good enough. I know using a dream sequence is the biggest cliché in moviemaking. (*Look, it didn't happen, it's only a dream!*) Yes, I'm being lazy and not very original, but my goal is just to get a base hit, not a home run, and move forward.

With this film, I mainly want to show my class—and my instructors—my kids. They are such an important part of my life, and I want to use this film as a two-minute brag session. When I plug the camera into our television set and we watch the completed film, Maria beams. Sophia claps. Even Lara agrees her annoying little sister did a good job.

If this is film school, I think, *this is not hard.* For my two-minute film, I did no more than twenty different setups. That works out to six seconds a shot—a pretty slow pace. Watch any TV show or film and count how long each shot lasts. In television, it's rare for a shot to last more than four seconds on-screen, most are less than that. My short film is a slow-moving affair, and, if I remove my bias, it's actually pretty dull. But I'm happy. I'm guessing film school is a game of attrition: I just need to survive to fight the next battle and not flame out early.

The next week we show our two-minute films in class. The Zemeckis classrooms have large pull-down screens and overhead video projectors. As we sit in the dark, our videos play out on the screen, larger than life. The smallest details are enormous. It's the first time I've seen my camera work displayed on such a large screen. Small bobbles of the camera make images look like they are going through a magnitude 8.7 earthquake. Flaws in lighting, in acting, in set design all jump out.

No one has a masterpiece. Most are, like mine, silly things. I feel relieved watching them spool out on the big screen that I'm not completely outclassed. Fee Fee, a production major in college, features a woman being chased, horror-movie style, by what turns out to be a fluffy stuffed animal. This is par for the course.

My film has the effect I hoped for on my classmates. I hear *ooohs* and *aaaaaahs* as my three daughters appear on the screen. My five female classmates seem especially appreciative. I get a nice round of applause. I feel like I've got a two-minute family talent show on the screen. Von Trapp Family Singers, watch out.

The lights come up. FTC clears his throat. He holds a long dramatic pause. He is frowning. His lips are tight.

Finally, he speaks. "Steve." He exhales. "Steve . . . Steve . . . Steve." He shakes his head.

He looks at me for several seconds. I look back, confused. Did the story not make any sense? Is he going to hammer me for using the lame *It's Only a Dream* concept? Did my technique stink that much?

FTC finally speaks. "Did you have a studio teacher?" he asks.

My brain races. I do a quick mental survey of the term *studio teacher*. I had read about them in some of the material we received in class. They make sure actors under eighteen don't work beyond union-specified time limits on a set, and they're also supposed to make sure a child actor is tutored while on set if a shoot takes place on a school day. A studio teacher costs about $400 a day.

Did he really mean I needed to spend $400 to hire someone to watch me shoot a video of my kid riding a bike at the playground?

"No," I answer, slowly. "I used my wife. She *is* a pediatrician." I smile wanly.

"That's not good enough," FTC snaps. He stares straight at me. "The rules here at USC are very explicit. You needed a studio teacher. You did not have one. This is a very serious breach of filmmaking."

He pauses, then adds: "The rules say you are to be expelled from school for doing what you did."

The room is silent. Completely and totally silent. I feel every face in the class staring at me. I can hardly see FTC's eyes under his cap. He jaw is set.

I feel my face flushing. My heart, which has been beating fast, now starts pounding. *Oh, Lordy, I'm about to get kicked out of film school for making a home movie.*

3

The Backstory

How did I get here, at USC, as a graying father of three? Part of the reason I'm loath to say much during our classroom introductions is because I can't imagine turning on the spigot and explaining my background. When I applied to USC, I had to write several essays. One was a personal statement. It started like this:

> On a sweltering August morning in the 1960s my mother is in a Minneapolis hospital, about to deliver her third child. That would be me. A young doctor feels her stomach and wonders aloud if the baby has two heads and one body. My mother is very upset. Luckily, a more experienced doctor goes into the delivery room and assures my mother I don't have two heads. My umbilical cord is wrapped around my head and I survive.
>
> My parents name me Stephen Gregory Boman. If I could have talked, I would have said: "I prefer Steve instead of Stephen. So many people mispronounce Stephen (Steff-en) it's kind of

embarrassing. Saint Stephen got stoned to death by an angry mob just for mouthing off. And that young actor named Steve McQueen seems like a good egg. So, please, just make it Steve."

I could not talk, of course, until much later, about the time my parents move north to Duluth, Minnesota. They have one more child and buy a small house. I now have two older brothers and a younger sister. My dad is a newly minted professor at the local university. My mom stays home. We have a pretty normal existence. I never came home to find the car on fire and my parents brawling on the lawn. My brothers and sister and I are outside playing constantly. We rarely watch TV. I am teased by my brothers, and I learn to use my mouth as a weapon (blame my namesake). I become the family joker. We are highly competitive. We have sibling competitions to see who can run the fastest, who can shoot BB guns the most accurately, and, among us boys, who can pee the farthest in the woods.

We all turn out pretty well. No jail time, no front-page scandals. Just the usual family sagas of marriages and heartbreaks and laughter and minor grievances. My oldest brother becomes an orthopedic surgeon, marries, has two kids. My other brother is in the Air Force for years, and then he, too, becomes a doctor. He has five kids. My younger sister is the brains of the family, a PhD in biophysics from Johns Hopkins University and a successful medical researcher.

I am the reader, the storyteller. I am always curious about the outside world. I read Papillion in the fifth grade, and give a book report about it. My fifth-grade teacher, Mr. Johnson, has also read the book. He does not ask me to explain to the class some of the finer details in the story, such as how prisoners stuffed valuables up their assholes to hide them.

When I am in high school, the school guidance counselor sits me down during one of his rare bouts of sobriety. We go over my

record: I have been a good student. I have been a jock. I play trom-
bone. I act in plays. He wants to know what I want to do. I have
my choice pretty well narrowed down. I don't like science. I am
very good at math. In junior high, I wanted to be a forest ranger
but mainly because I wanted to drive around in a Jeep all day.
But by high school I have ruled that out. I tell him I want to be a
writer. He nods vacantly.

Duluth, the town I grew up in, is then a town on the skids, just
like my guidance counselor. It's a blue-collar town with a recently
closed steel mill, high unemployment, and limited options. My
idea of being a writer probably sounds dreamy and stupid, like
students saying they're going to be a rock star or an NBA player.

The counselor doesn't give me any advice, or any that I remember
anyway. With all the wisdom that seventeen-year-olds have, I
know—absolutely know—the best way to pursue my career is
to load up a motorcycle and head west and work as a menial
laborer. I am going to spend at least a year traveling, working,
and, most important, renting a really cool apartment somewhere
in the Rocky Mountains where I can work during the day at a ski
resort and write fascinating stories in the evening as Count Basie
plays on the stereo. I assume there will be many beautiful women
visiting. I imagine I will be smoking a pipe, like a young Hugh
Hefner.

I go on the trip with my former seventh-grade locker partner,
Scott. Scott has his own beat-up motorcycle, a bike even more
prone to breakdowns than mine. We work as dishwashers in
Wyoming. We live in a single tiny room in a trailer. We work full
time and spend most of our wages for food and rent and motor-
cycle repairs. I don't write one word. Then it starts to snow. We
are cold. We dump the idea of working as ski-bums. (What were
we thinking? We were on two-wheelers.) So we ride toward Los
Angeles where Scott has relatives . . .

Feel free to cut and paste it for your own application essay. It wasn't the whole story. I didn't write about how I was a disinterested and bored student who spent much more time dreaming about motorcycles than on finishing school assignments.

In contrast, my sister, Annette, was focused like a laser. She was just a year and a half younger than me, and in many ways we were yin and yang. I ducked out of class as often as possible; she got perfect attendance marks. I spent my summers on a ladder painting houses, dirty and sunburned, to earn money for college; Annette was on a full-ride scholarship and did research at the Woods Hole Oceanographic Institution. When I graduated from college, I owned a motorcycle and a few suitcases of clothes, and I started looking for work. When she finished college, she headed to Johns Hopkins for graduate work, and she was invited to Stockholm to witness the awarding of the Nobel Prizes. She interviewed several of the Nobel winners for a Swedish television program. She asked them about their thoughts on God, which sounds a bit presumptuous, but she was so young and straightforward that the people she interviewed answered her with great earnestness. She got a PhD from Johns Hopkins in biophysics when she was twenty-six. She wanted to be a scientist, you see.

I n 507, we are to make five films. The first has landed me in hot water. During a class break after the screening of my little two-minute bicycle dream, I approach FTC. He isn't eager to talk. I tell him I had no clue I needed a studio teacher to oversee my own kids for such a simple shoot. He tells me the rules are what they are. I ask him if he's going to have me expelled. I'm not pleading or begging. I just want to know what's going to happen.

He pauses. Then he says no, he's not going to bring up the issue with the school. But he warns me that he could have me expelled—and I'm left with the realization I'm on thin ice.

I go get a drink of water. I can understand his position. He doesn't know me—for all he knows, I'm a stage parent who would push his infant into a cage of hungry polar bears if it meant a chance at fame. He doesn't know my wife and he doesn't know anything about how I treat my kids. He's only spent a few hours with me in class, and he saw that the first film I did used minors, without a studio teacher. I don't blame him for coming down hard on me. I thought the studio teacher rule wouldn't apply to me for this small exercise, in part because of the genteel nature of the shoot and also because I figured my wife is a better monitor than a hired studio teacher and because we were filming under the agreement that our work wouldn't be publicly shown. We could use copyrighted music without permission on these little exercises, for example, something we couldn't do for later films. The bottom line, I learned, was this: the rules are not to be ignored. When at USC, follow the playbook.

I'm also learning the role I'm starting to play in 507. Just as Casper is using me as a foil in his film history lecture, I get a strong sense FTC is using me to set examples. I'm guessing it's because both instructors expect I'm not going to go sobbing into the hallway when I am criticized. For better or worse, I come across as a durable guy. Whatever role I'm being cast in, I'm not going to fret about my relationship with FTC. He is very direct, which I appreciate. If he doesn't like me, so it goes. Besides, I have to prepare for my next project.

Our next four films in 507 are to be much larger in scale. Each film can be up to eight minutes long. We will edit on AVID and have three weeks to do each film. One week to write and produce, one to shoot, one to edit and mix. On screening day, we will show our films to our class. The three-week schedule allows each person in the camera partnership to have a week with a camera and a week with our computer hard drive for editing. In my case, I'll be shooting second in the rotation. Thus, a third of our 507 class will finish and screen a film one week, a week later the second third will screen theirs, and the final third will screen the third week. Then we'll repeat it all over again until the end of the semester. Each week, we'll watch five or six films, and spend thirty minutes or so discussing each one.

This is how the semester will go: sixteen students showing five films each. During the semester, I will watch eighty short student films, comment on them, study them, critique them, make them.

It seems at first like a luxury of time. Twelve weeks to make just four short films? It sounds almost routine. Easy, in fact. Until I start making them.

In the past, I'd burned up eight minutes of film shooting a birthday party before the candles were even blown out. That, I quickly learned, is not making a short film; that's recording something, just as jotting down a list of things to be picked up at the grocery store isn't the same as writing a short story.

Now, just a few weeks into classes, I'm already feeling a time crunch. In film school, I spend a lot of time in classes, more than twenty hours a week. Add a few hours of getting to and from those classes, standing in lines (waiting for equipment or an editing booth or food), and thirty hours a week is down the drain before doing any actual filming. I also have lots of studying and assignments for my other classes. My screenwriting class requires me to write several scenes every week. My 507 sound class requires several hours of reading a week, and my 507 acting class takes up an astounding amount of time. For that class alone, I'm required to memorize scenes from various films, practice acting with small groups of students, and direct scenes with the same students.

Of all my class work, my acting class eats up a disproportionate amount of time. The school wants to have student directors know what it's actually like to act, and USC puts a heavy emphasis on understanding acting theory, especially the theories put forward by the well-known instructor Uta Hagen, author of *Respect for Acting*. It's a dandy idea, but I'm one of the few students in my 507 class who has done any acting. In high school, I wrote and acted in a few silly comic skits and got the lead in a one-act comedy. I spent a year at Exeter University in England, and I got a role in a student production of *The Merchant of Venice*. I played the foul-mouthed and hot-tempered Gratiano. I even got talked into playing, ahem, a horse in *Equus*. I've also got good friends who are actors, and I've been behind the scenes on stages and at readings. I feel I can communicate pretty effectively with actors.

Luckily, my Casper film history class hardly eats up any time outside of class, at least for now. I'm supposed to do prelecture readings, but I don't do them. My knowledge of postwar history is good. I hope it will be good enough because Casper knows my name. Every other bit of time goes into my next 507 film.

In college, I underwent a transformation. I studied. I worked hard, really hard. It paid off. I even got a National Endowment for the Humanities scholarship to Tufts University to study the rise of Hitler.

When I graduated, I wanted to tell stories. I got a job at Minnesota Public Radio. On my first day, I was handed a tape recorder and a microphone and told to cover a presidential candidate who was making the rounds in northern Iowa. For nearly three years, I used the same tape recorder and the same microphone and covered hundreds of stories. I wrote fifty-second news stories; I wrote eight-minute feature stories. I voiced my own stories and produced them and was eventually made news director and anchor.

I learned many things, among them the cardinal rule of journalism:

don't expect to get paid much. I started at $12,000 a year and lived in a $180-a-month apartment. I shared my bathroom with a mentally ill man who lived next door.

But money didn't really matter. I was single. My girlfriend lived in Germany. I didn't care if I shared a reeking bathroom. I liked journalism. And journalism was starting to like me. More of my stories went national on NPR, and I won a few moderately prestigious awards.

Then an odd thing happened. One dreary winter day, I drove with my German girlfriend to Chicago. She had pals there. The husband of one of her friends was a transplant coordinator for the University of Chicago. *What kind of a job is that?* I asked him.

He explained he retrieved organs from brain-dead people all over the country and brought them back to the surgeons in Chicago, where they were transplanted into sick and desperate patients. *That's an odd job,* I said.

In class, FTC is explaining that we can focus on specific aspects of filmmaking on each of our films. If we want to emphasize lighting, that's great. Or if we really want to work on our cinematography, ditto. He says we don't need to be constrained by traditional ideas of filmmaking. Feel free to experiment, he adds. But, he tells our class, we have to follow these rules:

- In our second film, we can use only one spoken word on-screen.
- In our third film, we can feature one sentence on-screen.
- In our fourth film, we can feature one short bit of dialogue—no more than a paragraph.
- In our fifth film, we can have more dialogue but no more than a page. (A script page equals roughly a minute of screen time.)

There's also a wildcard: We can do one documentary if we wish as a substitute for any of the fiction films. The documentary has no dialogue limitations. It can be up to eight minutes long, just like our fiction films.

FTC explains that the smaller the box we work within, the easier it is to focus on the art of filmmaking. Hearing the limitations causes me to experience a wave of anxiety. One word in an eight-minute film? I'm a wordsmith, for cripes sake! Words are the only thing I know! I've never done pictures. I've never been a photographer, and my drawings are pathetic, worse than a preschooler's scribbling.

I am obviously going to have to focus on my weaknesses. I desperately wish I had known these were the rules for the first semester. I had come to USC with dozens of ideas in my head for film. All of them were wordy—and, it turns out—all of them were overly complex and too difficult to produce. Had I known I would be doing essentially silent films my first semester, I would have been a lot better prepared. I'm a bit frustrated by my own ignorance. And now I need to come up with a plausible story for my next film.

Before I left Chicago, the husband of my girlfriend's pal asked if I was interested in joining him as a transplant coordinator. I thought he was joking.

Two weeks later, I completed my morning anchor shift at the radio station and raced out to the Rochester airport. The husband of my girlfriend's pal had chartered a plane to fly me to Chicago for the afternoon. I spent the day being interviewed by some of America's most elite doctors for a position I knew nothing about. I was an English major in college and a radio reporter. I knew nothing of surgery. I was twenty-five years old.

For reasons that remain inexplicable to me to this day, the University of Chicago hired me. They paid me much more than MPR ever had. I would live in Chicago. I would retrieve organs from dead people.

My second 507 film presents me with a dilemma. Before I came to USC, I jotted down lots of film ideas, aided by friends and family who pitched me stories. In my time in newsrooms, I was never at a loss for ideas for stories. I was normally a one-man story-pitching machine. Now I have to make an eight-minute film that includes only one word, but every idea I have involves lots of chatter.

I spend several days jotting new ideas down and then throwing all of them away.

Finally, I come up with one that seems workable: A young man goes to a funeral for his father. Afterwards, he gets the will. The father's handwritten scrawl claims he hid some treasure. The will includes a crude map. The letter and map look as if they were created by a crazy person. The son, a straitlaced young office worker, goes on a long journey to find the hidden treasure. By the time he reaches the map's end, having overcome various obstacles, he's a dirty mess and he finds . . . nothing. But he has become as insane as his father appears to have been. The one word the son will utter is "DAD!"

It's a dark comedy. I name it MY CRAZY DAD.

Early in my shooting week, I find a funeral home willing to let me shoot inside their parlor. The funeral home director is even willing to drive his hearse for me.

I discover a gorgeous Catholic cathedral just a few blocks from USC. With a few shots, I figure I can approximate a funeral.

For the treasure hunt, I'll shoot in the mountains above Malibu. The area has a gorgeous state park, filled with hiking trails I've taken my kids and Julie on many times. I know a site with an abandoned windmill—it looks like the remains of a farm. The park has a valley with uninterrupted vistas—no power lines, no houses, no roads on the horizon.

For the son's workplace, I have an office I can use at USC.

I have everything I need . . . except an actor. My other classes are taking up more time than I planned, and the first few days of the week quickly pass as I start searching for talent. I need someone for a full-day shoot.

Tuesday comes and I'm able to go to the funeral home and shoot some amazingly authentic scenes, just me and my camera and the tripod. A real dead guy is in a casket, awaiting a memorial service. The funeral home director discreetly closes the lid before I roll the camera, but otherwise he offers me the run of the funeral home. He says he appreciates I'm an older family man who has returned to school. I am careful not to disrupt his business. The hearse looks great, too, and he agrees to act for me a bit, shutting the doors to the hearse.

At the start of the week, I put out some calls to student actors at USC who had advertised their willingness to work for student directors. I need a full day from an actor. But none of the student actors I speak to are game.

I go through books of actors' headshots inside the USC Student Production Office—SPO, as the students call it. I'm new to the casting game, and I'm clueless. No one returns my calls. I'm told to put a casting notice online, but I put it off, hoping to get a USC acting student.

When Thursday comes, I'm still actor-less. I have to shoot Friday—it's when the office I'm using is open—and I've got nothing. I feel the pressure rising. I was hoping to spend the weekend with my family in Camarillo. I feel the tension grabbing my innards. With my first little exercise, I was able to use my kids. Now I'm coming up with nothing for film #2, and I know FTC is watching me closely.

I feel surreally out of my element. I'd spent a decade as a reporter convincing people to be interviewed; I spent a year organizing life-and-death transplant operations; I've raised three kids . . . and now I'm starting to freak out because I can't find an actor willing to spend a day in front of a camera, in Los Angeles. And only have to say one word.

In my 507 class on Thursday afternoon, I'm thoroughly anxious. In class, I ask a few classmates if they know anyone who could act for me. They shake their heads *no*.

As class lets out, I feel awful. The sun is going down. I feel my time is running out. S., the comic kid with the red hair, asks me what's wrong. I tell him I can't find an actor. S. shrugs and says, "I'll act for you."

I want to hug him, plant a kiss on his forehead. I don't, but suddenly the sunset takes on a beautiful glow. The cracked sidewalk leading from Zemeckis becomes a gorgeous pathway. I run down the sidewalk to my car. I have some clothes to buy for my character, and now I know what size to buy.

Friday morning dawns sunny and clear. I understand why early filmmakers loved this city. The weather so predictable, so stable, that it means one less worry when making a film. The cloud cover is exactly the same as it was Tuesday, when I shot at the funeral home, and Wednesday, when I shot at the cathedral. Now, Friday, S. meets me at Zemeckis at 9 A.M. I bought some clothes for him the night before at a T.J. Maxx. I have a white dress shirt and a pair of dress slacks. I brought my own black shoes. S. changes into the clothes, puts his pile of red hair into a tight bun, and the transformation is total. The alt-rock artist is now a conservatively dressed white-collar worker.

For the film, I ask him to be very reserved, not to display any emotions at the cathedral for the funeral or when he's reading his father's handwritten scrawl.

In the earliest days of film a century ago, actors really projected their emotions: a character about to be run over by a train emoted by overamping the screams, the knuckle biting, the arm waving. Today, to our modern sensibilities, it looks comic.

But in the twenty-first century, student films have their own version of overacting. Most student films are dramas. Many of the dramas are about breaking up with a boyfriend or a girlfriend. In student films, a woman who discovers her boyfriend is leaving her will generally do one, some, or all of these:

1. Sob uncontrollably while holding a breakup letter.
2. Stare out the window, with tears flowing down her cheeks.
3. Sob while clutching a pillow.
4. Smoke and stare at a picture of the former boyfriend, then drop her head and sob some more.

The remaining dramas generally involve bad dads—overbearing and narrow-minded assholes, guys who spend their evenings like I do, watering their pathetic little patch of suburban grass, a beer can in one hand and a garden hose in the other.

In the bad-dad films, the male actors playing Dad glare like their eyes are shooting death-beams. I had no idea of the prevalence of bad dads until I came to USC. They're everywhere! They're always glaring and finding ways to make their children's lives miserable— they're probably not even paying the tuition for film school.

I don't want S. to overact. I don't want him to sob or glower. I want him to underact. I want a dry comedy.

As the day goes on, we shoot our film. I'm shooting it pretty much in sequence because I don't have extra costumes. We drive out of L.A., S. behind the wheel of my car. I film him driving: expressway, two-lane highway, narrow road, dirt trail. Then I film him hiking, following the map. He climbs a mountain, the trail getting ever harder. His slacks and white shirt become dirty. Soon there's no trail left. He gets more desperate, tripping, falling, running up hills. He gets to the windmill and can't find anything. He frantically digs with his bare hands, looking for the treasure.

I'm now asking S. to act as if he's going out of his mind with frustration. He's throwing himself into the role. I'm laughing so hard I have to take a break from shooting. We're losing daylight and, with the last minutes of sunlight, I direct S. to lie in the dirt, filthy, and utter his one line: DAD!

I'm shocked at how much effort S. puts into the role. In class, he's always laid-back, seemingly low energy. Out here, he's going nutso in the dirt. And he's nailing the part.

As we walk down the trail in the twilight, S. explains he went to Columbia College in Chicago, studied filmmaking, then applied to USC. His knowledge of hands-on filmmaking far exceeds mine—which is why he gently offers me advice as I'm shooting. ("Steve, you should check your white-balance again." "This would be a great time to use a tripod. I don't think you'll be able to handhold this shot very well.")

On the drive back to Los Angeles, I query S. about his background. This was the first time I'd spent considerable one-on-one time with any of my classmates. We were already three weeks into the semester and I'd had lots of group discussions and plenty of short one-on-one chats, but I never found myself with much extra time to just . . . talk. I always feel like the White Rabbit in ALICE IN WONDERLAND. *I'm late. I'm late. I'm late!*

Now, on our postshoot road trip home, there is time to talk. As we drive along Highway 101 in the darkness, S. admits he comes from a show-business family. He says he doesn't want to name-drop. After some prodding by me, S. sheds more light on his background: his grandfather was a well-known actor who ran a well-known acting studio for comics until he died in the 1980s.

S. says his father is also in the business. He's a director, won an Emmy, and is now doing feature films.

In the dark car I glance over at S. I tell him I had no idea about his background—none. I'd never heard a word of gossip on campus. S. says he doesn't want to be treated any differently in class. He says he wants to be judged on his own merits.

I drop S. off at his yellow SUV and thank him again. When the door shuts, I breathe a huge sigh of relief. I can spend the weekend at my own house, seeing my kids and Julie. I have studies to do, but I'll be home before midnight Friday, and I have enough footage to cut together my second film. I feel I've dodged a bullet.

B eing a transplant coordinator is a bit like being a firefighter. Long stretches of quiet are punctuated by frantic action. It was an odd job, no doubt.

I oversaw an organ harvest in a small hospital that was running on emergency backup generators because tornadoes were sweeping through the region. Another time, I scrubbed in and assisted a surgeon doing a dissection of a liver during a then-experimental living donor operation on Christmas Eve at the University of Chicago—a time when the hospital was short-staffed. Over my tenure, I learned how a handful of surgeons—well-meaning, talented people—would bend the rules to help their patients or, sometimes, their careers.

I knew my experience of being swept up in the excitement of the transplant world was a good story. It was too good to be limited to a small story. I held my experiences close to my vest, waiting for the right venue.

What didn't wait was romance. While working in Chicago, I fell in love. She was a gorgeous woman with long brown hair and big brown eyes named Julie. She was just back from the Peace Corps.

We had both gone to Gustavus, but we were both dating others and the mutual attraction had never burst into flame. Then she came to visit me in Chicago. We went out one night and—poof!—just like that, we were engaged. She was going to go to graduate school in ecology at the University of Pennsylvania. Our marriage was a happy place, filled with laughter and kisses and dancing.

And then a little surprise occurred during our honeymoon. She decided she wanted to go to medical school instead of pursuing a PhD in ecology. With love-sparkles in my eyes, I said, *That sounds like a great idea, honey! I would love to support you. Medical school sounds fantastic!*

In the film version of this book, a scene of two newlyweds kissing would now dissolve. We would hear a small child crying. A title card would announce: *Nine Years Later.* And the next scene would be Julie heading off to the hospital, stethoscope around her neck, white doctor's coat bulging with notepads and pens and pagers. She would have dark circles under her eyes. There would be a four-year-old girl at a breakfast table. I would be holding a baby in my arms. I would need a shave. I would be wearing Winnie the Pooh slippers and an old T-shirt and shorts. Julie would give the girls a kiss, peck me on the cheek, and rush off to work, her pager squawking. As soon as the door closed, there would be silence. The four-year-old would ask me: "What are we going to do today, Daddy?"

Editing MY CRAZY DAD is conceptually easy. There's not much reordering needed, just trimming the long minutes of footage into an eight-minute journey. My story is simple, probably too simple. When I get to the Zemeckis editing room with its dozens of computer stations, I find I'm all thumbs. The computers are running AVID software, an industry standard, but I have little experience using it. Like all modern editing software, it's nonlinear. Final Cut Pro, iMovie, Windows Movie Maker, OpenShot, and others are similar nonlinear programs.

I'm used to linear systems. In radio, way back in the twentieth century, when I wanted a cut from a piece of tape, I'd literally cut it out, with a blade. If I wanted a cut from the back of a reel, it meant winding through the whole reel. Like walking down a long dirt road, it took time.

Film worked the same way. Linear film editing was in place for a century. Editing rooms would be filled with hundreds of pieces of film, hanging from racks. A film was built, piece by piece by piece, all spliced by hand. Editing was slower; editors worked with the original source material, and going back to a previous cut was time-consuming.

Since the early 1990s, film editing has moved nearly universally to nonlinear systems. Imagine that same long dirt road but instead of having to walk from beginning to end, you could push a button and—zap—be anywhere on the journey.

With AVID (as with all nonlinear systems), it's possible to find a cut by moving a computer mouse or hitting a few keystrokes. In an instant, you can be at that particular spot, make a virtual clip, label it, and move on. With nonlinear systems, you can move from the beginning of a film to the end in a heartbeat.

The computerized system is much faster, and it makes it possible to move clips around, trim or lengthen cuts in an instant, save multiple versions, do a cut and immediately reverse yourself, and save multiple versions.

It's similar to using a computer versus using a typewriter. (My children have never seen a typewriter. They are mystified by a machine that uses thin metal rods that slam down a metal key on an ink-covered ribbon that hovers over the paper. As a cub reporter, I wrote all my copy on an IBM Selectric typewriter.)

I find AVID a hindrance. I'm not being a Luddite: I love my laptop. I'm just extremely slow when I first use AVID. Compared to my editing-savvy classmates, I feel like I'm going to journalism school without ever having learned to type. It takes me hours just to download my tapes and figure out how to create "bins." I'm the slowest editor in my class. I console myself with the realization that we students all have various strengths and weaknesses. I like to think I'll have a leg up in other areas, like writing and directing.

I start to make a list of things I would do differently before enrolling in film school. Top of the list is spending time on a non-linear editing system.

I'm slow as molasses at editing, but I appreciate the importance of it. Good editing is an art, maybe the most underappreciated part of filmmaking other than sound. The great Robert Wise, director of WEST SIDE STORY and THE SOUND OF MUSIC, was originally a film editor. And Stanley Kubrick, director of 2001: A SPACE ODYSSEY and FULL METAL JACKET, explained that he loved editing more than any other part of filmmaking. He also noted that editing is unique to moving pictures. The other components of moviemaking—writing, photography, music, and acting—all predated motion pictures.

When I finally finish cutting together MY CRAZY DAD, instead of feeling relieved, I feel a bubbling sense of anxiety creeping back into my gullet. I have barely completed the film on time—I spent every available hour in AVID lab for a week. It had just one primary actor. A couple of different locations. What happens when I start shooting more complicated films? Maybe the doctor-turned-film-student was right. Maybe it was harder than medical school.

I had watched my wife go through medical school. That was hard, no doubt. But I saw her divide each week up into manageable sections. If she studied, she would pass the test, and move onto the next subject in lockstep with her classmates. Medical school is highly regimented, and students all follow roughly the same path. As long as they stay on the treadmill, they keep moving forward.

In film school, there is no lockstep formation. We're more like mice in a corridor trying to get to the next room before the cat comes back. Most of us are going in the same direction, but we're arriving at different locations, going at different speeds with vastly different talents. Some of us are moving backward, some are cleaning their whiskers, some are eating fermented berries. And there never seems to be enough time to get down the corridor! I think about the cat. I wonder if I'm going to get eaten by the cat.

I also wish USC put more emphasis on editing right off the bat. It seems a little absurd—we're making films from week one—and there's almost no instruction in the basics of editing. It seems they assume everyone already knows how. I'm definitely in a program that emphasizes trial and error . . . and I'm making plenty of errors.

When I finally finish editing the film, late the night before it is due for class, I show it to the husband of a classmate. I tell him it's a comedy and give him my headphones so he can watch it on the monitor. As he watches my little film, he starts laughing. I go to bed late that night, excited about my second film's prospects. I'm hoping the audience in my 507 class reacts the same way.

The screenings always follow a specific ritual. The students and instructors sit in a semicircle facing the projection screen. We watch the film. Then when it's done, the director goes to a chair in front of the entire group, and waits while everyone silently writes critiques on standardized 8½" x 5½" pressure-sensitive forms that we've all purchased from the USC equipment department. The double-sheeted forms, which look a bit like blank parking tickets, seem like throwbacks to the 1950s. They're white on top, yellow on the bottom. We write the director's name, film title, and date, then the following:

- Intention
- Synopsis
- Strengths
- Weaknesses

Then, after five or six minutes of jotting down comments, the writing stops. And the talking starts. We critique the films, reading to the director what we wrote. *Critique* is derived from a Greek word that means, roughly, *to discern the truth or value of things*.

While this is going on, the director sits in a chair facing everyone.

At first, we're all leery of being too negative. Our criticisms are laden with positives.

It doesn't take long for FTC to lose his patience. He urges us to be harder hitting with our criticism. This is not a popularity contest, he says. He doesn't want to hear soft praise ("I just loved that! It was great!") or flattering commentary. FTC is quite exasperated.

Once again, I don't entirely disagree with FTC. I don't mind being direct—my editors in the past were pretty direct. Mike Waters at the *Daily Southtown*, a great editor, once whipped a phone to the ground in disgust and swore a blue streak at me when the *Chicago Tribune* beat me on an important story. Once when I was a radio reporter, I was sent to the Dominican Republic to do a story and blurted out over the air, live, that women in an overcrowded and filthy birthing hospital "really squirt their babies out." When I returned home, my boss yelled and threatened to fire me. But both those bosses were also free with their praise when I didn't mess up.

In 507, we start hitting harder. It becomes a bit of a sport to see who can have the smartest critique.

THE BACKSTORY ■ 71

Directors on the hot seat cannot speak until the very end, after the class and the instructors have spoken. (In addition to FTC, we have a student assistant and a quiet cinematography instructor.) Then the directors explain what their intent is. If their intent matches what the *audience* thinks the intent was, the director has succeeded in one very important area.

When the time comes for me to present MY CRAZY DAD, I'm really surprised by my nervousness. I spent a decade writing articles for thousands of people every day. A news story of mine on National Public Radio would play from coast to coast. Now I'm doing a short film for fewer than twenty people. And I'm nervous. This feels much more personal.

The most rewarding part of the screening is watching the audience. It's something I rarely got much of as a reporter. When I wrote or voiced a story in the past, it was consumed by people I rarely if ever saw. I occasionally wished my stories would be read simultaneously by a stadium full of people. I wanted to know when they laughed, when they groaned, when they lost interest, when they fell asleep in their Cheerios. I see why comics want to do stand-up in front of a live audience and why actors love the theater. It's the immediate response.

So when MY CRAZY DAD starts playing on the big projection screen, I'm stoked when I see appreciative nodding. The footage from the funeral home looks very good, and what a location! Then S. appears on the screen, and he gets a big laugh of recognition. So far, so good. Only a few people in class have any idea what the film is about, which is normal. We don't really know what the others are up to during the week. We might get a sneak peek at someone's project on an editing screen or hear gossip about it, but generally the film on-screen is new and fresh for everyone.

This creates a dilemma. For us student filmmakers, there's no advertising our film beforehand. That is, no one knows if a film is supposed to be a drama or a comedy, serious or flippant. The directors don't announce to a class: *this is my comedy!* It's an artificial situation. After all, everyone in the real world has some idea of what a movie is about before they see it in a theater or rent it from Netflix, especially today, where even the most casual moviegoer has ample opportunities to find out every detail about a new film.

In our case, no one knows what will be appearing on the screen. As a result, no one knows whether to laugh or be serious. Our small audience is reserved and waiting. They're looking for obvious clues—certainly no one wants to laugh at a film that's supposed to be serious. With MY CRAZY DAD, there's no outward evidence this is a comedy. There's no comic music, no bug-eyed acting, no pranks or pratfalls. There's S., looking buttoned down and serious at a funeral. There's nothing funny about it, at least on the surface.

When S. goes on his journey, the audience is silent. Only two people in the class have an idea what is coming—me and S. Finally, there's some chuckling as S. begins his hike and begins to fall apart. The location is awesome, and a shot of S. walking far in the distance through a large field, his bright white shirt glowing in the setting sun, gets some appreciative murmurs. Finally, when S. begins digging in the dirt, scratching at it with his bare hands and failing to find any treasure, there is some laugher. It's not the kind of raucous laughter I had hoped for.

But it's enough. At least people aren't sitting on their hands. The lights come on and I get a round of polite applause. S. gives me a thumbs-up.

I move to the hot seat. I'm facing a dozen-and-a-half of my classmates plus FTC.

FTC asks a couple of students for their synopses of the film. That brings some chuckles because the film couldn't be more straightforward. The students duly note the plot.

When FTC asks for suggestions and critiques, a few others speak up, suggesting the pace could be faster, with less walking. I agree with them. Eight minutes is a long time. A few others chime in with concerns about some soft focus at times, and a couple of instances where my exposure was off. But the tone from the students is positive. One student notes I have "lots of control over your craft and good performance from the lead actor."

I sit in the hot seat feeling good.

Then FTC clears his throat. Uh-oh. Here we go again. I wonder what I did wrong this time. He's frowning. He doesn't like the film. He tells me very directly. Here's the entirety of his written notes:

The continuity of the shots are very clear. So I followed the sequence of events very clearly. But at the end I knew no more than I knew at the beginning—a son (?) looks for treasure (?) with a map. Who is the son? Why does he want the treasure? What was his relationship with his mother? With his father? Was his father crazy? Does it matter? Why did we watch this?

Please have reasons that are evident in the film for your next go-around.

A few months after Julie and I got married and moved to Philadelphia, I received an offer from the *Philadelphia Inquirer*. They needed a part-time freelancer. I said *yes* immediately. Julie was deep into her graduate studies in biology at the University of Pennsylvania, even as she was readying her application for medical school. We moved into a tiny apartment in Center City Philadelphia.

Two weeks into my gig, I was assigned a feature story about a kayak race in eastern Pennsylvania, on a Sunday morning. No other reporters were eager to take the assignment. Lucky for me, the temperature was below freezing. Ice lined the river. I got a great feature story and my first front-page Metro story, and from then on I was a go-to guy for human interest stories. Within a few months, the *Inquirer* promoted me. I covered a county courthouse, crime, and cops, and did a lot of feature stories. It was swell working for a place that had a good reputation and deep resources, and where if you put a phone call out, it generally got returned quickly.

Meanwhile, Julie planned to finish a master's degree in ecology, then go on to doctoring. She was accepted to some very good medical schools. Her favorite was the University of Chicago. Perhaps she had fond memories of the time I sneaked her on the plane to a liver harvest.

With love-sparkles still in my eyes, and while in my second year at the *Inquirer*, I started applying for reporting jobs in Chicago.

Yet I didn't get a nibble from the big Chicago papers. Yes, the *Inquirer* liked me, but the recruiters at the *Tribune* and *Sun-Times* didn't. *The Wall Street Journal's* Chicago editor called me, said he liked my clips, and invited me to lunch but emphasized they weren't hiring. I had offers from newspapers in New Jersey and North Carolina and Pennsylvania—places where Julie was also accepted to medical schools—but no offers from any of the big Chicago media outlets.

Yet one newspaper in Chicago did offer me a job: *The Daily Southtown*, circulation fifty-five thousand. It covered Chicago's South Side and the southern suburbs, a working-class paper for a working-class audience. It was a big step down from the *Inquirer*, which had nearly ten times the circulation. It was supposed to be a temporary gig. I ended up working at *The Daily Southtown* during all four years of Julie's medical school. I called it *The Daily Saltmine*.

And the characters in the newsroom! There were foul-mouthed miscreants, neurotic workaholics, the politically connected, the very talented, the inebriated. And those were just the women.

What the paper lacked in prestige, it made up for in character. The newspaper's billboards on South Side Chicago expressways showed a toilet, a razor blade, and a rolled-up *Southtown*. The not-so-subtle message: a shit, a shave, a *Southtown*.

I had great friends at the *Saltmine*. I think being at such a journalistic underdog made us tighter. My colleagues and I played tennis at 6 A.M., dealt cards at night, went to dingy South Side bars on weekends. And never underestimate the skills of people at a smaller paper. Two of the people I worked with have since won Pulitzer Prizes, journalism's highest award. Michael J. Kelley, who hired me at the *Saltmine*, later became managing editor of the *Las Vegas Sun*. Under Kelley's hand, that paper won a Pulitzer Prize for Public Service in 2009 for investigating the high number of construction worker deaths in Las Vegas. And my fellow reporter and sometime-lunchmate M.L. Elrick later moved on to the *Detroit Free Press*, where he won a Pulitzer for Local Reporting, also in 2009. Elrick, funnier than most professional comedians, reported on the text-messaging scandal that resulted in the jailing of former Detroit mayor Kwame Kilpatrick. In addition, my *Southtown* pal David Heinzmann is now a big wheel at the *Chicago Tribune* and an acclaimed crime novelist. (In the spirit of full disclosure, Dave wrote one of my letters of recommendation for USC.)

Working at the *Southtown* put me in some of Chicago's most crime-ridden neighborhoods. Once, while working a night shift, I covered the story of a young woman who had worked her way out of a bad neighborhood only to be shot in the head outside her new job in the supposedly safe suburbs. The shooter was her ex-boyfriend; he hid in her car and ambushed her.

I was sent to interview the woman's mourning family and neighbors in the heart of a South Side ghetto. It was dark. I was the only reporter on the scene. When I got out of my car, I was approached by five men, all older teens. They demanded to know what I was doing there—a white guy wearing a dress shirt and tie. I explained I wanted to learn more about the woman and her successes. They listened, five gangbangers. They told me they knew the woman well and that she never gave anyone any trouble. They were sad and, it seemed, furious. I drove back to the newsroom physically untouched—but emotionally touched—and wrote the story. I made my hundred bucks for the day, and saw another hard example of life in Chicago's South Side.

Julie got pregnant in her third year of med school, and I told Kelley I wanted a cushier job when the baby came. He moved me from the news desk to the features desk. No more breaking news, but I had an easy nine-to-five schedule. It was, however, yet another step down in the journalism world. When our baby was born, a lovely little girl we named Lara, Julie could take only a few weeks away from school. I took three months off work to stay home with our infant. Raising a baby seemed so much more important than covering the news.

When Julie graduated, she received a residency position at the University of Minnesota. For my going-away party, my reporter pal Heinzmann wrote an invitation touting me as "St. Paul's brawniest soccer-mom."

He was wrong on one point. We moved to Minneapolis, not St. Paul.

I thought paradise awaited us. I even planned to write a film script.

I was wrong on the paradise part. Residency for Julie meant ninety-hour weeks, working overnight at the hospital every fourth night. That went on for three years. I freelanced and juggled the domestic duties.

Our bright spot was when we had another daughter, a beautiful girl we named Maria.

The different levels of talent in our 507 class are starting to show. In the first class exercise, the little two-minute film, we all did roughly the same kind of work. Now that we're on the second film, we see a real difference in quality.

J., the guy with the great story about his dying grandfather, remains an enigma in class. He's opinionated and irritable at times, supportive and friendly other times. His second film is a revelation.

It's a play on the silent films of the 1910s. A lady and a robber meet and have a relationship. It's a great-looking work. He's using lots of locations and several actors, all in early-twentieth-century period costume. The video looks very film-like, and the acting and editing seem lifted from 1915. It's very amusing, and the class loves it from the first few seconds. We start clapping and shouting during the film, we're so impressed. The film uses old-fashioned title cards to get around the use of the one-word-only restriction, and the number of the title cards keeps increasing until by the end of the film, title cards are literally raining down on the characters. It's a postmodern take on early silent films, and it's breathtaking how much effort J. put into the film. In a final scene, the characters dodge dozens of three-foot by two-foot title cards that appear to be falling from the sky. When I watch it, I'm wondering how many people J. had helping him throw title cards. And how did he print that many cards in the first place? I'm impressed, and so is the class. My comments are typical: "Very funny and VERY clever."

J. is beaming in the hot seat as he hears us students talk. We are all, I think, taken aback by his talents. I know I feel suddenly unworthy. *Who is this guy?* In the back of my mind, I know that somewhere in our class there may be a real talent, someone who will later turn out to be big, someone in the pages of *Variety*, someone we'll see interviewed at the Oscars. When I watch the film, I can't help but think, *Damn, this guy is good.*

As always, we students critique first, then the instructors get the last word. J. is beaming when FTC begins to talk. FTC is not smiling. In fact, he looks positively angry. He's angry at J., and he lets loose a tirade against the film. The gist of it is this: FTC thought the film was just a clever exercise in getting around the one-word rule. The longer FTC talks, the more upset he becomes. He accuses J. of mocking the process, of not taking the film or the class seriously.

When FTC is done, the class is silent. So is J. He looks shell-shocked. I'm wondering what the hell FTC is talking about. Yes, J. did get around the one-word rule, but incorporating title cards into the action of the film was brilliant and funny. It was raining title cards! In my notes, I had told J. it was "sort of cheating by using all those title cards." But FTC seems to be going overboard. Way overboard. J.'s work was fantastic, and FTC had not a word of praise for it. Could FTC have felt threatened? Jealous? Upstaged by some cocky student with an outlandish story about his dying grandfather and a big helping of talent who makes it look easy?

After screenings, our class gathers for a dinner at the 2-9 Café, a restaurant just a few blocks off campus. The dinners had started a week before, and they were a nice way to spend some time together and socialize. For those screening films, Thursday nights marked the end of an often-frantic three-week push. I drive Fee Fee from the Shrine parking lot to the restaurant in my Oldsmobile, and we talk only about J.'s treatment at the hands of FTC. Neither of us understands it. At the restaurant, we are all there—all but J. We sit at an outdoor table and wonder if he is going to show up. Perhaps he's going to lick his wounds in private.

Fifteen minutes later, J. enters, looking downcast. Almost in unison, we rise to our feet and give him a standing ovation. We are loud, and we hoot and high-five him. I start chanting his name. He looks extremely glad to be surrounded by us. In class, J. had been rendered mute by FTC's criticism. Now in the outdoor bar, he loosens up.

I look at the group of us, smiling and cheering on J. We are cohesive as a group in a way we never were in the first weeks. It seems to be the happiest I've seen any of us. We're having beers, talking excitedly, and the sense of togetherness is tangible. I wonder if FTC staged the outburst as a way to build unity among the class, the same way a drill sergeant will harangue new recruits to create a brotherhood in the barracks. I doubt it, though. My guess is he was just angry.

As we roll into the second month of school, I'm getting to know my 507 classmates a little better. I'm at a real disadvantage going home on weekends to Camarillo. Most of the shooting, and almost all socializing, takes place on weekends. I hear my classmates talk about events on Monday that happened over the previous weekend and I know they are getting closer. I don't share in those events, which makes me feel even more like the odd man out.

Even though I'm missing out on class-bonding time, I am getting to know my two camera partners better.

I'm fascinated at the differences among the three of us. Fee Fee is pretty, but she tends to disappear in our class. She slumps into her chair, seemingly hiding, and often wears baggy, oversized clothes that drag on the ground. Fee Fee doesn't talk much in class, and she sits in the corner, like a shy spider.

My other camera partner is Shorav, the Indian exchange student. He's a PhD student with a thin wisp of a moustache. When he holds court in class, which he does often, he moves his arms and hands as if he's trying to shape his words out of the air. His voice is very high and lilting. I nickname him Showbiz, a name that quickly catches on with the whole class. Showbiz likes his nickname and embraces it. The name is intentionally ironic because he's the furthest thing from a Hollywood player. Showbiz is an academic and he's a free-spirited freethinker. He's so free-thinking none of us knows what he's thinking, and it's compounded by the fact he seems stoned much of the time. Showbiz is always late for class, and he always arrives wearing a satisfied grin. His films—collages of often badly exposed, out-of-focus, seemingly random images—are as far from the mainstream as one can imagine. In class, he gives oddly looping monologues in heavily accented English.

Showbiz admits to me when we exchange the camera one afternoon that he's taking the production class because he's on a scholarship from the Indian government, and if he stretches out his schooling by taking some production classes, he can delay his graduation. He really likes a chance to make experimental film, he says, and he doesn't need to prove himself. For him, it's an adventure, and a free one, thanks to taxpayers in India. He's going to get his PhD eventually in critical studies and, I suppose, teach in India, where he'll confuse and mystify his students just as he confuses and mystifies us.

Showbiz's second film is called L.A. It's a film about people getting on and off a bus, set to music. Some of the shots are out of focus. The scenes are shot on a real Los Angeles city bus, and the characters are just regular riders. It's interesting though, in the same way that sitting on a bench on a busy street and watching people is interesting. There is no story, however, no plot and no actors. Is it a documentary? An art film? A collection of images taken on a bus ride? Yes to all of them, apparently.

In contrast, Fee Fee spent her undergraduate years making films. She has a very good sense of how to use a camera, how to edit. The physical parts of filmmaking don't intimidate her, and her work is glossy and focused.

But her second film is pretty dull. A woman gets a call from her boyfriend and it's apparently a breakup call because she cries a lot and we see flashbacks of the couple. It looks like a music video. It's a standard Film School Drama.

Fee Fee looks out at the world with large eyes that remind me of the oversized eyes on animated Disney characters. She sometimes wears a My Little Pony T-shirt. Her first film was about a cute little stuffed animal that chased people. Her second was the crying woman dumped by the boyfriend.

Then she shows her third film. It hits us like a cast-iron skillet to the skull.

In Fee Fee's third creation, a gorgeous young woman masturbates in bed. The camera puts us viewers *right there* into the action. The woman wakes her hunky young boyfriend. He looks like Adonis, and he is inexplicably uninterested in having sex with her, despite her intense efforts to arouse him. The scene causes several of us males in the class to elbow each other during the screening and whisper how that sure wouldn't happen to us, no-way, no-how.

Then Fee Fee's lead character leaves her hunky boyfriend and goes to a sex-toy shop, where she peruses various latex wear and adult toys. Then she has sex with another hot young woman.

The film is graphic, and looks like arty soft porn. Her film leaves the class as speechless as Showbiz's but for entirely different reasons. We're not prudes, but we're just stunned at the film because it comes from quiet Fee Fee.

And the credits and titles in the film are super-dazzle spectacular. The credits cite Fee Fee's company (there is no company, all of our films are owned by USC) as Rock Star Productions!

All of us look at Fee Fee in wonderment. I thought she was a quiet kid who went home to do needlepoint.

4

Superbabe, *GeezerJock*, and Steve All Fall Down

It was December 2000. Julie and I walked along the beach in Ventura County, California. The Pacific *was* pacific and the air was warm, amazingly warm to us, coming from the freezing Midwest. Families strolled on the picturesque Ventura Pier. The sun was going down. It was a gorgeous evening. All was mellow.

Julie and I were about to move to California. We had left our two daughters in snowy Minnesota and had flown out to look at real estate. We were elated. Life looked so good. For years we had scrimped and saved and both worked around the clock. She had done her medical residency, and I had freelanced all sorts of crud—technical writing, business writing, speech writing. I ghost-wrote a book about home repair for *Popular Mechanics*. And even though I had no idea what I was doing, I had produced a few safety videos for Cargill, the same agribusiness I wrote speeches for. All of it was to earn enough money to pay a mortgage, raise two kids, and support her dream of being a doctor.

Now Julie was going to be working her first real job. It was at a clinic for migrant workers in Oxnard, about fifty miles northwest of Los Angeles. Julie spoke Spanish and loved the location.

And me? I would be launching a magazine that my *Daily Southtown* pal Sean Callahan and I had dreamed up. It was called *GeezerJock*. It would be a snappy, beautifully illustrated monthly magazine dedicated to master athletes—those forty and older. *GeezerJock* had attracted the attention of a deep-pocketed New York publishing investor. He was going to pay us to develop the magazine in exchange for a minority share of the company.

Julie's nickname, given by one of my favorite *Southtown* reporters, was Superbabe. In the fading sunlight on the California coast, Superbabe looked especially superbabealicious. Her long brown hair caught the sun. Her big brown eyes were liquid.

One year later, I sat and watched the ocean from the same place. Huge waves smashed into the Ventura Pier, spraying water high into the air. A storm in the Pacific was calving these monsters, the biggest to hit the coast in years. How different the scene was from a year earlier, when the ocean was so tranquil. How different our lives were.

GeezerJock was dead—the deep-pocketed New York investor had bailed out. The World Trade Center towers were piles of rubble. We had sold our house at a loss when our money ran low. We moved into a rental house. I was making zilch. And Superbabe was now recovering from cancer surgeries. What a year it had been.

Our first clue was the nausea. Julie had gotten pregnant when we arrived in California. She never had much morning sickness during her other pregnancies, but this time she had a *lot* of morning sickness. And most of it came in the evening. Every single night, as predictable as the tide, she'd head for the bathroom and kneel by the toilet and barf. And barf and barf and barf. The pregnancy was very hard. She wondered if it was because it was child number three or because she was now past thirty-five or because she was exhausted from her long residency.

But it was from something different. Late in her pregnancy, Julie felt a lump in her neck. Doctors had to wait until she delivered to operate; it was too risky to do so while she was pregnant. On a sunny warm January day, beautiful little Sophia Rae Boman entered the world. Four days later, Julie went under the knife and surgeons removed half her thyroid.

The lump on her thyroid was cancerous so, less than a week later, Julie had the rest of her thyroid removed. During her second thyroid surgery, an inexperienced surgeon at the Ventura County Medical Center damaged the main nerve to Julie's left vocal cord, leaving her rasping and choking on her own spit. She couldn't talk. She couldn't swallow. She had big bandages around her neck. She no longer had a thyroid gland, and one of her vocal cords was paralyzed. Sophia was two weeks old, Maria was twenty-six months old, and Lara was five years old. I wasn't making any money. Julie was at home, recovering. She received no pay from the clinic while she was home. Within two months, she returned to work. She had to wear a portable loudspeaker on her hip and a microphone around her neck so her patients could hear her thin and damaged voice. She gasped for breath while walking up stairs. I stayed home, taking care of the kids, meeting Julie at doctors' appointments, changing diapers, doing laundry. We'd been in California for less than a year. We had no family within two thousand miles. Few close friends lived nearby. It was a lonely, frightening time.

We watched our money drain from our savings. An earlier last-ditch effort to rescue *GeezerJock* fell short when a story Callahan and I had been asked to write by *The New York Times Sunday Magazine* was killed in the post-9/11 chaos, ending our hopes that the *Times* publicity would be enough to bring *GeezerJock* back to life. Our story was about a fifty-six-year-old grandmother who was banned from international sporting competitions for doping. It was a good story, and we were reduced to dumping it on Salon.com for a few hundred bucks. Google it if you like.

Julie still had to go through radiation treatment. She kept losing weight.

These were supposed to be the good years.

Casper's film history class continues where it left off. I had hoped that Casper would have forgotten my name after the first week, but such was not the case. At the beginning of each class, he calls me out for special attention and often calls on me during lectures.

And then I decide to wear glasses to class, a first for me in grad school. Normally I wear contacts—but the lenses irritate my eyes when I'm spending long hours in front of a computer, which I'm doing every day. My glasses are horn-rimmed jobs, very studious looking. When I enter the auditorium and take a seat, Casper spots me in the crowd. He puts his hands to his mouth in mock shock. Students are still filing into the large hall, and it's several minutes before class begins.

Casper loves being the center of attention. He approaches me. "Look at this. Look at *this*!" he says. "Steve, you look *lovely*." He's playing to the crowd, of course, and nearby students are laughing. I'm his straight man, and he's the comic. He's wearing a wireless microphone, so his voice is projected through the auditorium's loudspeakers.

He takes my glasses off my face and puts them on his. He strikes a pose like a Milan runway model. I don't think he can see a thing—my eyes are really terrible and the glasses have lenses powerful enough for the Hubble telescope—but he doesn't seem to care.

"What do you think? I think they're lovely. Wonderful. You should wear them more," he says.

He takes them off and hands them back to me. Then he turns to the one hundred-plus other students in the class. "Did you know Steve wore glasses?"

It's a rhetorical question, of course. Most of the students in the class have no idea who I am, other than I'm that older guy Casper likes to pick on. Casper turns to me. He appraises me with mock seriousness. "No, I take it back. You have blue eyes. You definitely should *not* wear glasses."

I notice that in this whole exchange I've never had a chance to say a single word. It's all Casper, and it's extremely entertaining. I've never experienced anything like this in an academic setting or in *any* setting. Casper is the most interesting lecturer I've ever heard. He is intense, for sure, but he puts himself into his lectures in a way that is fascinating, and it's often more one-man performance art than academic lecture. If ever there is a Church of the Blessed Angel Doris Day, Casper will be the lead acolyte. It doesn't take much of a spark for him to praise her honors and all-around wonderfulness. And if there is a figure that represents for him the inner circle of hell, it's Barbra Streisand. If Doris Day is heaven-sent, Barbra Streisand shares a smoke with Lucifer. Casper will stand onstage and belt out a few bars of Streisand's signature tunes, singing loud and woefully off-key and waving his arms like a drowning swimmer. Then he'll spend a few moments discussing her awfulness before returning to the lecture at hand. He's funny, opinionated, and erudite—so erudite that many of his comments go flying over the heads of his younger students.

His comic interludes are little breaks to cleanse one's palate before he launches again into his lectures. His talks are so intense that if anyone tries to slip out to go to the bathroom, he'll demand to know why they're leaving. During one lecture, Casper called out a student who tried to sneak up the aisle and chided him for not being able to "hold his water." Some lectures go on for two hours, without a break. I quickly learn not to drink too much water or coffee before a Casper lecture. I later discover a website called Rate My Professors that has more than one hundred comments about Casper. One student posted: "If you like eccentric entertainment while learning at the same time, Casper is for you! But *don't* raise your hand unless you're ready to be *grilled.*"

Later on the same day as the glasses performance, Casper is discussing the post–World War II involvement of the U.S. government in the film business. In the 1930s, the Federal Trade Commission had been investigating Hollywood. The Feds were concerned about the movie industry's vertical integration. That is, the studios made the films and also owned many of the theaters where they'd be shown, thus guaranteeing an outlet for their product. After the war, nearly half of ticket sales came from studio-owned theaters. The Feds under President Roosevelt thought this was monopolistic and sought to bust it up. In 1945, the Feds sued the studios, and the case went to the U.S. Supreme Court. In 1948, a court that had been shaped by the heavy hand of FDR ruled that the studios had to sell their movie theater chains. The case was titled *United States vs. Paramount Pictures Inc. et al.* The ruling marked the beginning of the end of the Golden Age of movie studios.

Casper jots notes on a blackboard. He writes "Paramount et al" and, without missing a beat, asks why Paramount was named the defendant, when there were seven other studios also in the government's lawsuit.

He asks Susan.

Susan silently shakes her head. She doesn't know. Casper asks a nerdish loudmouth who sits in the front row, a guy who always wears a fedora in class. The loudmouth wants to say something, anything, but before he can formulate an answer, Casper points to me. *Steve, tell them why Paramount is named.*

It isn't a question; it is a command. I hadn't read about the specifics of the case, but I had spent more than a year in Philadelphia with the *Inquirer* going through every single court case, criminal and civil, filed in the Bucks County Courthouse. I am familiar with lawsuits.

I answer firmly and loud: "Paramount was named because they were the biggest, most powerful studio."

I don't know if it is the right answer. It is a guess, but I need to *act* like I know it's right. With Casper, sounding like you're guessing and having a rising inflection at the end of a sentence is the same as being wrong. Therefore, I answer as if I'm 100 percent sure.

I'm right. Casper smiles. "We need everyone to see how smart Steve looks with his glasses. Don't they look wonderful? Yes! Paramount was the *largest* studio and thus was named the lead defendant."

And so it goes, another lecture from Drew Casper in film school.

After class, I do a little research into Dr. Casper. I know he teaches several classes, and he's got a nice sideline business doing commentary for DVD releases of classic films (more than twenty at last count). He's close to members of the Alfred Hitchcock family, and he's holder of the Alma and Alfred Hitchcock chair at USC. He's literally written the book about this era of American film (*Postwar Hollywood, 1946–1962*). Early in the semester, Casper tells us he'll be teaching a course on Hitchcock the following semester. He warns us to sign up early because the class fills up quickly. I look around the cavernous 341-seat Eileen Norris Cinema auditorium. I do a little math. The Hitchcock class is four credits. At nearly $6,000 a student, the amount of tuition paid to USC for a semester of one Drew Casper course is more than $2 million. Two million dollars in box office for just one class! He teaches other courses, too. Casper's classes raise an astounding amount of money for the university, and it is all the more noteworthy because it's based on meritocracy. Very few of Casper's students are required to take any of his courses. His Hitchcock class is an elective for nearly everyone who enrolls in it. Even the survey courses—such as the one I'm in, American Post-War Film—are taught by other critical studies professors as well as Casper. If Casper stunk, students could avoid him. And Casper's popularity isn't because he's an easy A. The same online grading site gives Casper low marks for "easiness." Casper is popular because he's good, because he's entertaining, because at the end of a lecture given at machine-gun speed, you feel a connection to the topic you didn't feel before.

That week I take Casper up on an offer he made to us in class. Our grade will be based on a single term paper. The paper will focus on one film, which we can choose from a long list he hands out. He offers to meet with us individually and give us advice on which film to pick. I meet him at his office, and we engage in ten minutes of small talk about Philadelphia, about my background, about his Jesuit education. Then we switch to the topic at hand, which is picking a film for my research paper. He snaps his fingers. "Clark Gable and Doris Day. TEACHER'S PET. He's a newspaper editor who goes back to night school, and she's the instructor. They fall in love. I think it will be a *perfect* film for you."

I tried not to roll my eyes. TEACHER'S PET it is.

For a short, sweet time after J.'s virtuoso display and FTC's tongue-lashing of him, our class is cohesive.

And then it starts to unravel. We're a dozen-and-a-half people with different backgrounds and different temperaments. We work together closely all week long. We begin to get sick of each other. I start hearing complaints. *Did you know so-and-so really screwed you-know-who? Did you know that he did that?* The comments in critique sessions become edgy at times, cutting and personal.

It's all understandable. There's simply not enough time in the day to do everything. The first semester of film school is a constant time-management struggle. Because everyone is rushed, everyone at one time or another becomes irritable.

For me, the biggest blot on my schedule is acting class. We have a good instructor. He's a very empathetic guy, very knowledgeable. But the workload is immense and way out of proportion to other courses. During the semester, we only meet once a week, but the three projects we are assigned are killers. In one project, I'll direct. In the other two, I'll act. We rehearse scenes from famous films to be performed onstage, with lighting, props, costumes.

My first assignment is to play a scene from SEX, LIES AND VID-EOTAPE. It's a fight scene, and I'm cast by the director (a student I'll call H.) as the guy who gets beat up. Another student, P., is cast as the guy who beats me up.

H. has us rehearse for several hours every week. P. is a nice guy, but he's pretty stout, and we ad-lib our fighting scene. It starts innocently enough, but H. wants more drama, more action. He wants us to wrestle. We shrug and follow his direction. It's how we're playing the game. The director is in charge. We're acting as he directs us. Because I'm playing the part of a guy who is passive, I let myself get wrestled to the ground, thrown around a room, kicked in the back. P. is about my weight—close to two hundred pounds—and I feel every pound when he lands on me as I cower on the ground. I really play the passive guy to the hilt. I try to keep myself from getting hurt.

H. seems to get satisfaction out of watching us fight. He has us repeat the scene over and over. A couple of his films have a sado-masochistic bent, and he never expresses any worries or concerns as P. and I crash to the ground in a rehearsal room.

The acting takes its toll. After several weeks of rehearsals, I have a large, oozing, open wound on my elbow, and my knees are skinned enough that I've begun wearing rollerblading kneepads under my pants during rehearsals.

I'm not hating the rehearsals, however. I used to love wrestling as a kid. Our fighting rehearsals are like intense aerobics, which I rather enjoy. However, as P. tosses me onto a carpeted floor, my elbows dragging, I realize I'm paying USC hundreds of dollars to wrestle like I did with my pals in seventh grade. And I am realizing that H. really likes to watch us wrestle.

When the day comes to present our scene in the theater, P. tosses me to the floor and starts his beat-down. The instructor is aghast. "Whoa! Whoa! Whoa!" he yells. "Let's stop that right now." We're sprawled on the ground, panting. He asks us if we had any instruction in stage fighting. We say, no, just real fighting. He shakes his head. I've got a big bandage on my elbow, and my knees are battered. The instructor gently gives the class a tutorial on how to fake a punch and how to push someone against a wall without any impact. "It's all in selling the move," he says. It's all so simple, of course, and I feel foolish that I've been playing a rag doll for weeks.

The instructor then pauses a moment and asks us to reverse roles.

I take a few seconds to compose myself. Then, following the script, I bang on the stage door, and as soon as P. opens it, I burst through and grab his shirt in my fists and lift him a half-foot off the ground. P. is now suspended in the air with my face pushed next to his, and I'm snarling out my lines like I am *pissed*. He looks genuinely frightened (maybe it's just good acting). For several weeks, he's been the aggressor and I've been the wet noodle. Now that the roles are switched, I'm playing the aggressor with everything I've got. The class lets out a nervous gasp.

Our instructor applauds and tells us to "Cut!" I let P. down.

The instructor then lectures us on the importance of learning stage fighting and the greater importance of casting correctly. The instructor pats me on the back, chuckles a bit, and sends P. and H. and me back to our seats.

As I start planning my third film, I fret again about having enough time. I feel the familiar squeeze of anxiety. It feels like some unseen force is very slowly kneeing me in the balls. I see why I put up with weeks of getting beat up by P. It certainly took my mind off my own films. I find the only way to keep the anxiety at bay is to work, and to check off some of the tasks that fill my schedule. I get up every day at 6 A.M. and work until 10 P.M. or later, at which point I have a snack or a beer and then read. I try to get some exercise every day, but some days there's simply not enough time.

My schedule is completely different from that of most of my classmates. I get up hours before they do and go to bed just as they're getting into their groove. I like getting up early because my commute to USC is bearable if I leave before 7 A.M. If I leave after that, I double my commute time. On bad days, the seventeen-mile commute from La Cañada can take an hour. I also get up early because I'm used to it. My kids never sleep in.

With the increasing pressure, I find I'm dwelling on school late at night . . . and getting insomnia. Then one evening, I pick up a copy of *Hot Rod* magazine at the grocery store. I recall reading old copies in my sparsely stocked junior high library. I flip through the pages and find an odd comfort in the discussions of cam durations for Chevy big-blocks, so I buy a copy. In bed that night, I pore over the magazine and lose myself in an article that has nothing to do with film school. I sleep like a baby.

The next morning I size up my next obstacle. I've got a film to shoot, less than three weeks to do it, and I don't want to repeat the near-debacle of my previous film, where I didn't have an actor lined up until the eleventh hour. So this time I tap my easiest source: my mother-in-law. She quit her job at a nursing home back in Minnesota and moved in with us in Camarillo while I go to school. I tell her she's going to act in my movie. She has no choice. She's reluctant but agrees.

I'd rather use a real actress, but I don't want to film in Los Angeles. I'm going to film in Camarillo, fifty-five miles away, and from what I've learned, it's hard to convince actors to travel all that distance and work a long weekend for no pay for a USC 507 project.

Thus, my mother-in-law. She's in her sixties, so she'll provide a decent bit of the all-important *diversity*. Most 507 films feature friends and roommates of the students. Thus, almost every actor is young. My lead is a grandmother. She's available for forty-eight hours of shooting, and, best of all, I won't need a studio teacher.

I don't have a story yet. I begin thinking like an old-time studio honcho who has a star under contract and needs to find a film for him or her. What would my mother-in-law do well?

My brain seems remarkably dense. It is hard to explain this to someone who hasn't gone through film school, but here is the reality for me: prior to coming to USC, I could shoot out good story ideas as easily as breathing. In a newsroom, I'd rattle off what seemed an endless supply of decent script ideas. I was always good at finding and pitching stories. Now, however, in the pressure of school, with a deadline approaching and class assignments filling my schedule, I can't think of a thing. My brain seems to be as responsive as a car out of gas. I turn the key and . . . nothing.

A major drawback to creativity in 507 is the lack of partnerships. We are all flying solo. I don't know anyone well enough in my class to spitball ideas with . . . and even if I did, everyone seems too busy running around to be of much help. I like working in partnerships and bouncing ideas off of other people. I feel alone at USC.

I call some of my former newspapering friends and we talk, but they, too, are not accustomed to having to think of stories without words. They are as flummoxed as I am.

With the clock ticking, I devise a story that has echoes, unfortunately, of my previous two stories. I will cast my mother-in-law as a Dumpster-diving homeless woman who is shunned by everyone she meets. Then, she finds a lottery ticket in a Dumpster. She looks in the newspaper and sees it is a winner. She's rich. Jumping up and down, she imagines the future: social acceptance, a nice house, sobriety. We see her sweet future along with her. But when she goes to reclaim the ticket and collect her riches, the clerk at the convenience store tells her sorry, she had the wrong day's paper. Her ticket is worthless. She trudges back to the Dumpster, and the film fades to black.

This is my one-sentence project, and the sentence is uttered by the clerk who breaks the bad news to her.

It doesn't take much dime-store psychology to realize I might be projecting just a wee bit in these films. A character facing financial hardship dreams of finding a better life through some magical act? Shocking.

I'm looking forward again to shooting near home. I can spend weekend evenings with my family, and frankly, it's far easier to shoot away from Los Angeles. L.A. is home to an incredible number of film shoots. True, there are more and more films and television shows shot away from Los Angeles than in past decades, but the city remains a hotbed of filmmaking. Student films, porn films, low-budget films, television shows, blockbuster films . . . you name it. And because of that, everyone in town seems to be a filmmaking expert, including the police, and merchants, and neighbors, and even that guy walking his dog down the street. As a result, shooting even an incredibly small student project means you are dealing with:

- Police who want to see a film permit. Los Angeles police operate under an ordinance informally called the "rule of three," which means that no permit is needed for shoots that involve three or fewer people, as long there is no disruption. However, there are lots of stories of police shutting down a shoot that doesn't have a film permit, despite this informal rule. And getting a film permit in Los Angeles means you have to deal with FILM LA, the city's awful permitting agency. FILM LA marries Stalinist warmth with south-of-the-border efficiency. Imagine the slowest, least motivated employee at your local post office counter or city hall office. Now, put them in a cool shirt, expensive jeans, and add a big helping of smug "I'll be out to lunch for the next two hours" attitude. They hate dealing with film students. They'd clearly rather be setting up permits for the next Jerry Bruckheimer film than talking to another nervous and ignorant film student.
- Residents who want to "help out" or offer advice or simply want you gone because the last student film crew in the area urinated on the bushes or left behind garbage or did whatever unseemly things students do. Then they'll call the police, who will arrive and ask where your permit is.
- Merchants who figure they can get paid.
- A dog walker who will stop and want to watch, while the dog starts barking. Its owner will explain that it's a free country, and besides, do you have a permit?

I'm gearing up for the weekend when I get bad news. Julie's brother, who is mentally ill, has disappeared from his halfway house. Julie's mother is beside herself with worry. I decide to skip Casper's class and drive home to help out, and I selfishly worry that the issue will affect my weekend shoot. Then my brother-in-law turns up. He's fine. I focus on my weekend shoot. The next day, Julie comes down with the flu.

I had planned on using her mother for two days of shooting while Julie watched the kids both Saturday and Sunday, but I have to trim the shot list to one day. Julie feels lousy with a 102-degree fever.

My plan to use an antagonist goes out the window, as do several locations. I'm feeling frustrated at the bad luck and what feels like my nonstop family drama. I feel so burdened with family obligations compared to my single fellow students. It sounds like a joke: well, my brother-in-law went AWOL from his halfway house, and my wife came down with the flu, and I have to take care of my kids 'cuz my mother-in-law needs a little break. If we had a dog, I'm sure he'd eat my homework.

I feel sorry for myself, and I'm concerned about Julie. She rarely gets sick, even though she is surrounded by sick children all day at her clinic. I'm learning that cancer survivors get jumpy about any routine illnesses.

The film is a disappointment. It is so short, with so little material. I edit it together—a snap—and title it LESS THAN I EXPECTED.

When I screen the film in front of my classmates, they give it a tepid response. It looked good in the first few minutes, just like MY CRAZY DAD, but it is as filling as water and rice cakes. The film is only four-and-a-half minutes long—barely half as long as other class films. My classmates are diplomatic. I sense everyone is underwhelmed. Even FTC doesn't say much about the film.

It just slips under the water like an exhausted swimmer.

Three films so far, and all three have been barely adequate, nothing more. I'm guessing how other students view me: I'm the guy who knows all the answers in Casper's film history class but on the screen puts up mediocre films. I leave class that day biting my lips in frustration. I want to kick a garbage can (or a Dumpster).

I'm more than half done with the semester and my films all have roughly the same story line: a person imagines something better, and it either turns out to be untrue or just a dream. If there's any consolation, it's in seeing that the rest of the class is struggling, too. J.'s third film is a disappointment—as a class we have huge expectations, and the film is a simple affair about a businessman sharing food with a homeless guy. It looks no better or worse than the class average.

After my third film, I can feel my reputation in 507 starting to congeal like turkey fat. I'm falling on my face. I came to USC with dreams of doing incredible films, real stunners, and all I've done so far is make three forgettable snoozers. I console myself with the realization that no one in 507 is a Mozart of the film world. Some of my classmates are immensely intelligent and driven people. Yet no one is making consistently great films. It shows just how hard the process is. In 507, the films are very simple exercises. The crews are tiny, and in theory it should be possible for a good film student to make a series of good strong films.

In reality, it doesn't turn out that way. The semester turns into a slog. The only real surprises come from Fee Fee. One day she brings a swimsuit calendar to class. It's got a dozen bikini-wearing Asian women. The calendar is the kind you'd find in mechanics' bays or college dorms. She giggles and shows us one of the months. There she is, in a tiny suit, strutting her stuff for the camera. She looks nothing like she does in class. The straight guys pick their jaws off the ground and paw at the calendar. She later tells us she's a DJ at a downtown club. We should come, she says. She starts her shift at midnight, she adds.

That week when I enter Casper's class, I'm in for a treat. I had missed the previous class what with my missing-brother-in-law/ill-wife family issues. I'm walking down the aisle when Casper spots me.

"Oh, how nice to see you, Steve!" he says with a bite in his voice. "It seems you chose not to skip today like you skipped last week. To what do we owe the pleasure?"

He's mocking me, of course. And he's wearing his microphone. I have no answer, and even if I did, there's no way to be heard without shouting. He knows how to own the room and how to use the elements of power. I go to my seat and get ready for the lecture.

That day, as the lecture goes on, Casper repeatedly chides me in front of the class for missing the previous week, but he never asks me a question. Several times he makes references to the film the class saw seven days earlier, and then adds: "Of course, *Steve* wouldn't know that."

It's very funny, and I take my lumps. I know he enjoyed testing me in previous classes, and I assume he took it as a sign of disrespect that I missed the previous class. During a break I debate approaching Casper and explaining why I missed the lecture, but I don't. I dislike people offering excuses short of death or disfigurement. I missed the class, period. I made my choice. Now I suffer the consequence. I'm in Casper's doghouse.

In Ross Brown's writing class, I get no such guff. Ross is always upbeat and grinning. I realize partway through the semester I'm on an easy first-name basis with him. Whereas Casper is Dr. Casper, and Tomlinson Holman is Professor Holman, Ross Brown is . . . *Ross*.

As our 507 class gets more edgy every week and the students get more testy, my writing course becomes a little oasis of support for me and for others in the class. In the first few weeks of writing class, I disliked going. The writing from my classmates seemed juvenile and crude. Then . . . the class got better. The writing improved, at least a bit. Mainly, we talked about how we felt relief to be away from our other 507 classmates. It wasn't that there was anything toxic about the people in my 507 class—or apparently in the other two 507 groups—but the constant interaction and the constant critiquing in 507 wore on us all. We were like soldiers on a long march. The writing class was a little island of calm. We shared our stories and laughed and critiqued in a way that was less caustic than in 507.

In the days after 9/11, I was a house dad. I changed diapers, cooked, cleaned, and walked Lara to elementary school, taking the others along for a ride in their stroller. The days became weeks, and the weeks became months. Julie underwent radiation treatment. Then she had a third surgery on her neck at UCLA, where doctors attempted to repair her damaged vocal cord. Life became a series of dirty diapers and doctors' appointments. Even little Sophia seemed to want to get in on the action, as a small sore she was born with on the small of her back became a large bleeding sore, which didn't scab over until she was nearly a year old. Diaper changes often became a bloody affair—which just added to my feelings that life was spinning out of control.

One night in 2002, Julie and I sat down to talk. "You're going stir crazy here," she said. I agreed. She noted I had written a script, done some freelance video production, and had enjoyed both immensely. I agreed again.

"I think you should apply to film school," she said. I blinked. Film school? It did have a nice ring to it. "There's some good film schools right in Los Angeles," Julie added. "Right?"

Yes, there were. I researched them all and one place kept rising to the top: USC. So I applied, ignorant about what I might face and blissfully unaware of how unlikely I was to get in.

Applying to USC's production division is all about words and test scores.

The application required several essays, one a personal state-ment. Mine was sixteen pages long. It started with the observation that, when I was in high school, the idea that I might go to film school seemed as likely as becoming a flying monkey. It ended with the following paragraphs:

This is one of my dreams: I look at my arms. They're hairy, intensely strong, and I'm holding a banana. I am on the edge of a cliff. I jump and then . . . I start gliding through the air, my hairy wings gently beating in the sun. I am a flying monkey.

In another dream, this happens: I am admitted to USC. I do well. I write and direct many good short films. I write screenplays. I sell a screen-play. A studio knows I have attended USC, and they give me a chance to direct the film. I am well trained, so I agree. I direct the film. The film is very good. I hold a statuette at an awards ceremony and thank USC.

And as I walk away from the podium, my hairy monkey wings quietly slide out from underneath my tuxedo, and I flap into the air.

Another essay asked for a character study. I wrote the following, a character for a script I had sketched out, using some of what I had learned hauling human organs for the University of Chicago.

John Calvetti is a thirty-nine-year-old former cardiac surgeon who was ousted from the medical profession three years ago after he was convicted of felony narcotics possession.

Perhaps you saw him on the news. The cops stopped him for run-ning a red light in Baltimore. They found a half-dozen doses of med-ical morphine in the glove box of his BMW and two rocks of crack on the floor. The bigger problem came when Calvetti, stoned and sitting in the back seat of a police cruiser, told the cops they had better also check his trunk. The police found more than 600 doses of morphine he'd stolen from a hospital pharmacy. His face was in all the papers.

The headlines said those who knew Calvetti were "shocked." It was true. He was known as a meticulous person. Always perfect. At high school in a little town in Western Pennsylvania, Calvetti got all As. He did the same in college, at Penn State: a perfect 4.0. He was stunningly focused. At medical school at the University of Pennsylvania, he continued his streak. Calvetti was smart, there's no doubt, but he made his mark by studying harder than anyone else. Calvetti liked to say he would even outwork the Asians.

Calvetti wasn't a popular guy. He was too cocky, too arrogant, too smart and—to prove there is no justice in the world—much too handsome. Calvetti was distantly friendly with nearly everyone he met, but he had no close friends. No wife. No ex-wife. No long-term girlfriends. After his arrest, his lawyers told him to call on his best friends to be character witnesses. He didn't come up with a single name. In court, his lawyers brought up the fact that his mother had died when he was young, that his father, a nursing home administrator, drove him hard as a boy. The jury returned a not guilty on intent to distribute but guilty on felony possession and theft. Calvetti was sentenced to six years' probation. He lost his medical license.

Calvetti first became addicted to painkillers during his residency at Johns Hopkins. He was visiting the room of a seventy-six-year-old patient, a guy who was hardly lucid in the best of times. A nurse came in with a pair of painkiller tablets, but Calvetti shooed her out before she could give the pills to the patient. She left them beside the bed. Calvetti hadn't slept in three nights. He'd been in the hospital for eighteen of the past nineteen days. For the first time in his life, Calvetti admitted to himself that maybe he was drowning, that maybe he couldn't reach the surface fast enough to fill his lungs. Calvetti stared at the pills for several long seconds. And then, carefully but quickly, he swallowed one of the pills. He started taking more pills, and then discovered morphine on his rare off days, and then cocaine on his on days. The spiral was in motion.

The predictable happened after his conviction. His former acquaintances reveled in his misfortune. They laughed about him at the bars, at the sports clubs, at medical meetings. John Calvetti was just wound a little too tight, they would say, chuckling at their own good fortune. But they all thought Calvetti would bounce back, that he would take his licks and come back a chastened surgeon. He was a great one with his hands, they said. He'll come back.

He didn't. He found cocaine just too strong. He loved crack. He loved the way it made him feel, the smartest guy in America, stoned out of his mind on a shitty street in the ghetto. He felt powerful at first, in total control of his destiny, and then, slowly, he just felt wasted.

He sold everything. His guilt and his pity drove him on a two-year journey into the gutter, which is where he was when the twelve-year-old was shot. The boy was a crack runner, innocent as the morning, who got a bullet in the chest when a buyer started waving his Glock around and the thing went off. Calvetti, coming off a high and sitting on the curb, just watched the boy bleed to death.

When the police cleared the scene, Calvetti walked away, puked, and took a bus to his old hospital, where he checked into rehab and made his first attempt at staying clean.

He failed, and failed a second time.

It was after his second drop-off into crack that John Calvetti, one of the best heart surgeons in America, met in a Burger King with one Jose Cardinal, who had an offer: one million dollars if Calvetti would sober up and perform a heart transplant on Luis Mercato de Silva, the vicious and ailing drug kingpin of Tijuana.

USC also wanted an essay about an emotionally powerful moment. I wrote about the day Julie gave birth to Maria, without sedatives, and tried chewing on my arm because she was in so much pain.

USC also wanted my GRE scores, transcripts from my undergraduate days, and at least three letters of recommendation. The essays were easy to do. Taking the GRE was not. I hadn't taken a math class in decades. So I picked up a study guide at the local Barnes & Noble and spent several weeks going through it while the kids napped during the day.

I figured I might have a leg up on the all-important diversity issue, as I guessed not many middle-aged suburban family men applied to film school. The thought that I might be a minority candidate made me smile with a sad sense of irony. In my days as a reporter, there was always the blunt and rarely discussed reality that it was hard to get promoted or hired as a white guy in newspapers. Newsrooms had plenty of old white men, and hiring editors didn't want more if they could help it.

Still, diverse or not, I figured my chances of getting admitted to the production program were still very slim. I had only one real ace in the hole: my letters of recommendation. The USC guidelines state an applicant must provide at least three letters of recommendation, with one being from a former instructor. I thought if three were the minimum, I would send ten.

And what letters they were. I had letters from a Milwaukee television news anchor; a *Chicago Tribune* reporter; a friend who wrote about third-world poverty; a designer with a piece in the Museum of Modern Art's permanent collection; a lead actor on the TV series SPORTS NIGHT; one of my brothers, a former air force captain who was on the flight crew of the world's fastest ten thousand kilometer flight; a pal who'd worked for National Public Radio and now taught at Duke University; my former college English teacher; a former *Saltmine* pal who worked at *Vanity Fair*; and finally, my old college traveling chum named Tom, who had been the best man at my wedding. They all knew me very well, and all of them wrote exquisitely funny and touching letters. My age was an advantage here. I felt bad for my fellow applicants who didn't have such a deep bench.

I sent my application package off to USC late in the summer. I would find out in the spring. Meanwhile, there were diapers to change, meals to cook, bathrooms to clean, laundry to ruin, and bills to pay. Life went on as normal, whatever that was.

I n 507, time moves forward with amazing speed. We receive a lecture about the next semester, and the next big production class, 508. With 508, we leave behind solo filmmaking and work at all times with a partner. The quality in 508 is expected to be much greater, as we'll be spending more than five times as long per minute on our work. Instead of shooting on a relatively cheap video camera, we'll be shooting sixteen-millimeter color film. We are told to think wisely about choosing partners. Whatever the stress of 507, the stress of 508 is worse, we are told—much worse.

We learn a few details about 508. We will be locked at the hip with our 508 partners. A 508 partnership shares the same grade. If one fails, both fail. If one partner quits, the other partner is out for the semester and has to repeat the entire class again.

It's a tremendously high-stakes partnership, and we're asked to make our choices after only a few months in film school. Like others in the class, I hardly know anyone from the other two 507 sections. It's like dating within a very small pool of potential partners.

As class lets out, I walk from Zemeckis with S. The sun is setting, and it's a really beautiful evening in Los Angeles. I tell him I'd like to partner with him for our 508 class. We share an overall comic world outlook, and I tell him I am impressed he does not have any apparent issues with sadomasochism or ego or heroin. He is surprised I am asking so quickly in the mating ritual, as the deadline is several weeks away. I explain I don't like to wait 'til the last minute on anything, much less something as important as a 508 partnership. Despite our age difference, we enjoy each other, and he agrees we'd make a good partnership. I think: *That's easy! A partnership! Whoooo!*

As I walk to my car I feel lucky. I don't know anyone else in our class who would be as good a partner as S.

Having to find a partner emphasizes the fact that our 507 class has become less cohesive as the semester goes on. Turnout is down at the Thursday-evening gatherings at the 2-9 Café. We're all tired, and it seems some of the more biting comments and critiques in class are taking their toll. We are becoming cliquish. I make an offhand comment to S. that *critique* is French for "rip the shit out of someone." We all seem to take joy in snapping at each other's throats.

We are also learning more about FTC. He shows favorites, which becomes fodder for gossip after class. He likes the women in our class, and jokes and offers them support, but with the straight men he's colder. During a break in class one day, I ask him directly—I feel like a reporter again—if he feels hostility toward heterosexual men. "Yeah," he says, nodding. "I do. I consider straight men to be the enemy."

He says the worst are older straight men. "They have been disruptive in class in the past," he says. He feels they've been hardheaded, and he implies they carried an antigay bias.

I ask him if I'm being disruptive. He shrugs and smiles slightly. "Not really, no. You're different."

I'm surprised at his honesty. It's refreshingly direct. Yet I can't imagine an instructor at USC expressing antigay views with the same intensity. If an instructor said, "I don't like homosexuals, I consider them the enemy," he would likely be bounced from campus.

Still, I find myself liking FTC the more he expresses himself. It was blatantly obvious I bugged him from the first moment I showed up in class. At first I thought it was *me*, the individual. Now I realize he disliked what I represented: all the straight white males of the world. One day not long after that, I met him by chance outside of class on a campus sidewalk. He was walking to lunch. I was walking to lunch. We talked easily and even joked a bit. The tension of the early days had mostly dissipated . . . and I thought of inviting him to get a burger with me. But I didn't invite him. I figured he'd consider either me or a Fatburger XXL (or both) too unpalatable. Or maybe I didn't invite him because I still harbored a slight grudge against him for his behavior in class.

Favoritism and outbursts aside, FTC talked about some very important things. His chief tenet in class is: have a point of view. During this period he's writing a film in which the lead character shouts: "I wanna kill every straight fucking asshole!" This character eventually moderates his stance and urges his new lover not to kill *his* heterosexual parents with a bomb, but rather to shame them with a little PDA. "You can't get rid of them with their weapons. I tried that," the lead character advises. "But if you really want to fuck them, all we have to do is kiss, because when two guys kiss, it's like a bomb going off in the straight world."

The promotional material for the film says the characters free themselves "from the homophobic bonds of an oppressive American society."

FTC most certainly has a crystal-clear point of view. He's deliberately stationed himself on the outer edge of queer cinema (a genre term, not my name). In his work, gays are good and straights are very bad. It's us vs. *them.*

The more I learn about FTC, the more I understand him. And the more I feel, well, a little sorry for him. All the heterosexuals in this film are violent or dishonest scumbags. All parents are unaccepting at best, abusive at worst. He's obviously got a worldview different from mine. I do find it slightly ironic that the guy who complains about oppressive American society is an instructor at the world's best film school. That's a pretty good gig. I apparently represent to him the oppressor class. Yet I'm the one without money in the bank, without a job, without power. He's the teacher, I'm the student. I wonder if he sees the irony.

The more I ponder my relationship with FTC, the more I learn about the USC School of Cinematic Arts administration . . . and *my* point of view toward the place. The leadership, so sensitive of doing the right thing, tends to turn a blind eye to reverse discrimination (Lord, how I hate that term) from some key faculty. In my time at USC, I learn that certain people are fair game for jokes and mockery from a handful of instructors. The list is short: white males, blue-eyed blondes, Mormons, political conservatives, religious Christians. Especially Mormons. In an environment where I never once heard a joke or criticism aimed at Jews or Muslims or Buddhists or freethinkers or New Agers or blacks or, heck, even Canadians for that matter . . . it seems the only outlet for venting is against people who live in Utah or go to church or have very little melanin in their skin. When I hear one of these occasional broadsides, I sigh at the predictability. It's so tired and timid. Where's the creativity and boldness in that?

The prevailing attitude coming from the administration seems to be that all of the above (white males, etc.) represent Repressive Power; therefore, fighting the power, whatever exactly that means, puts one on the side of the angels. The student body at USC is a mosaic of colors and sexual orientation, with every class of incoming film students a perfect Benetton commercial. There is diversity in everything at USC, it seems, except diversity of opinion.

At USC's film school, the fashion is to say that America is a corrupt and villainous empire, with injustice under every rock. It is as if the 1960s were sealed in amber. I hate to use the word *irony* so much, but it is ironic that in this bastion of wealth and privilege and luxury, I hear almost unrelenting criticism of the society that creates all this wealth and technology and freedom of expression. I notice the loudest critics often have perfectly straight and dazzlingly white teeth. Sometimes these opinions seem more often based on the desire to be cool than on clear-eyed political analysis.

I'm different from most of my classmates, I realize. My worldview is different. My former girlfriend grew up in East Germany. Her father was imprisoned for five years by the East German government for the crime of speaking to the American Red Cross. She knew what it was like to be monitored by the secret police. My wife worked for three years in an Ecuadorian village where squalor and corruption were endemic. For better or worse, I've spent a lot of time interviewing people, cloaked in the full power of the First Amendment, and I take complaints with a grain of salt. Only in America can a guy like filmmaker Michael Moore get stunningly rich and powerful by continuing to play the underdog card. So, in film school, I sigh quietly when I watch and read a seemingly endless stream of stories that depict (choose a topic) American GIs torturing innocent prisoners, square suburban bourgeoisie squashing someone's dreams, buzz-cut cops brutalizing innocent kids, villainous corporate types, and, of course, bad dads. It truly is the minor leagues of whiny Hollywood, and I often think (as a buzz-cut suburban bourgeoisie former corporate speechwriting dad) *you don't know how good you have it.* I'm guessing most of my classmates didn't grow up in rough-and-tumble towns like Duluth, a place where my eighth-grade shop teacher had us build gun racks and where the biggest employers in town when I was a kid included a U.S. Steel mill, an air force base, and the Duluth shipping harbor.

To magnify my differences, I'm also a bit of an outlier when it comes to gender politics because I've lived the progressive dream, and it gave me a chomp in the ass. To wit: I put my career on the backburner and supported Julie through medical school and residency and her postresidency payback so she could become a doctor and we could have a family. I became the supportive spouse, a feminist's dream. I shunted my career onto the mommy track as her career took off. Then Julie got sick, and she had a very basic desire: she wanted to work less and stay home with her children more. By then, my earning potential had crumbled. We were broke, and I couldn't get a decent job. That's what led me to film school.

The fact is, I had started our marriage as Mr. Public Radio Liberal (but one with a couple of nice rifles in that eighth-grade gun rack). Then I began to realize I had been hoisted by my own petard. I'm reminded of the old joke: *What's the definition of a conservative? A liberal who's been mugged.* I began tuning out public radio. I started subscribing to *The Wall Street Journal*. My views put me in a very small minority at USC.

Now I certainly wasn't expecting anyone on campus to be humming Lee Greenwood's "God Bless the USA," but I often roll my eyes at the reflexive anti-Americanism on campus, and the lack of historical perspective of my classmates, and, well, the simple absence of life-lessons. Granted, some of my gripes are simply an age issue. I was much more idealistic/naïve when I was twenty-two, but my time at USC let me clearly see where the institution sits on the political spectrum.

In classes, discussions regarding the Hollywood blacklisting era are common, as are discussions about the current lamentable state of American democracy. The bogeymen are the standard punching bags of the American Left (McCarthy, Bush, capitalists). I understand their frustration, but I'm intrigued at the lack of a rounded discussion. For example, I never heard any mention of filmmaking conditions in other countries. Sure it's fun to complain, and people are absolutely right to expect nothing but the highest standards in American political discourse. But a *little* comparative analysis would be helpful in film school. Consider Boris Shumyatskiy. I bumped into his name while I was doing a paper on early Soviet filmmaking. Shumyatskiy was the head of the Soviet film industry and the boss of filmmaking greats Sergei Eisenstein and Dziga Vertov. Unfortunately for Shumyatskiy, he failed to please his boss, Stalin. In 1938, Shumyatskiy was executed by firing squad, a blacklisting that was undoubtedly more permanent than the one accorded screenwriter Dalton Trumbo. And on that tiny vexing issue of Islamic radicalism, there was silence on campus, at least from my perspective. From what I witnessed, the only terrorists in student films and scripts were Americans in uniform. Given that my dad was an army officer before getting his PhD, and my brother was a captain in the air force before he went to medical school, it rankled me a bit. I never witnessed a discussion about the fate of Dutch filmmaker and provocateur Theo van Gogh, who was shot, stabbed, and nearly decapitated in 2004 by Mohammed Bouyeri as a protest against van Gogh's criticism of Islam. That's a subject apparently too prickly to broach, as was the controversy that resulted when the Danish newspaper *Jyllands-Posten* printed a series of cartoons depicting Muhammad. From my perch, I witnessed only nothing-to-see-here whistling from ostensibly daring filmmakers. If van Gogh had been murdered by, say, a pale and fleshy Kansas Baptist, ideally a banker at that, I can only guess how many student films would have been spun from that narrative.

So, in the halls of the film school, George W. Bush quite naturally is reviled constantly as a gun-packin' cowboy. Yet a *real* gun-packing cowboy, Che Guevara, is seen as a stud. Che Guevara shirts are popular here. I find it disquieting, and illogical, that historical figures who represent the very antithesis of artistic and academic freedom are often the ones who are enshrined by the academics and artists. Sometimes there's even a passing appreciation of Mao that gets aired. So strange.

The writer Tom Wolfe was right about radical chic. Many filmmakers seem to love asshats like Mao and Che, both in film school and in the real world, and they generally ignore the current messy reality of Islamic fundamentalism. Imagining a film student wearing a T-shirt depicting, say, a Lincoln or Churchill or George Washington is supremely laughable. Che? He's cool. So what if he jailed gays, banned free elections, hated free speech, and unloaded his pistol into people he didn't like? What matters is that his hair was sexy, and he looked great in photos, the hard-Left's Christ.

5

Annette

When I put my application package for USC in the mail, it was early fall 2002. I wouldn't hear whether I was accepted until March. My life went on as normal: getting the kids ready in the morning, walking Lara to school, coming home and doing laundry and going shopping and changing diapers and cleaning the house and putting the kids down for a nap and picking Lara up from school and feeding them snacks and getting dinner ready. I know the thrill and joy and utter monotony of being a stay-at-home parent. I loved being with my kids, and I valued deeply the time I had to share with them and play with them. I was glad I was home with my kids, raising them, reading to them, guiding them.

Yet I didn't have a Plan B. *GeezerJock* was dead in the water. Julie had another year in her government-mandated job. Newspapers were laying off my friends.

Month by month, Julie got stronger. That fall, I took her and the kids down to USC, and we explored the film school. It seemed such a foreign place . . . all these film students who seemed so familiar with each other, smoking and sitting on an old rickety picnic table and talking. I walked by with my family and the film students ignored us.

One Saturday night, Lara had a friend over to watch a movie. During the film, I got a phone call from my parents. They were crying. My younger sister, Annette, was in the hospital in Duluth. She had leukemia, diagnosed just that evening.

Her cancer was very aggressive. She had two young children, a boy and a girl, and a husband.

When we were young, Annette and I would pour water on our sloped driveway and watch the rivulets stream down toward the curb. We named the rivulets and urged them on like we were watching a horse race. With the peculiar logic of preschoolers, our favorite names were Nixon and Snoopy, both dogs in our world. We'd stand there and yell, "Go, Nixon! Go! Go, Snoopy, faster!" I don't recall us choosing sides. They were just two water rivulets slowly running down an asphalt driveway.

In early March I traveled back to Duluth with my three daughters. During the day I was a sad Pied Piper who led around Annette's two small children and my own kids. At night I would visit Annette in the hospital. She was very sick. Four months earlier she had been a vibrant, healthy woman without a hint of problems.

She died a painful death. It snowed hard the day before her funeral. It was late March.

When we flew back to California after the funeral, we seemed to be on the other side of the world. The sky was blue and sunny, and the temperature was in the seventies. Our mailbox was stuffed with bills and junk mail and catalogs. Then I spied it: a thin letter with the USC logo. With a shock, I remembered my application.

I ripped it open. It was a form letter, thanking me for applying, but the length of the letter itself had already told me all I needed to know: I wasn't accepted.

I tried not to show my disappointment. I realized that the sun was shining, my kids were healthy, and Julie was healthy. After all that had gone on in the previous few months, and the death of Annette, graduate school at USC seemed a petty issue. Maybe next year, I thought.

That night I tossed and turned. I dreamed about a surreal journey that involved me being in film school—it was a fantastic place—and when I woke I felt a painful ache in my chest. I wasn't going to film school. That was reality, just like Annette's death. I didn't want to admit to myself how disappointed I was by the rejection. The next day it was back to normal: Julie went to work, I walked Lara to school. A few more days like that went by. Then there was another letter from USC. I ripped it open. Longer this time—it said I was *accepted* to USC. I read it slowly. I called USC's admissions office. A nice woman answered the phone, and I asked her in my most mellow radio voice if the letter was legitimate.

Yes, she said.

I asked her about the previous letter. She apologized and said there had been a clerical error and that some people on the acceptance list had inadvertently gotten rejection letters. (Some of my classmates later reported the same thing.) She apologized again. I thanked her, hung up, and jumped around our living room, whooping and pumping my fist into the air.

Three-year-old Maria and one-year-old Sophia, both with big eyes, started mimicking me. They pronged around the house, excited. Maria finally asked me what I was yelling about. I picked her up and held her high in the air. "I'm going to USC, honey, the best film school in the whole world!" She squealed and laughed as I tossed her in the air.

When I put her down, she asked me another question: "What's film school?"

My fourth film is coming up and I want finally to hit one out of the park. The three 507 groups hold an informal film fest, but I'm too embarrassed to show any of my first three films. On the night of the screenings, nearly every 507 student is there. I don't want to go. I make up an excuse not to be there. I feel like a complete outsider.

Meanwhile, the 508 partnership dance has been quietly going on behind the scenes. We don't have to formalize the partnerships until after spring break, but from what I'm picking up on, most people are already in partnerships.

One day at the end of Holman's sound lecture—the only class that has all three groups of us 507 students in one place—a trio of students takes the podium. They're from the previous semester and they're looking for 508 partners. They go onstage, one by one, and give short speeches that explain their predicaments. They give rather pitiful "choose me" pleas.

The presentations drive home the point about how serious these 508 partnerships are. Three students from an earlier 508 class are forced to beg to find new partnerships, all because their original partners failed to make the journey all the way through the semester. Wow. We understand USC isn't joking about this joined-at-the-hip thing.

I'm glad I've got my partnership set up. I'm also pleased with my progress on my fourth film. I'm going to get around the language barrier by using animals as actors and having human voice-overs. I'm going to create a doggy detective film, shot as a noir film. I'll have a dog-napping with a Sam Spade-like dog detective on the case. I intend to shoot it in black and white. I spend hours day after day on the phone, calling dozens of animal trainers in the area. L.A. has a *lot* of animal trainers who provide cats and dogs and mice and elephants and bears to the moving picture industry. Think of it the next time you see a cute little kitty in a commercial or a bear in a movie. Someone in L.A. is training that animal, and transporting it, and hoping it acts on command. I cold-call these places and pitch my idea. I tell them I want to use their animals, for free. I finally find a dog trainer who is willing to play along. She has several younger dogs she's training for Hollywood roles, she says, and they could use the practice. She doesn't have a lot of dogs, just three that would work. I'm ecstatic. This will be an awesome film.

This is what happens to people in the middle of 507. They think absolutely terrible ideas are brilliant. At least this is what happens to me. I've got my shooting weekend coming up and I'm swamped with work and I'm going to make a film using dogs. What a knucklehead I am! There's a long-running joke in Hollywood: never work with kids or animals. My first little film was with my kids. Now I'm planning to work with animals.

My schedule is just jammed. I'm rehearsing a long scene from THE PLAYER for my acting class. I'm doing a recording exercise for sound class and catching up on class reading. I'm writing fifteen pages for Ross Brown's screenwriting class. In Casper's class, I have the class term paper due at the end of the semester, and I'm setting aside time to do research at the Academy of Motion Picture Arts and Sciences' film archives museum on Vine Street. My paper on TEACHER'S PET needs to include the production history, social impact, historical setting, and critical reaction to the film.

Spring break is fast approaching, and I'm going to be taking part of it to drive to Arizona to meet up with my brothers and parents. We're gathering on the first anniversary of Annette's death.

The stress is getting to me. One morning as I drive to USC, I think about Annette. I'm lost in thought when I arrive in University Park, but I see I need gas, so I pull into a service station near USC. It's about 7 A.M., and as I push a nozzle into the Oldsmobile, I see a good-sized guy in shabby clothes approaching other people filling their cars. He sneaks up on people as they pump their gas and corners them against their cars. He's an extremely aggressive panhandler, and I watch him receive several dollars from a smaller woman who seems frightened. From where I'm standing, the situation is on the razor's edge of robbery.

The panhandler is maybe thirty, handsome, and amazingly strong-looking for a junkie hitting up people at a Shell station. As I watch him, I feel a flash of anger. How come this guy is still alive? My sister got a horrible form of leukemia and died. She spent her life helping people. She had her own research lab and, in the irony of all ironies, had just gotten a nearly one-million-dollar grant to do research into the type of cancer that killed her. She didn't extort money from people at dawn at a gas station near USC.

As the guy walks toward me, I step toward him. I want to fight. I feel rage and sorrow well up in my chest. I want him to absorb the unfairness that was dealt my little sister. I get in front of him and unleash a stream of colorful and insulting profanities.

He stops in his tracks. I don't think he's used to this from USC faculty. He's about my size, and we stand just a few feet apart. I want him to try to hit me. I'm just itching for him to make the first move. I know the gas station has the parking lot videotaped, and I want him to give me a justified reason to kick his ass. I insult him, tell him he's pathetic. I know if he moves toward me, I'm going to hit him hard, right in the ribs, and I know he'll drop like a stone.

A little voice in my head is aghast. I'm not a guy who picks fights. But part of me—a big part—now wants to battle with something tangible, and I want to fight this douchebag who's putting the lean on fifty-year-old women refueling their Civics.

He's surprised, and he starts backing up. He shakes his head and calls me crazy. I follow him out of the parking lot, calling him a litany of colorful and profane names. I *am* crazy.

Later, when I park on campus, I take a few minutes to compose myself. I realize picking fights at gas stations with druggies at 7 A.M. is not good behavior.

Meanwhile, others in 507 seem to be losing it, too. One of the women in class goes to the hospital for an extended stay because of a kidney infection. She blames it on overwork and her non-stop consumption of Red Bull Sugarfree. One of the men suffers from a bad bout of food poisoning. He says his immune system is down. Everyone looks tired. When we do short assignments in class, Fee Fee says she just wants to sleep. The dynamic in 507 is becoming more confrontational. My elbow still oozes blood from the "acting" I did under H., so I can't look at him without questioning his judgment. The fundamental fact is we are tired of each other. We are in class together seemingly all the time. Ideally, we could be gelling as a group, but we're not. At least, I'm not gelling with the group.

On Wednesday, I get a call from the animal trainer. She says "something came up" and has to postpone. I tell her I don't have any flexibility in my shooting schedule. I consider pleading with her, but that same little voice in my head says: *It's a really stupid idea anyway, Steve.*

So, on Wednesday afternoon, just before Casper's lecture, I shift gears. I'm going to shoot a documentary instead. It's the only thing I feel I can do in the short time I have. Casper, as usual, calls me out in class—thanking me with great sarcasm for showing up—and then ignores me. He goes so far as to stroll between the rows of seats, asking questions, and then pauses in front of my seat, glancing past me as if I'm not there.

In 507, I notify FTC I'm changing my plans. I'm going to shoot a documentary about the hard-core sport-bikers who use a public highway in the foothills above Los Angeles as their personal racetrack. He's fine with that. Perhaps surprisingly, our relationship has warmed considerably. I've gotten to the point of joking with him, and he's gotten to the point of laughing at my jokes, at least a bit. It's a far cry from the icy reception I got in the first weeks of the semester.

After class, I'm feeling better, and I talk to S. about sealing the deal for our 508 partnership. We need to submit some paperwork in the coming days. He stops and tells me he's going to partner with someone else.

"What?" I feel like I've been kicked in the privates.

S. says he's going to work with the Goth girl in our screenwriting class. She's a smart student and a hard worker, so she *would* make a good partner. She's funny, too. Her most recent 507 film was a massive undertaking, and she pulled it off. Then S. reluctantly volunteers that he really *likes* the Goth girl, in that boy-likes-girl way. I understand it now.

I'm stunned, however. And upset. I ask him why he didn't tell me earlier. He says he just didn't want to break the bad news to me. He *looks* like he feels bad. I'm angry at him, not for choosing someone else but for waiting so long to break the news. I'm angry at myself for assuming we had a partnership, and the definition of "assume" pops into my head: *an ass out of u and me*. I know most people have sealed a partnership deal already. I shake my head, take a deep breath, and wish him luck.

Over the next twenty-four hours, I approach a handful of my classmates. They've already partnered up, as I suspected. One classmate bemoans my timing. "I just made an agreement," he says, and adds that he'd rather work with me. I take the last comment with a grain of salt. It's the kind of thing you tell someone to let him or her down easy.

I feel awful. It's embarrassing. I strike out again and again. Everyone I could imagine working with is paired up. Because the hour is late, I approach people with the subtlety of a used-car salesman. I tell myself it'll be okay, that I'll find a good partner, *any* partner, but S.'s decision and my fruitless search make me feel like crap.

On Friday, I approach one of my classmates in Ross Brown's class. She's in her thirties, a lesbian, and pleasant, straightforward. I ask her outside of class. "That's *so* nice, Steve. I'd really love to, but . . . "

I dread the "but." She has a partner already. I make a list of people who might be available. It's a very short list. A couple of my classmates assure me that people aren't shunning me because of my abilities, which makes me feel a *little* better. It's clear, however, that I'm not a desirable product. I'm gone a lot on weekends. I'm older. My films have been ho-hum. I think Che is an asshat.

Even Casper has been ignoring me.

After Ross' class, I stand on the sidewalk with several students. They give me a pep talk, tell me that everything will be okay. I've heard these optimistic speeches before. I heard a lot of them at Annette's bedside, just before she died.

That night should be a celebration. Spring break has started. Classes are off for a week. And I feel absolutely miserable. The more I look at it, the more I feel bad about the long term to come. Whoever I eventually partner with—*if* I can find a partner—is likely to be a less-than-ideal fit. I'll be spending four months with that person. It makes my entire film school future look bleak.

That night I drive to Carl and Irene's home. I'm planning to interview motorcyclists in the morning for my documentary. I'm working into spring break because my talking-dog fiasco put me behind schedule. I call Julie and she tries to cheer me up, but I'll have none of it. I avoid Carl and Irene. I don't want to waste their time bitching about what feels like being shunned for the high school prom. I sit up that night drinking bourbon by myself, a Friday-night lonely loser.

Later, I hardly sleep. I realize the hole I'm in. I ponder my options. No 508 partnership = no going forward. Bad 508 partnership = bad experience and mediocre films. The reality sinks in. Nearly three months in film school and I realize where I stand in our classes' pecking order. I'm that chimp on the outside.

On the day of my documentary screening I am pensive. I don't know how it will be received. I had hours of interviews and B-roll, and condensing it into an eight-minute film with a coherent message took dozens of hours. For the entire week after spring break, I lived in the editing lab.

I named my film WHEN GOLF IS TOO SLOW after one of the riders, who explained that he had no taste for sedate sports like golf. He liked going 170 miles per hour on a motorcycle instead.

I chose the topic because I felt a kinship with these riders. When I was a teenager, I traveled by motorcycle. I loved motorcycles, and I rode them fast. I read everything I could find about them. I subscribed to four motorcycle magazines and memorized bike statistics the way other kids memorized baseball trivia. My brothers owned bikes, I owned several, even my dad bought a little Honda sport bike and commuted to work on it.

When my friend Scott and I traveled to California as eighteen-year-olds, we were both on motorcycles. At the time, I had heard about the Angeles Crest Highway. It was described in motorcycle magazines as some sort of spiritual place, offering riders a glimpse of either heaven or hell. One day, I rode my Kawasaki on the Crest, and it scared me. It's an unforgiving, narrow road with blind corners and rock slides and sheer drop-offs. It's also a hugely popular road with motorcyclists, who see it as a test of their skill and daring. Every year, many are injured on the road and several die.

I want to find out what attracts these riders to the Crest. When I edit my little documentary, I want to be able to explain the attraction to outsiders. I'll attempt to tell the story from an insider's perspective. I have no narrator's voice-over, just the words of the riders. Even though I haven't written a word in this film, it feels very personal.

When the screening gets done, there is a moment of quiet from the class. It is a reaction that normally comes after a really bad film, when everyone waits for someone else to clap first.

This isn't the case. A split second later the class breaks into loud applause—very loud applause. The class loves it. The reviews are a love-fest. There are some comments about doing a better job lighting some of the subjects and adding more and better B-roll, but everyone seems to feel connected to the film.

Especially FTC. "Wow! That was excellent. I thoroughly enjoyed this film. Interesting topic, well presented," he wrote on his comment sheet. "More visuals would have been nice but taken longer to shoot it too, so this will do. Excellent film. Well done!"

I leave the screening walking on air. This is only the second documentary in our class so far, and it is by far the best. I have my mojo back.

True to form in my first semester of film school, the highs and lows quickly are swapped. It's an amusement-park ride, a veritable manic-depressive's paradise. Everything went great for WHEN GOLF IS TOO SLOW. Now, in acting class, I'm feeling at the bottom of the curve.

In my rotation as a director in acting class, I'm in charge of doing a scene featuring J. and one of the women in our class, a very polite and soft-spoken novelist. J. is, simply, a pain in the ass to direct. He's extremely nervous, which I find odd because he seems to have no lack of confidence when he's behind a camera. He is constantly, always late—a common film student malady. On this day I've had enough. The novelist and I have been waiting for forty minutes when J. shows. He hasn't gotten his lines down. I'm upset with him and tell him. I'm also upset for reasons other than J.—it's the weekend, and I'm on campus instead of home in Camarillo because of this rehearsal. I miss my family, and I'm feeling a pang of *what the hell am I doing here?* We start to argue. He yells at me, I yell at him. We jawbone at each other for a few moments, then we both calm down. We continue our rehearsal. Not only is he chronically late, he's jumpy about acting. The nervousness I can deal with. I can't deal with the inability to budget time.

Student film shoots are notorious for tardiness, you see. The issue stems mainly from the notion held by many students that artists don't watch the clock because they don't *need* to watch the clock. Apparently, they think creativity can't be forced. Thus, the notion goes, only conformists who don't "get" creativity pay attention to time. What it means in film school is that a great many students are perpetually late. And when they show up, they ignore deadlines. Thus, a student-led event scheduled to run from, say, 4 P.M. to 8 P.M. will actually get going at about 4:40 and run 'til 9:30.

It drives me bonkers. I know I'm different from the other students in this regard, and it's not an obsessive-compulsive thing. It's just that I've been watching the clock my entire career. Radio news is every hour, on the hour. Stories are written and produced to the second. Organ transplants are a life-or-death operation where every second counts. In newspapering, the presses run like clockwork. When a paper goes to press, there's not much that is going to hold it back. (Yelling "Stop the press!" *is* a romantic notion, however.) And I've got three children who follow a pretty basic schedule of mealtimes, bedtime, wake-up time.

Of all the aspects that define me in film school—age, race, sexual orientation, cinematic taste, world outlook, etc.—my punctuality sets me most apart from my classmates. I show up on time for all my classes, and rehearsals, and shoots, and meetings. I get impatient when classes or rehearsals or shoots or meetings run long. I don't mind spending more time on an important project—if it really warrants the time—but most projects in school don't.

I think another underlying reason many students are late is because they've never had to be punctual. They're mostly single. Many have never had a boss tapping a watch or an editor demanding a story or a hungry child waiting for lunch.

The issue of timeliness is not just a bugaboo of mine. Our instructors constantly chide students for being tardy, and they explain that it simply won't fly in the working world. They repeat over and over: "On a movie set, if you're on time, you're late." I always feel patronized when hearing this. I think, "Well, duh!"

This is the issue between J. and me. J. is late, and I'm upset. We discuss, and agree to do things differently in the future.

By the next class, however, the gossip mill has turned our argument into a full-blown fistfight. "Did you and J. start hitting each other?" my classmate Rebecca whispers to me.

I roll my eyes. No, I explain, we did not punch each other. We both yelled a bit, that was all. Rebecca doesn't quite believe me.

During this time, I also find a 508 partner. She is a fat and quiet woman who took the stage during Sound class to explain her predicament. We met, and we instantly agreed to be partners after a short conversation over coffee. We are both 507 survivors floating in the ocean, and we both feel lucky to have found someone, anyone, to partner up with. We are an odd couple, and I know next to nothing about her. We agree it should be an entertaining ride.

My fifth and final 507 film is fast approaching. I'm learning from my mistakes. My great friend Tom wants to act for me, and he's willing to fly out to Los Angeles to do so. He was my best man, I was his, and through the years of our friendship, he would occasionally lament that he was not pursuing his artistic side. Tom went to law school, practiced overseas, and works as an executive coach but had no acting experience. I now give him his chance. I write a script about a lawyer who has a drug problem and eventually kills himself. Tom doesn't do drugs and so far he hasn't committed suicide, so it's only partially casting to type.

For my character's wife, I put a notice on NowCasting.com. I'm looking for a woman from the age of thirty to forty-five for one day's shooting. I state that I'm a USC student, shooting a low-budget student film.

I get 176 postings from actresses interested in the part.

I know Los Angeles is filled with hungry actors, but I can almost smell the desperation as I click through page after page of headshots. USC has an agreement with the Screen Actors Guild that allows SAG members to act for free. Most of the women sending me postings are not SAG actors, but a few are. What makes a USC film appealing is that actors hope to meet with a director who will be a rising star.

I know a considerable number of people in the industry say wannabe filmmakers would be better served by spending their tuition money on just making a movie without going to school. The writer/director Robert Rodriguez even wrote a book about it, *Rebel Without a Crew.*

Rodriguez makes a compelling case, but it's not going to work for me. I'm not connected enough with like-minded people, and I don't know how to do the mechanical filmmaking steps without some guidance. As a film student, I get access to things like SAG actors and liability insurance, without which it's impossible to get a film permit at many public places. Rodriguez shot in Mexico, where he didn't need any stinkin' permits, and where he shot incredibly cheaply.

Tom arrives, and together we look through the electronic head-shots. There are pages of beautiful women. Tom is agog. We agreed this would be an incredible way to meet women—if we were single, and younger, and interested in that sort of thing. Thinking of Tom's marriage and my own, I bypass the hotties and contact a pleasant-looking but overweight actress. She's eager to work.

I look at my shooting schedule. What a joy! I have three full days: Friday afternoon through Monday morning. In my four previous films, I felt intensely pressured by time and shot each film essentially in one day. No wonder my fiction films were so weak—there was simply not nearly enough time to shoot a simple eight-minute student film, no matter how good the preproduction.

Film students at USC have a pattern. Classes are clustered on Tuesdays, Wednesdays, and Thursdays, with a few courses offered on Monday evenings and Friday mornings. It's a schedule that allows film students to have the maximum amount of time for shooting and editing on weekends.

In the afternoon, Tom and I go over the script over glasses of iced tea at an outdoor table on a cloudy and remarkably humid day. We feel very *Hollywood*. I explain that in this film he'll play a strait-laced lawyer with drinking and drug issues whose life unravels. His wife leaves, he loses his house, he loses his job, he finally kills himself. It's meant to be dark and sincere, and I'm finally joining the crowd. This film will be about drugs and depression and death, the holy triad in film school. No more comedies. I'm going to show my classmates I can go dark with the best of them. I figure it will be my magnum opus, and after my mini-triumph with the motorcycle documentary, I'm on a roll.

That evening we begin filming, and the actress joins us. She's a sweetheart, and the three of us shoot until well into the early morning.

Tom is easy to work with, and he throws himself into the role. Like my stage fighting, he blurs the line between acting and being.

Thus, when I ask him to act like he's throwing up, he actually barfs into a toilet. When I ask him to act like he's snorting cocaine (in our case, some white flour), he inhales it. On the first night of shooting, with our actress present, I ask him to act like he's a bit tipsy. Tom takes this one to heart. He starts getting liquored up.

In fact, the more Tom gets liquored up, the more relaxed he gets. A scene calls for Tom's character to have an argument with his wife. He's fairly drunk at this point. In his first take, he's sedate. I gently tell him to "amp it up." In his second take, he's still sedate. Same with the third. I tell him I want more. I want him to show his crazy side. Tom takes a big swill of bourbon and prepares for the scene. I stand behind the camera and remind him to really let go.

This time Tom unleashes. He's screaming so loud I'm afraid someone is going to call the police. His face is beet-red and it looks like he's going to blow a gasket. Spit flies from his mouth. He looks absolutely enraged.

When we play back the scene on my video monitor, we all fall to our knees with laughter. His teeth flare like a howler monkey in the midst of a death battle. I can't tell if Tom is channeling Richard Burton in WHO'S AFRAID OF VIRGINIA WOOLF? or if he's channeling something he saw on Animal Planet. So much for seriousness.

For the screening of this film I've cleverly called THE LAWYER, I bring Julie to class. It's the first time she's seen any of my classes in action. She takes a day off work and we drive to USC. When class starts, I introduce Julie to everyone in 507. They are all, in a word, impressed.

FTC seems especially impressed. And I'm also not surprised. Gay guys seem to go gaga over Julie. It's something I've witnessed since we've been married. They treat her like a more stable Liza Minnelli.

As a result, with Julie present, the dynamic in the room is very different. Everyone is really *really* nice, and their critiques are kind. But the reality is THE LAWYER falls flat as a pancake, and no one wants to be too blunt. The critiques from the students are uniform. They praised me for effort but not for subtlety. As FTC writes in his critique:

> *I very much respect the strengths displayed in this film—the well-cast actors, the locations, the serious ideas. So, excellent work on all that! What would make your film even better would be a more subtle approach to material—although the plot is clear, it also has certain issues up front how to make a story we kind of know new or especially interesting. Perhaps using the wife as the main character or developing the story in a new way . . . something different and revealing.*

During my time in the hot seat, I'm gently reminded that my lawyer didn't act like a guy messed up on coke. I'd edited one scene so the lawyer snorts coke and is next seen sleeping. To the drug-savvy hipsters in class, the scene proves I'm an idiot.

I confess on the hot seat I've never seen cocaine. A few classmates try not to snicker. When I later show Tom a copy of the film, he laughingly calls the scene "the snort and snooze." Just when I think I'm making a film cool enough for film school, I show my true colors. I'm just not cool. I'm not worthy of wearing a Che shirt.

As Julie and I drive back to Camarillo, an obvious thought hits me: my best film, by far, is one I know something about. I know what it's like to ride fast on a motorcycle and what drives those sport bikers. The class loved my documentary. All my other films were on subjects I know little about.

I realize I've been ignoring the most basic tenet of Writing 101: write about what you know. That night, Julie and I get to Camarillo in time to tuck the kids into bed. A few hours later, Maria wakes up with an upset stomach. At 4 A.M., she throws up. I stay up with her, rubbing her back and cleaning up after her, and at 7 A.M. I drive back to USC for my Friday-morning screenwriting class. I am very tired. I don't want to miss the class, which I have grown to love.

When Ross Brown overhears me telling Paulo about staying up during the night with Maria, he chides me for coming back to USC for one class, but then he chuckles and tells me how he spent many times holding one of his young daughters' hair so she wouldn't get vomit stuck in it.

Brown is the one instructor I have who likes to share small talk about family. In that regard, he's an odd duck among my teachers— the majority of whom are wedded to their careers.

As I sit in class, I ponder this observation. Brown is an optimist, and he's obviously made a nice pile of money in Hollywood and he's very family-centric. Also, in his class, we critique our writing in a way that's much more supportive than the critiquing we do in 507 screenings. There, we often act like little pit bulls that seem to relish tearing each other apart.

During a class break that day, the other students and I discuss how we consider this screenwriting class a refuge from the pressures of our 507 classes. I'm not alone! "God, I'm really tired of that class," states the affable lesbian, who is in a different 507 section. We all nod in agreement. Everyone seems sick of the dynamics, of the workload, of the constant need to be "critical" of the work of our classmates, and of the dual pressure to both be tough and yet supportive. In screenwriting, we share eagerly, and we are much gentler in our criticism. I know Brown could tear our writing apart if he wanted to, but he doesn't. He emphasizes ways to improve our scripts, which range from the sublimely awful to the pretty good.

I look back at some of the critiques I wrote in 507. As I reread them, I'm struck by how pissy I can sound.

To M.: "I was confused; therefore I AM confused, and can't say shit."

To S.: "Way too dark in disco and outside . . . Oh, yes, one other thing: learn to spell. 'Their' is not 'thier' and punctuation could also use help. Oh, and it was confusing."

To J.: "Too over-acted. Too much weeping and anguish."

To A.: "Very jumpy camera. I don't know if you wanted that or not, but it was very distracting. I didn't see the connection in shots . . . Also, exposure and focus were off in places."

To M. again: "Gee, where to begin? I liked your previous films a whole lot. I didn't like this'un though. Didn't believe the actors, didn't buy the plot. I think one group of female assassins per generation is enuf, and Quentin T. beat you to it. Some strong sixty-cycle hum on your sound, too. Perhaps more use of 'fuck' would help."

To Showbiz: "Story weak. I didn't know what was happening, other than people riding a bus, which I don't really like doing much anyway. Some bouncy and out of focus shots."

To J. again: "I don't know what this is about. It was Fellini-esque but without his bigger sense of story. The biggest problem: what in the hell was this about? I like foreign films a lot and most of the time I don't need subtitles to know what is happening. Not the case here."

Those are just the written comments. The verbal comments were less diplomatic.

With my final 507 film done, I focus full attention on my term paper for Casper's class. I spend several days at the Academy museum library. There I found a thick file of fifty-year-old production notes from TEACHER'S PET. I spent hours poring over them, realizing how similar my travails are to those faced by the producers of this film, albeit on a vastly smaller scale. I read how the director, George Seaton, took ill one day, causing production to be halted. I learned that Doris Day was despondent over the death of her brother, who had died of a cerebral hemorrhage just days before filming. I read about the *five years* in delays getting the film made, mainly because the producers wanted Clark Gable for the lead role and they needed to wait for a gap in his schedule. I saw how much it cost to build each set. I read the contract and daily call sheet for Clark Gable, who started every day at 9 A.M. and was contractually obligated to be released at 5 P.M.

In the beginning of the semester, I had grumbled about having to write a term paper for a critical studies class. Now, digging into the Paramount production archives, I am gaining far more insight into real-world filmmaking than I had anticipated. I can't hide my eagerness. The policy of the museum is to allow nothing in the reading rooms but paper and a pencil. I write down page after page of notes. I'm doing original research, and it's much more satisfying than writing a paper citing a hundred barely understood, esoteric concepts. I even try to track down the last living crew and cast members of TEACHER'S PET for interviews but to no avail.

For a week, I work on the paper nonstop. The entire grade is based on it, and, more important than the grade, I'm doing it for honor. I want to see how I can do in Casper's class. I want to test myself against his other students, those who come from Stanford and Harvard and Yale. Nearly every 507 student is taking Casper's class. My movies have been erratic. Casper himself picked the film for me, and ironic or not, it is tailor-made for me to do something with it. Yes, I have a chip on my shoulder. My college isn't Ivy League; I worked long years as a reporter; and I spent longer years writing manure-handling test manuals for farmers and year-in-review speeches for food-company executives. I want to see how I measure up with my classmates.

Back on campus, we're doing our last acting exercises, and we're watching the last group of our 507 films. I was in B group. Now it's C group's time in the hot seat.

Eli shows a film that has seriousness written all over it. "Great casting, but, alas, the acting sucked," I write in my critique.

Showbiz shows another eight minutes of filmic mystery-meat. Once again, we're stumped.

Mitch, the Japanese student, turns in another adequate film. I'm amazed how well he functions. If I were in Japan learning filmmaking and spoke only rudimentary Japanese, I'd be sunk. Somehow, he survives.

The surprise of the day is Heather, the novelist. She unveils a film that is unlike any other she did. It is a slow-blooming film about a couple in their sixties selling a car. The casting is perfect, as is the acting by the two graying actors. Compared with the usual somewhat bombastic films we 507 students do about spurned girlfriends and zombies and mean dads and characters who wake up from dreams or kill themselves because of a drug habit, this film is about something much more subtle. The older couple in the film, we learn, is selling a car once owned by their recently deceased grown child. It's a slice of life so tender and so realistic I feel a lump gather in my throat. I know my own parents are still dealing with the unexpected physical reminders of Annette: dresses left in a closet, credit card offers addressed to her, her old skis in their garage.

When the lights come on and we're supposed to comment on the film, I find myself unable to talk. The lump in my throat is growing. I sit there, trying not to show any emotion.

After Heather's film, we take a ten-minute break. The students file out to smoke, take a bathroom break, and to talk. I remain behind. I don't want to face any of my fellow students in the hallway. I want to compose myself. I act as if I'm busy with paperwork as they all file out of the screening room.

FTC remains in the classroom. It's just him and me. Heather's elderly couple dealing with their grief has unlocked something I've been keeping tamped down all semester. I think of Annette. I think of her awful death. I think of the past year, of my pushing my emotions to a place where I can deal with them, categorize them, ignore them. I look down at my notebook, trying to see the pages.

I start sobbing quietly. Snot and tears fall from my face. FTC asks what's wrong. I can't say a word. He asks me again. Finally I speak, and then I start blubbering. Through my sobs I tell him about my sister. How she died, how she left behind a baby girl and a little boy. I tell him it seems so unfair. I feel just overcome by grief and stress and worry—and it all pours out. For long seconds I cry like a big baby, to the instructor who early on was my antagonist. At this point, I don't care that he once held a grudge against me for being one of his hated straight white males. I only care that he isn't a student, that he is about my age, and that he might understand the grief I am feeling.

FTC sits there and listens. He doesn't say anything, just listens.

Within a minute or two, my blubberfest is over. I wipe the snot and tears from my face and take a big breath. I am thankful no students have come back into the room. The end of 507 is in sight. The end of my first semester is in sight. I apologize to FTC and ask him not to mention my sob session. He agrees and says he is sorry about what happened to Annette.

Now, to set the record straight, I did not sob into FTC's shoulder, and he did not pat me on the back. We did not become best friends. Violins did not play. That would have been an easy melodramatic scene to imagine, but it didn't happen. Instead, it was an awkward moment of emotions exposed, emotions observed. And another day in film school class.

I breathe again and comment about the absurdity of bawling in class. I ask FTC if anyone else has cried in front of him. "Not this year, so far," he says. I wipe my eyes one last time and chuckle at his comment. FTC gives me a slight smile. The clenched jaw is history.

I duck into the hallway to get a drink of water and a breath of fresh air before the other students come back.

I'm done making films for 507. It should be a relief, but I've still got much on my platter for the last few weeks of school.

The production of 507 films takes what appears in retrospect to be an insane amount of time. When I look back, I question my sanity. Did I really spend several long days tracking down animal trainers? Yes, I did.

Early in the semester, I felt like we were mice in a hallway, trying to avoid a cat. I feel that way now more than ever. Looking back, I see how many wrong turns I made and how much time I wasted and how many mistakes I made. I realize the first semester of film school would be quite easy if I could only do it all over again.

Life doesn't work that way, of course. My experiences seem to be shared by my classmates. Many are very talented, and I'll admit it sometimes gave me a slight feeling of *schadenfreude* to see them stumble and make the same mistakes I make.

Some events that could be great instead become memorable for their awfulness.

Every semester in 507, all the production students participate in the Vagabond shoot. It's named after the nearby Vagabond Motel, where the shooting takes place. The idea behind the shoot is to let students work together for the first time and make a short film, together. It's the first taste of the system we'll see repeated over and over again in film school.

The rules are simple: the film must be filmed within the confines of the Vagabond Motel in one afternoon. We all pitch ideas.

I pitch a story of a young man and woman, the woman extremely pregnant, who walk into a room at the Vagabond where film students are shooting a sci-fi drama. The students and the couple both have keys for the same room. During the argument over who gets the room, the pregnant woman's water breaks. Surrounded by film equipment and costumed sci-fi characters, the now-screaming woman is aided by a lowly film student who was once an emergency medical technician. It's a scene in which the director and producers know nothing, and the lowliest grips and costumed actors save the day.

The kicker comes when other film students, peering into the room and unaware of what's really going on, compliment the woman in labor for her acting.

Students vote on the pitches. Mine doesn't get chosen. Instead, we choose a script that hits the film school high notes: a young couple shoot heroin in a cheap motel and talk about breaking up.

The Vagabond shoot takes over much of the motel for two days. One day is pre-prep and rehearsal. The second day, a week later, is the shoot. I'm recording sound for the shoot, a job I volunteer for because I want to spend as little time as possible involved with a film about a couple talking about heroin and breaking up.

Our story is very simple and contains almost no movement or action. The day of rehearsal, the two actors show up and they know their lines. We run through several rehearsals, check the lights, check the sound. It's all good.

At this point, I come up with what seems an obvious suggestion: let's shoot the scene, I say. We have our actors, we have all the equipment. Let's strike now while the iron is hot! I gather our group together and explain my thoughts. I'm not the director, however, and she doesn't want to. She wants to wait a week. I'm mystified—it seems to invite disaster. What happens if one of the actors doesn't show up in a week? Plus, I point out that all of us are busy, so why don't we do this shoot now and have a free day to work on our other projects. My fellow students look at me like I'm speaking in tongues.

We don't shoot. We instead sit on our hands and run through several more rehearsals, not shooting any video. I feel frustrated.

A week later, we gather in the same room. Luckily, the actors show up. Unluckily, the day is hot. We have to turn off the AC while shooting because the cheap AC unit roars and blots out our sound. Given that we have roughly a thousand watts of extra lighting in the room, it quickly becomes stiflingly hot. It also soon stinks—there are eight of us in the small room. We spend the next four hours shooting take after take after take of the same scene. From my perch next to the bed, holding the boom mike over the two actors and listening to the dialogue through my headphones, I try to discern if there are any noticeable changes in the acting or if we're just recording the same thing over and over. The hours tick slowly by. Sweat runs down my back. Eight hours total shooting time over the two weeks, and we have a very short, one-location, one-scene film.

As I watch my much younger classmates agonize over every minute detail and spend long stretches trying to decide what to do, I formulate an observation based on something I learned long ago in chemistry. Nature abhors a vacuum, and film students will often use every minute of time they are given. Give some film students an hour to pound a single nail, and they'll spend fifty-nine minutes discussing how to hold the hammer before swinging it.

It's an oversimplification, but I'm so sick of being in the motel room I want to scream. At the rate we're shooting, it would take six months to wrap a low-budget feature film. When the shoot finally ends, I leave as quickly as I can, carrying a heavy load of sound equipment the block back to Zemeckis in the heat. I'm hot, I'm dehydrated, I'm glad to be done. When I return my load to the equipment room, a student technician inspects it. He shakes his head over the badly coiled electrical cables and a microphone wind cover that is in pieces. "Who did this?" he demands. I just want to get out of there. "Showbiz," I say. Everyone knows Showbiz.

He shakes his head. "F'ing Showbiz."

My paper on TEACHER'S PET is finished. Casper wants twelve pages. Mine is twenty-nine. I have gone overboard, and when I drop it in a cardboard collection box, it hits the bottom with a meaty thud.

I take Holman's sound exam. I'm sure I pass it easily. We study the textbook he authored, *Sound for Film and Television*, which has become standard reading material at most film schools around the country. I've read the entire book, some parts twice, because it gives an exceptionally clear-eyed view of sound and the physics of sound. His teaching shows the importance of sound—and its woeful underappreciation by the public. Just reread my last two sentences: I describe sound in entirely *visual* terms: *clear-eyed view* and *shows the importance*. Sound doesn't even get any respect in the English language. But Holman's class emphasizes how vital good sound design is.

Holman worked for George Lucas, and he's the man behind the Lucasfilm THX sound system. Holman jokes in class that if he got a nickel for every time the THX promo appears at the start of a film, he'd be so rich he wouldn't be teaching at USC. And then he adds that he probably wouldn't be as happy, either. Holman likes to teach. He heads the sound department at USC, and he won an Academy Award in 2002 for Technical Achievement in Sound.

Most of the class is technical. It reminds me more of an engineering class than an art class. It's objective material. Sound is wavelength, which we can learn to our advantage and ignore at our peril.

There's plenty of artistry displayed in the class, however. Holman brings in the dailies of famous films to emphasize his points. One day he brings production dailies from STAR WARS. The dailies have the sound recorded on set. He shows the scene where the storm troopers take control of Princess Leia's starship. It's the opening battle scene, familiar to anyone who has watched STAR WARS, and it introduces us to Darth Vader. But in the dailies the sound is atrocious and comic. The storm troopers sound as if they are running on plywood, which they are. The voices are dreadfully bad. Darth Vader sounds like a skinny asthmatic talking from under a mask. There are no sound effects for lasers and explosions and beeping robots. It *sounds* like a really low-budget sci-fi film—and because of that it *looks* like a really low-budget sci-fi film.

When Holman shows us how different STAR WARS looks with good sound, we understand a bit more about the importance of our ears. He also gives a few insider tidbits, like how some of the sound effects of that film were recorded within earshot of the USC campus.

He continues the demonstration with a scene from RAIDERS OF THE LOST ARK. First we watch the scene with no sound. In the scene, Indiana Jones takes the carved head from the pedestal inside the cave and makes his escape, avoiding darts and spears and a chasm and a rolling boulder. With no sound, it's a somewhat dull scene. Then we watch the scene with successive layers of sound added. The darts now have some zing. Indy's whip cracks with authority. The boulder sounds enormous. Over and over we watch the clip. Each time the sound becomes more rounded. Each time the action gets more exciting. Finally, we watch it with dialogue and music added. By the time we see the final version, we want to keep watching, which is to say, listening.

Holman's class makes me feel like I've learned something truly exciting, a bit of moviemaking magic. To laypeople, filmmaking is always about the image. Film schools capitalize on that. Every school advertisement I see shows people operating a camera. Sound? That's not sexy. In class one day he asks how many of us want to direct. Nearly everyone in class raises a hand. He tells us the straight truth that only a tiny handful of us will ever actually make a living as directors. Holman gives us advice: if we want to make a living in Hollywood, work in sound.

Holman's sound class is an example of why film school is worthwhile. The director Robert Rodriguez famously spent just $7,000 to *film* EL MARIACHI on sixteen-millimeter film, but the Internet Movie Database (IMDb) estimates a total of $220,000 was spent in postproduction, and much of that was to improve the original film's soundtrack.

I like Holman's class because it is primarily technical, but it often veers into the realm of art. Holman's class lifts the veil on a lot of the magic of movies.

Earlier in the semester I had a discussion with several students and FTC about the notion of art vs. technique. I explained I came to USC for practical reasons: I wanted a more stable career, and I wanted the hands-on training to do that.

"If you want that you should have gone to a technical college, that sort of place," FTC said to me. "You'd be better off getting that training there." I disagreed with him. I thought USC should be putting as much of an emphasis on teaching technique as any technical college does.

FTC shrugged. He said film school is there for us to find and pursue our artistic vision.

The idea chafes at me. Implicit in that idea seems to be that, although technique is teachable, art can't be taught. Art is, according to this view, something that flows from a mysterious source. To extend the view further, either you've got *it*, or you don't. Those without the genius are doomed to mediocrity, to non-art, to being hacks or replicators. Those with the genius are the *Ubermensch*.

This argument was put forth most prominently in the eighteenth- and nineteenth-century Romantic movement, by Byron and Keats and Blake. And that movement, the belief in the artist as a gifted *Ubermensch*, has been lapped up ever since by the creative class. And no wonder! In this view, artists are special, with a genius that comes from elsewhere, and thus can't be understood by the unwashed nonartists of the world. The masses don't have that *it*, whatever it is.

There's a serious side effect to this, of course. It breeds elitism and gives the artist a ticket to behave anyway he or she wants, for better or worse. Artists, in this view, are temperamental like Lord Byron, and it just can't be helped. Hollywood seems to embrace this because the list of directors and writers and actors who behave poorly is long. It is a Romantic conceit, this notion that the rules of society stifle and bind the true artist. It's a notion that emerged only a few centuries ago, long past the era of William Shakespeare and Leonardo daVinci. DaVinci was a scientist, a mathematician, an artist, a teacher . . . and he was fully enmeshed into his Florentine society. Shakespeare, for what little is known of him, never trashed a hotel room.

On the last day of Casper's class, he takes the stage and explains his grading. He says he's sick and tired of grade inflation, and he's grading accordingly. He warns people that a C means average work, that he's giving out a handful of Ds and only a tiny sprinkling of As. He tells us to be happy if we get a B.

His assistants hand out the papers. Our grades on the paper will be our grades in class. It's a chaotic scene in the auditorium with 120 students milling about and excited to see their grades.

One of Casper's assistants stands on the stage and points at me. "Are you Steve Boman?" I nod and work my way to the front of the milling crowd. "That was quite a paper," he says. I hope he means that in a good way . . . and when I look at the back of my paper I see my grade: "An Easy A," it says. I feel my chest expand.

Everyone in the auditorium spills outside to compare notes. A handful of undergraduate girls are crying. My 507 classmates gather in a clump and I join them. They want to know my grade. I reluctantly show it—I don't want to gloat, but it does feel mighty good. A serious-minded classmate who did a stunning stop-animation film, a guy who already had an MBA, also got an A. The others got Bs or Cs, and there were a lot of Cs in our group. Some of those who got the grade are angry; one woman wipes away tears. One guy wants to confront Casper.

I look at my classmates, and the very informal polling of grades doesn't surprise me. I know some people hardly put any time into the paper. I put in a lot of hours. The USC School of Cinematic Arts has an annex in the basement of the massive Doheny Library, and I had a pretty good idea of which ones were putting in some serious time working on their papers.

My last class of the semester is a Friday, with Ross Brown showing the film THE THIRD MAN. Our class wants to throw a party, and we ask Ross if there is anything wrong with celebrating over pizza and beer. He thinks it's a great idea. So we bring in a case of beer and watch Orson Welles in black and white and eat pizza. I drink only one beer, simply because I am so tired that if I have any more I know I will fall asleep. I have my Friday-afternoon slog through traffic to get home to Camarillo. Attendance in class is sparse. It isn't that much of a party. And then the semester is done.

Over the summer, Julie and I packed our furniture, left our rental house, and moved to Minnesota. Julie has a job that pays twice as much as she made in California. I'm going to commute to USC from Minnesota. Now I am going to spend seven days a week in California while going to grad school. I'll fly back home once or twice a semester. It's a plan held together by duct tape and crossed fingers. We're not broke anymore, but money is still extremely tight. Julie's mom will be living with her, helping with the kids.

That next fall, I fly into Los Angeles International Airport at 10 A.M. When I arrive in Los Angeles, I feel a knot in my stomach.

I've got my orientation for 508. I go to the same meeting room where we gathered for 507, but this time I know many people. Everyone is partnered up. Only one person is not there: my partner.

I sit through the orientation with a red face, the seat next to me empty. It was bad enough to have to be shunned during the 508 partner dance, and now I find the woman who publically begged for a partner is missing. I call her cell. She doesn't answer. I hide my frustration and worry and calmly explain to an instructor named Pablo that everything should be fine. It's a serious breach of protocol not to show up on the first day of class. Pablo is not happy.

A few hours later, I get a call from my partner. She sounds breezy, and explains she was running late and didn't bother to come to orientation. "It's not that important, you know," she says. My knot grows larger.

The next day, my partner shows up on campus. We meet with a directing instructor and go over our 508 film ideas. My partner is going to shoot first. She explains she wants to shoot a film with dancing zombies. I make certain I hear her correctly. *Dancing zombies?*

Along with angry dad films and breakup films, zombie films are a staple of USC student film subjects. It's easy, I suppose. Get some actors. Put some whiteface on them, make their mouths drool blood, and have them shuffle. Bingo, instant zombie. Such films strike me as not funny and not clever. What worked for NIGHT OF THE LIVING DEAD has gotten very stale.

She explains she wants to create a dancing zombie movie to dispel, she explains, "the negative connotations of zombies."

I want to put my head in my hands when I hear this.

That day we also go to our first class. We're given the schedule for 508. We are expected to work seven days a week for every week except Thanksgiving. We shoot every weekend, on Saturdays and Sundays. We have class every day of the week.

That night I sit beside the pool at USC and listen to the swimmers splash their laps. My family is now two thousand miles away.

I decide to quit.

I can't take four months of 508 in Los Angeles with my tardy partner, with a film about dancing zombies, with a group of people I just don't feel close to. I love so many aspects of film school— the instruction, the creativity, the freedom—but the good does not outweigh the bad. I'm spending way too much money. I'm too far from my family. I don't want to be with my partner for four months.

I meet with Pablo, a friendly, bearded professor who reminds me of the actor Richard Dreyfuss. He's head of the 508 program, and when I explain to him I want to quit, he simply looks at me and sighs. I'm sure he deals with this often. I then tell him I'm not going to quit until I can find my partner a new partner.

"I don't want to burn any bridges here," I tell him, "and I certainly don't want to leave my partner high and dry." Pablo sighs again and gives me the name of a woman whose partner bailed out on her. I call the woman and my partner and ask them to meet at Pablo's office. Later, they both show up, unaware of what is going on. I meet them and say, "You're going to be partners for this semester. I'm quitting."

Pablo looks satisfied—a potential logistical mess was averted. I thank them all, shake Pablo's hand, and fly back to Minnesota.

I have spent $17,000, made five little films, started a feature script, and I feel a tremendous amount of relief and sadness. I remained enrolled in my screenwriting class, and the instructor is gracious enough to let me complete the semester-long class from two thousand miles away. Still, there is no mistaking what I am doing: I am walking away from the best film school in the world.

TAKE 2

6

Surprise!

I am driving down a freeway in Minneapolis on a gorgeous spring day with Sophia, who is now four years old. It's just after noon, and we're heading home to get some lunch after her morning at preschool.

Since I quit USC, life has stabilized. Julie has been in great health, and she took a new job at the best pediatric hospital in Minnesota. We have nice neighbors. Lara and Maria walk to the nearby elementary school. I take Sophia to preschool several times a week. I'm splitting my time between being a housedad again and working on *GeezerJock*, which has risen from the dead. A new financial backer put some money into the machine, and our monthly circulation is approaching sixty thousand. We're still not making a profit, however, and there's only so much a person can write about sweaty old people before running out of ideas.

Today, Sophia is chatting away, telling me about a boy who was hogging the swings at outdoor playtime when a car coming toward me in the northbound lanes skids sideways and flips into the air.

Pieces of metal and plastic and glass go flying. The car cartwheels along the freeway toward us. The cartwheeling car settles on its roof in a puff of smoke. It has skidded into the concrete dividing wall separating the northbound and southbound lanes. I stomp on my brakes and pull quickly over to the right. I'm directly across from the smoldering car.

I turn to Sophia: "I'm going to help. Do *not* get out of your seat. Do you understand?"

She nods her head solemnly. *Yes.* She is strapped into her car seat.

I dash across the three southbound lanes and jump the low concrete dividing wall. The car is a mess. It's an older Chevrolet Cavalier coupe. Smoke and steam pour out of the engine.

I go to the passenger-side window and get down on my knees, expecting the worst. There is a small gap between the roof and the doorsill. I wince as I peer in.

There is one person in the car and, amazingly, she is alive. She is a tiny Vietnamese woman, about sixty. She is suspended upside down in her seat belt, still behind the steering wheel. She is crying softly.

"Are you okay?" I ask.

No answer. Just constant sobbing.

A big-bellied black guy in coveralls and steel-toed boots arrives at the scene. He is breathing hard. Lots of people are watching from the sidelines, but he and I are the only ones next to the car.

"She looks okay. I wanna turn the ignition off," I say to him. "I think I can get through this window."

"I'll hold your legs," he answers. "If you need to get out in a hurry, I'll get you out."

I get down on my belly. The driver is still weeping. I wiggle into the overturned car through the broken passenger-side window.

"Hey, there. My name is Steve. I'm going to be turning off your car, okay?"

The woman keeps sobbing.

I search for the ignition. Being in a crushed upside-down car is disorienting. Finally, I find the keys and turn off the ignition. I take a closer look at the sobbing driver. One leg is clearly broken—it makes an impossible kink below the knee—but she isn't bleeding from her head or torso. All the safety gear worked.

I don't smell any gasoline. I take her hand. It's tiny. "You're going to be okay, okay? I can get you out of here in about one second flat if we need to. Okay?"

I'm talking to reassure myself as much as her. Her seat belt release is a few inches away from my head, and with me and Steel-Toed Boots jacked up on adrenaline, removing her in a hurry won't be a problem. I'm struck by something ironic: when I do military presses, my weightlifting pals and I call them the "pushing-up-the-roof-of-the-collapsed-car presses." Now I'm in that collapsed car. But I'm not doing any pushing. Just talking.

I still smell no gasoline. Given that I'm a guy who doesn't like being in small elevators, the fact that I'm not claustrophobic in this small space proves adrenaline is powerful stuff. I tell the driver I am going to leave her in her seat belt until rescue crews arrive. I don't want to unfasten her belt and have her fall to the roof on her head.

The lady doesn't answer. She just keeps whimpering, sobbing in little tiny breaths. She must be in shock.

I call out to Steel-Toed Boots: "I'm going to stay in here for a little bit."

I start chatting to the driver again. "Wow, that was sure a pretty amazing accident. You're going to do great. You look in great shape."

Without a risk of fire, I think it best to wait. "Do you understand English?" She doesn't answer. I give her the same optimistic pitter-patter I use on the sidelines of a soccer fields when I coach kids. *Oh, yeah, you're looking good. Doing awesome. Really, you're gonna do fine.*

I have no idea if she understands me. The thought passes my mind that maybe she's weirded out by this strange man who keeps yammering on and doesn't do anything. After a few minutes of more chattering, I finally hear sirens. "Hey, they're almost here," I tell her. "They'll get you out and you'll be home in no time." More gentle moaning from her.

Suddenly, I remember: *Sophia!*

I feel my heart jump into my throat. I yell to Steel-Toed Boots that I want to come out. With him pulling, I wiggle out in a jiffy. The police have to inch their way through gridlocked traffic to get to the accident scene, but they are close. Suddenly, I don't care about some groaning woman suspended in her Cavalier. I stand up and look across the freeway to my Suburban.

There, framed in the back window, is Sophia, her little moon-shaped face looking out with very big eyes. I realize if she unclasps herself from her car seat and opens the door she will almost certainly be hit by a car. I have been out of sight for long minutes. She couldn't see anything that was happening behind the concrete median barrier. She can hardly see the overturned car.

My heart, which felt so calm in the overturned Cavalier, suddenly feels like it is going through my chest. I put my hands up and motion to Sophia: *stay put!* I vault the concrete wall and run to the truck through the southbound traffic. I get to our Suburban. As soon as the door is shut, I turn to Sophia. "You did a great job, honey. A great job. You were such a good listener." I can hardly catch my breath.

Sophia asks where I have been for such a long time. She couldn't see me, and I had never left her in the car alone before. I tell her I was helping a woman hurt in the car accident. She is satisfied with the answer. I ask her if she was scared being alone. *A little*, she says. She is very quiet.

Ten minutes later we pull into our driveway. My hands are shaking. I notice I have blood on my forearms and elbows from glass cuts. The cuts don't hurt, but I feel awful. My head aches. I can't believe I had left Sophia alone in a vehicle on the shoulder of a busy freeway so I could run toward an accident scene. What kind of a knuckleheaded moron am I?

Yes, Sophia is extremely well behaved, and she does a terrific job of following instructions. But still . . . what if she had gotten out of the car? What if some distracted driver had plowed into our parked Suburban? What if I had been blown up by the smoldering Cavalier? She would have been stranded in a truck parked on the shoulder of a busy highway. Eventually, she would have succumbed to curiosity or fear. And then . . . ?

With a sick feeling in my stomach, I realize I had let my desire for action overshadow my primary responsibility, which is to get my four-year-old home safely from preschool. In ten short minutes, I have exposed a genetic failure in myself. I had done the equivalent of leaving my offspring unprotected in a cave while I charged out of the entrance with a club in my hairy paw, like some Neanderthalic idiot.

Julie never would have done such a thing. A hired nanny probably never would have done such a thing. But I did, and I did it because I am hardwired to seek out more challenges than simply playing Candy Land and washing endless numbers of tiny dresses and listening to stories about a boy who was hogging swings at playtime. And writing touching stories about elderly athletes.

A few nights later, I am complaining to Julie about a young film director I had read about.

"I think you're just jealous," she says over a glass of wine. I pause. "Yes, I probably am," I answer.

"Have you ever thought of going back to USC?" she asks.

I pause again. My mouth flaps a bit. "I can't imagine they'd ever . . . I mean, why would they let me back in? It would never happen. I quit, remember?"

Julie just shrugs. Soon she goes to bed. I walk down into the basement. I push aside a big pile of the latest *GeezerJock* magazines by my desk. The kids are older. I *do* wonder what would have happened if I had stayed in the program. I miss the filmmaking. I miss the faculty—Casper, Brown, Holman . . . even FTC. I sometimes even miss the other students. I wonder what would happen if I were to have another go at it.

I look up Pablo's email at USC and write him, asking what it would take for me to be readmitted.

Six months later, I am driving our 2002 Suburban, the Boman Family Truckster, to California. I am going back to film school at USC. I'm going to restart 508.

This time, in the back of the truck I've got my bicycle, books, a huge box of beef jerky, cans of Spam, a portable DVD monitor, gallons of water for when The Big One hits, tools for set building (even my sawzall), clothes, shoes, video camera, potato chips, and a cooler of soda. Compared to my first attempt at 508, when I arrived a few hours before classes in a rental car and carrying only a suitcase of clothing, this time I'm loaded for bear. And this time I've left the apple juice behind.

Two years earlier, I had a heavy heart flying to Los Angeles. Now, I'm excited. Nervous, yes, but ready. It's a so much better time for my family. Sophia, our youngest, is going into kindergarten. Lara is old enough to babysit. Julie loves her new job. She's healthy. No cancer for five years.

When I started film school, it was out of desperation. Julie was recovering from three hard surgeries. We were broke. Our kids were young. We were a long way from any family support. I needed and wanted everything to happen *now!* No wonder I was impatient with other students.

This time it's different. I feel more relaxed. Now I'm going to school for the long haul, not a short-term fix. I've thought a lot about my successes and failures in my first go-round. I figure I've got a better vision of what it takes to succeed.

I've spent the past two years writing a full-length feature script with the assistance of a writing instructor I had met at USC. It's a story about how a tough-as-nails but dying retired navy man tries to reconnect with his estranged and pacifist son by leading him on a wild goose chase over the beaches of South Florida. I'd also helped turn *GeezerJock* into a nationwide publication, and now the investors had sold out to a larger publisher. It was a perfect time to say *Adios, GeezerJock.*

The bottom line: Desperate Steve is history. Yes, now I'm *really* old, but that doesn't bother me. I'm feeling comfortable in my skin.

I've also got a new 508 partner. He's a honey-voiced Tennessean, almost half my age, and he's taking another whack at 508 because his partner quit on him partway through the previous term. He says she had a nervous breakdown. His name is Dan—I call him Dan the Man—and I'd flown out to Los Angeles to meet him during the 508 mating dance, and we hit it off. Under his sometimes-mellow exterior, I find Dan to be intense and focused. He seems to have a good reputation as a real filmmaker. Plus, he gets my jokes, I think. I get his. It's a very different relationship than my first 508 partner, ol' big-rump zombie dancer.

We're not two peas in the pod, that's for certain. Dan is half my age and looks about half my weight. If he were a boxer, he'd be a super featherweight. I'm at the very least a light heavyweight, maybe a cruiserweight, and by physical activity levels we're yin and yang. But we have started off well, and we hope it continues.

The only thing that causes me a bit of unease is my living arrangement. Carl and Irene again have offered a place in their house. It's an amazing deal—a studio apartment near USC goes for more than $800 a month—and I've got an entire wing of the house to myself. I park in a shady gravel turnabout. There's a hot tub. A big-screen TV. And Irene loves to cook. And she loves that I like to eat.

Still, I feel like I'm intruding on their lives. For my own pride, I tell them I'll do various chores around their house in exchange for rent. I know it probably barely covers the hot water I use, but still, it is something.

I drive west into the setting sun. I'm moving fast, driving out to Los Angeles in a bit more than two days. The Suburban, with its thirty-one-gallon gas tank, will go nearly five hundred miles on a fill, and I eat up mile after mile in Minnesota, Iowa, Missouri, Kansas, Oklahoma, Texas, New Mexico, Arizona, and California. At seventy-five miles per hour, I go five hours between stops or as long as my bladder will last.

I finally arrive in Los Angeles and, two years after I quit USC, move my gear back into my old bedroom. I plan to meet Dan for a couple of beers the night before classes start. It's our first extended face-to-face conversation since we agreed to become film partners, and we know we've got an adventure ahead of us.

We both know that among people who have gone through it, 508 elicits a knowing nod, a secret understanding of shared hardship. A little like World War II marines saying, "Iwo Jima." Or McDonald's employees whispering, "Oprah ate here."

A few hours before sunrise, I wake up feeling like crap. My head hurts. I feel woozy and vaguely hung over, but because I'd only had two cans of watery Bud Light with Dan the night before, I know I'm not suffering from bottle fever. I get up and shuffle to the bathroom.

Today is 508 orientation, and I'm not going to miss it even if it kills me. I shake out a couple of tabs of ibuprofen by moonlight, swallow them, and go back to bed.

At about 6 A.M., I get up. It's getting light outside. I shuffle into the bathroom, still feeling really crappy. From the corner of my eye, a mirror over the bathroom sink seems to shift quickly from side to side. *Weird.*

I think back to the day before. For much of the day, I had been at USC, getting my student ID, clearing up registration paperwork, standing in line after line. It felt very strange to be walking around the gorgeous USC campus again, yet I was exhilarated to have returned.

I think back to the evening before. I had spent my first extended time with Dan. We had a good time. We grabbed a dinner, then plotted our semester over those few Bud Lights. Dan is slight and very blond, and I learn when he laughs hard he has a high-pitched *bwaaaawaaaahaaahaaaa!* that sounds like a cackle a comic-book supervillain might make before immolating a major city. Dan and I know we will be outsiders. Some of our classmates apparently know a bit about Dan . . . they had heard stories of "that guy a semester ahead whose partner went nuts," but I am a completely unknown entity. I am just *That New Old Guy.* I am landing in the middle of a group of students like a parachutist at the Super Bowl. Dan and I find that, despite our differences, we share some core beliefs: we like the same kinds of films, we agree on our politics, and we both value hard work.

Dan graduated from Vanderbilt before coming to film school and he'd turned down a full-ride scholarship to go to another well-known film school for a chance to attend USC. He is much more mature than he appears. And he is smart as a whip.

And last evening, Dan and I had dinner at a diner on Sunset Boulevard—a greasy spoon populated by druggies and out-of-town tourists, a place where you can get pancakes and eggs for dinner. Later we went to Dan's apartment and talked.

My mind goes back to the restaurant. Our waitress was covered with tattoos and disappeared for long stretches during our meal. With my head aching, I wonder if I got slipped something. Did my waitress drop some acid into my drink? PCP in my eggs? I'm not a drug user, so I have nothing to compare it to. I try to dismiss the thought. It seems too paranoid. But . . . still, something feels very wrong with my head.

A little before 7 A.M., I pad into the kitchen and something is definitely not right. Carl looks up from his breakfast cereal and gives me a nod. I try to say, "Good morning," but the words don't come out. What comes out of my mouth instead is nonsense. It sounds like "flip tlock." Carl stops chewing. I focus my mind, hard. My mouth seems not to want to move. I finally get some noises out, but they are not words, just sounds. I need to get some fresh air.

I give Carl a quick wave and walk outside. There's my Suburban, parked next to Carl's Mercedes. I stare at the tires of my truck. The thick off-road tires have raised white letters. I had recently replaced the tires. My brain knows there should be a word—BRIDGE-STONE—spelled out in blocky letters. My brain remembers that I paid $220 per tire. My brain recalls what the tire salesman said to me about these tires. But when I try to read the letters, they seem to spell out RCTSMSSNOP. For long seconds I stand over the tires, trying to make sense of the lettering. I know the tires don't say RCTSMSSMOP! No one sells that brand! They should say something else, I'm positive, but I can't remember *what* they should say.

I walk quickly down the street. My head hurts. I don't notice the pebbles under my bare feet. I walk a block, then another. I'm in a panic, but I want to keep moving and stay calm. I walk back to my truck and try to read the letters on the tailgate. I stand in the morning light, squinting at CHEVROLET.

I try saying it aloud. *CHEBFLP.*

I look at Carl's car. I try saying the lettering on it: *MURCTA BAA.* I sound like an idiot. Now my heart is pounding hard. I quickly walk down the block again. I need to clear my system of whatever toxin I have in it.

Halfway down the block an older man is out for a morning walk with his dog. As he passes, he says, "Hello." I answer back, unconsciously, "Hello!" I sound perfect! I try to say it again. Nothing comes out.

I look at the No Parking signs along the curb. They are gibberish. I don't understand anything they say. Street signs. Address numbers. Stop signs. Nothing makes sense. I'm in a foreign country where nothing written is remotely close to English. I walk quickly back into Carl and Irene's kitchen. Carl is now concerned. "Are you okay?" he asks. I understand him. I can comprehend verbal English just fine. But I can't make sense of written words, and I can't talk. If I do force out words, they're mumbo-jumbo.

I nod and try to look as if everything is just dandy. I don't try to say anything. I just walk to the counter and get a banana. I point at it, smile, and nod like a bad mime. I figure some food will do me good. I give Carl an overencouraging thumbs-up and head back outside, leaving him clearly confused. I haven't seen him for two years, and now I come into his house and act like some misanthropic mumbling freak. Irene is still sleeping.

I take another power walk, my adrenaline surging, my heart pumping, my eyes not making sense of words. I feel I am living through a nightmare. I want to wake up. I am dizzy and scared.

After what must be about a half hour of walking through La Cañada, my brain slowly starts feeling a little more . . . normal. When I finally return to the house, Irene is waiting at the door in her bathrobe. She's frightened. "Are you okay, Steve? We're worried about you!"

This time, when I open my mouth, some words come out. I focus on every word. It is like lifting boulders. "I. Didn't. Feel. Good," I explain.

Irene has a big medical dictionary on the kitchen table. The book is open to a chapter titled "Stroke." She tells me I need to call my doctor, pronto. I shake my head. I don't need my doctor. I obviously have only a bad case of the nerves. I only need more bananas, a couple of big glasses of cranberry juice, and a little exercise to clear the cobwebs out of my head. I am going to jog it off. Then I lace up my running shoes and head out into the warming Southern California morning.

Later that day, I am flat on my back and being inserted into a massive MRI machine at UCLA Medical Center. I have driven myself to the Emergency Department at UCLA and explained to the triage nurse that I had briefly lost my ability to talk and read that morning. I act very casual when I tell the nurse this. I lean on the counter, suppressing a yawn. I figure if I'm not excited, she'll send me home and everything will be okay.

I did indeed make it to orientation that day. I drove myself to USC, sat through the same speeches as a few years earlier. I sat next to Dan. A woman asked me if I was a father. I took it she meant *Dan's* father. "I'm a father," I told her, "but not in the way you're thinking." That's about all I remember. My head was foggy, that's for certain. After orientation, my middle brother, an internal medicine doctor, caught wind of what was happening and ordered me to an emergency room. This put a fright into me, and I headed for UCLA. I got lost going there, even though I am very familiar with the area. At one point I pulled over to gather my wits, and after I wandered through Westwood I finally located the hospital.

Unfortunately, I didn't spend long in the waiting room. It's a bad sign when you're whisked ahead of the two dozen other people wanting to see a doctor.

Not long after I am put in an exam room, a nurse comes to see me. He's a muscle-bound black ex-marine, and he soon has a soft spot for me. We're the same age, we both have kids, and he's studying for his PhD in nursing. He is impressed I'm enrolled at USC. He knows what the doctors are looking for in my brain, and he promises me he'll watch over me. Before he leaves, he tells me his dad died of a stroke when he was just fifty-two.

The minutes tick slowly. I'm alone, waiting for the MRI results. Then the muscle-bound nurse comes in. He clasps my hand. "I saw the results. I wanted to be the first to tell you. You had a stroke." Tears well up in his eyes. We hold hands for a long time. I am terrified. A stroke? *Really?* It seemed unbelievable, inconceivable. I could understand getting cancer, or getting hit by a bus, or maybe being eaten by a shark . . . but a stroke? Gimme a break! I am healthy as a mule! Strokes are for old people, really old people, right? My dear grandmother had a stroke when she was in her late eighties and her arms were flabby and soft as pillows! I just spent a summer waterskiing at 5:30 A.M. and jack-hammering out a wall in my basement. I am fit as a freakin' fiddle!

Just then a female neurology resident skids into my exam room. She looks very young. I wonder how long she's been out of medical school. "I . . . hear . . . you . . . had . . . a . . . stroke," she says with deliberate slowness. "Can . . . you . . . understand . . . what . . . I'm . . . saying?" I debate mumbling some slurred nonsense to her, à la Jack Nicholson in ONE FLEW OVER THE

CUCKOO'S NEST. But I don't. For one of the few times in my life, I have no desire to joke. I just feel scared.

I'm wheeled in my gurney out of the emergency room into some elevators. I keep telling myself, "This is just a nightmare. This is just a nightmare." I pinch my legs to see if that will wake me.

We come out of the elevators. I see a big sign in the hallway: Stroke Unit.

The gurney's wheels squeak as we roll down the quiet corridor. I look into the rooms. I can't see much, a few legs under blankets. That's about it. Everyone is sleeping.

At the end of a long hallway, the nurse pushes me into the last room on the left. It's a shared room. I hear the beeping of a heart monitor from the patient in the bed next to mine. I hear my roommate stir. He moans a bit. I can't see him because of the room-divider curtain.

I feel super fucking agitated. I can't believe I'm here. I want to jump out of the gurney and run for the exit.

"How do you feel?" asks a nurse.

"I'm super fucking agitated," I answer.

"Would you like something to calm you down?"

Would I? Of course I would.

She gives me a pill. I swallow it. "This will help," she says.

With the two-hour time difference, it's now 4 A.M. back in the Midwest. Julie is on a trip with the girls to visit relatives in Wisconsin. Her cousin is getting married. Julie is staying with her grandma in a little two-bedroom house in a tiny farm town in eastern Wisconsin. The idea for the trip is to give the girls a little vacation away from home to soften the shock of my being gone for months at a time. I don't want to wake everyone with a phone call in the middle of the night. I'm not going anywhere, so why cause everyone more worry than necessary?

I lie in the bed, waiting. I think over my reality. I have had a stroke. It is an *ischemic* stroke. Something blocked blood flow to part of my brain. The doctors don't know what caused it. They don't know if I will get another stroke. I am hooked up to an IV with blood thinners. Because the symptoms abated quickly, it seems the clot dissolved before it did any lasting damage.

I know enough about strokes to know they should not happen to a forty-two-year-old man, especially a fit and healthy forty-two-year-old man. I don't smoke. I don't do drugs. I have zero risk factors for a stroke. I just ran eight miles in under an hour the week before I left for California, and it was an easy training jog.

And now I have had a stroke. None of it adds up. I wonder how it happened. My mind wanders to all of the stories I know where someone feels fine one day and the next they fall into an abyss.

My mother-in-law had died a year earlier. One day her legs started to hurt. Not long after that she went to the hospital. Within a few hours, doctors found massive numbers of blood clots in her legs, clots created by the cancer eating away her lungs. She never smoked, and had no risk factors for lung cancer. Three months later, she was dead. One evening, my younger sister, Annette, went to the emergency room because she had a painfully sore hip. Within a few hours, doctors discovered she had an aggressive form of leukemia. She lived for only four months. A decade earlier, my friend Shawn went to her doctor because she had a bad cold that wouldn't go away. She learned she had cancer. She died within the year.

I know cancer can cause blood clots. My mind keeps coming back to the word: *cancer, cancer, cancer.*

I wait for the pills to kick in. They don't. I hear my heart monitor beep. I hear my roommate's beep. I look at my watch: 2:30 A.M.

I speculate where my terminal case of cancer could be hiding. It wouldn't be something obvious, like a brain tumor or that would have been picked up in the scan. It was unlikely to be leukemia, I thought, because I had no other symptoms. I finally settled on my gut. It must be some quiet tumor growing silently in my liver or intestines or stomach, thriving on the junk I put into my mouth. Lord knows I feed it enough crap: Gummi bears, bourbon, Big Macs, sour cream 'n' onion potato chips. I don't like most green veggies. I don't eat an apple a day. I even lie to my dentist about flossing regularly. For years I've felt my body has been an unbreakable V8 that will run on whatever crud I put in the tank. I pour calories in, and it keeps going. Until now.

I wonder what my friends will think when they hear. I know they won't believe it. They think I'm an Iron Man.

I think back to when I was nineteen and my brother was in the air force. It was July. I had helped him move to Colorado Springs. In the back of the moving van was my motorcycle. After a morning of unpacking, I gave my bro a hug and I got on my Kawasaki and rode like a demon in ninety-five-degree heat, sometimes shirtless, at eighty and ninety miles per hour. I rode through the night. I made it to Minneapolis, 980 miles later, and ran the Hopkins Raspberry Run five-mile road race the next morning with my pals. Then we went to a pool party. The next day, I rode another 180 miles and returned to my job painting houses.

And now I lie on a hospital bed, wondering what is next.

The heart monitors beep.

I don't want to think about what my family will feel when they hear the news. When I think of my children, I begin to feel panicky, so I push the thought away. I don't want them to know Dad had a stroke. The thought sets my adrenaline rushing and overwhelms any effect of the sedative the nurse gave me. Five years earlier, Julie had gone through thyroid cancer treatment. I was the strong one then, the one who didn't get ill. Now I'm hooked up to an IV, and nurses come every few hours and check to see if I've had another stroke.

I feel guilty lying in a hospital bed. A blood clot got stuck in my brain. I can't believe it, no matter how many times I think it. How f'kn' lame!

Finally, my watch hands crawl to 4 A.M. That means it's 6 A.M. in the Midwest. I dial Julie. Her cell rings a long time before she answers. I woke her up.

Hey, honey, I had a stroke. I've been admitted to the UCLA hospital.
There is a silence on the line.

When I was in elementary school in Duluth, I had a friend who lived about a mile away. In between our houses there was a path that led through the woods. We played together almost every day after school, and no matter whose house we were at, we would walk together to the edge of the woods. In the winter, when it was dark, we would walk together into the center of the woods, trying to ignore the darkness and the fact that behind the trees there were almost certainly bears and wolves and crazy madmen waiting to rip us to shreds. Then, in the middle, we would part. We would yell to each other as we each walked our respective ways.

We maintained this call-and-response until we were at the edge of shouting distance. Then, one of us would yell: *Watch out for bears!* And with that, we'd start sprinting. Through the dark woods we'd go, running as fast as our eleven-year-old legs would take us. When we hit the lighted streets, we'd feel safe again.

I had hoped Julie's voice would make me feel safer. But when Julie collects herself and speaks, I feel vulnerable. I'm suddenly more scared than I ever was running through those dark woods in northern Minnesota. It was all imaginary fear then, and in my childish heart I knew that. Now it is real fear. I am in a hospital room in Los Angeles, two thousand miles from home. We have three young children, and here I am, failing them. I had convinced Julie it was a good thing for me to return to USC, and on the first day—the very first day!—I'm in a hospital bed.

She asks me what I need her to do.

"Oh, I'm fine. They could release me any time." I'm lying. I tell her to wait until I know more. I say I don't know what is holding up the hospital. A few more tests and I should be out, I say, adding that I'm really not that worried. Lie, lie, lie. It's depressing being alone in a hospital, but I didn't want to sound weak and needy.

We hang up and my mellow pill begins to kick in. I fall asleep.

I wake several hours later with a troop of doctors standing over me. I am stunningly groggy.

I keep blinking, trying to get out of the fog of my sedated sleep. I understand the scene: it is morning rounds, and the bored attending doctor, doing weekend call, is going to use me as a teachable moment to a handful of the eager residents.

In fact, fifteen years earlier I had been the object of a similar teaching moment. Then, it was funny: just a half year after marrying Julie, I crashed while racing a bicycle. After I picked myself off the pavement, I noticed blood seeping out of the end of my pecker. At the emergency room, doctors told me I had a "fractured penis." It is a true medical condition. Look it up. A week after the accident, my privates were swollen beyond recognition. I was referred to a urologist at Temple University in Philly. After I waddled into his office, he took one look at my distended manhood and asked me a question: "Could I show this to my residents? This is classic." A few minutes later, he led in a troop of young doctors just out of medical school. I was twenty-seven. They were about the same age. Four were women. The urologist introduced me, gave a quick explanation of what happened to me, and asked to examine me again. I stood up, and with as much dignity and gravitas as I could muster, lifted my gown, and showed the residents my massively bruised and distended manhood. "Ta-da!" I said.

Now, in a similar setting, I'm not feeling funny in the least. The attending doctor asks me to perform some cognitive and physical tests to see how my brain is working. He moves his finger across in front of my eyes to see if they will track. He asks me if I know where I am. "I'm on the stroke ward of the UCLA Medical Center here in the beautiful city of Los Angeles," I say. I'm tired.

On a sunny Saturday morning in August, these stroke doctors aren't full of cheerful banter. I suppose if you spend your weeks with brain-damaged people, it can get a little dispiriting.

The rest of that day is a misery. I am sent out for various scans. I keep waiting for a doctor to arrive with a solemn look and say, "I'm sorry, Steve, we found cancer in your liver/stomach/lungs/pecker."

My cell phone battery goes dead. The hospital phone at my bedside won't make calls out of state, but it will accept calls. I'm drowsy. Depressed. My roommate is a twenty-year-old recovering from an awful car accident. Along with broken legs and hip and a ruptured spleen and collapsed lung and a broken jaw, his skull is cracked. He can only mumble through his wired jaw. He looks like Wile E. Coyote after a run-in with the Roadrunner. But his brain seems fine underneath all the broken bones and wires. He mumbles to me that he was drunk when he crashed.

My parents call me. I hear the fear in their voices. I do my best to reassure them that all is well. They lived through the nightmare of their youngest child dying of leukemia just a few years earlier. I know they are panicked. They tell me they will arrange a flight for Julie to come out.

I need a little fresh hospital air, so I take a walk down the corridor. I stroll the hallway in my backless hospital gown and my two-toned cowboy boots.

What a depressing place! I see a guy in bed, drooling. A middle-aged lady is wearing a hockey helmet. Old people stare at the ceiling, oblivious to the TV blaring five feet from them. A dude my age in a wheelchair. It feels like a nursing home. I pass by one room and see teary-eyed family members surrounding a bed. I only see the feet of the patient. It looks grim.

The nurses give me a funny look, but they don't stop me. I don't think they're used to seeing patients stroll through the ward. The ward is surprisingly unkempt. Beds are double-parked in the hall. Medical equipment sits in the hallway. In some spots, there's barely enough room to get a bed through the corridor. The nursing care, I quickly learn, varies hugely by shift. When I was first rolled into my room just after midnight, I had a wonderful nurse—caring, efficient, quick.

But in the afternoon, my nurses are awful. I return to my room and watch some television, and an alarm by my roommate's bed goes off. It rings and rings. No one answers. He hits the nurse-call button. No one comes. I hit my call button. Nothing. Finally, I get up and put my boots back on and walk down the hall to the nurses' station. A trio of nurses are lounging at the desk. It sounds like they're gossiping. I tell them about the alarm. One huffs up from her chair and heads off to our room at the end of the corridor. I seem to be the only ambulatory patient on the ward.

At midafternoon, I'm wheeled down for an ultrasound of my legs. My doctors want to see if there are clots there. It's dreary in the hospital basement where the scans take place. The technician says everything looks fine with my legs.

Later, I'm rolled in my wheelchair out into a corridor and told to wait for a nurse to bring me back to the stroke unit. The nice ultrasound technician tells me I can't walk back to my room; I need to stay in my wheelchair. Hospital rules, she says. I kill time by doing wheelies in my wheelchair. After fifteen minutes of wheelies, I get impatient and roll myself to the elevators. I get in and push the button for the stroke ward.

I sense most stroke victims don't demand a lot of pampering. Still, I expect better, especially at UCLA, which touts itself as having one of the premier stroke centers in the world. Back in my room, I climb back in my bed and, feeling sleepy again, settle in for a nap. In the middle of my dream—I'm on a lake with Julie and the kids on a summer day, swimming—I'm awakened by a nurse getting my vitals. She's upset.

"You were supposed to wait for transport after your leg scans!"

I'm not a good fit for this stroke unit. The nurses seem to want me to be more brain-dead.

The day stretches on. Carl and Irene visit, and they have more bad news. Sometime Friday evening, a water pipe in the bathroom near my bedroom burst. They were both gone when it happened. It flooded an entire wing of their house, including my bedroom. The carpeting and sheetrock are destroyed. The confluence of events seems spooky and weird. My brain plumbing had a problem Friday morning. Twelve hours later, their house plumbing has a major snafu.

My parents call. They have a flight for Julie. She'll be driving home to Minneapolis from Wisconsin and flying out the next day.

As evening comes, the dreaded visit from a doctor never comes. There is no cancer diagnosis. I should be cheered up, but I'm not.

That night I have wild, strange nightmares. Without the sedative, I'm jumpy as a frog. I bolt awake. *Are my hands asleep? Or is it a stroke?* My vitals get checked every few hours. I hardly sleep, and then dawn comes and I doze off.

Sunday morning, another visit from the herd of residents and their leader. This time the attending doctor is a tall, older fellow. He lingers at my bedside, answering questions.

He explains that my blood clot was very small, and that I was very lucky to have dodged a bullet. "I think you'll look back at this and be very thankful this happened," he says. "It could have been much worse." He says the cause of the stroke is still a mystery, but he suspects I might have a small hole in my heart—a patent foramen ovale or PFO—that would allow blood to seep into the arteries that go straight to my brain. Normally, blood goes through the heart, into the lungs, where it is filtered of impurities and filled with oxygen, and then sent to the brain. With a PFO, some blood can take a shortcut straight to the brain. If there is a big chunk of impurity—a blood clot—it would play havoc with the tiny vessels in the brain.

He says I'll get a special ultrasound of my heart on Monday morning. He says nothing in my laboratory results or scans shows any markers for any kind of cancer. I feel a bit better.

I'm again waiting for time to pass. Julie arrives at LAX at 5 P.M.

At 4:30 P.M., I smell my armpits. I stink. I stink really bad. I haven't showered since Friday morning and it's now Sunday afternoon, and I've been through enough emotional turmoil to melt an entire stick of Old Spice. I learn there is a shower somewhere on the ward. I get a towel and roll my street clothes into the towel, like I'm planning a prison break. I take my toothbrush and razor and fresh underwear and a shirt that Carl and Irene brought me.

There's no indication the shower has been used in recent days. I scrub myself to a lather in the shower and start to sing. It feels so good to do something so ordinary. I shave in a foggy mirror. I wish I had some deodorant. I put on my jeans and the fresh shirt and look at my watch. Perfect. Shift change. The afternoon nurses on the unit are inattentive. I give myself a quick once-over and walk out of the shower and head for the elevator, my IV attachment taped to my arm under cellophane wrap. No one says a word to me.

Thirty seconds later I'm walking out of the elevators and heading for the UCLA Medical Center exit. A minute later, I'm walking across the hospital's sunny courtyard. I'm free! I feel terrific. After two days in the stroke unit, I have begun to feel like I should shuffle and drool so I can fit in with the other patients. Now I'm outside and the sun is warm and even the Los Angeles air smells sweet and beautiful.

Coming toward me is a familiar face—my night nurse! Unlike the lazy day-shift nurses, he's a champ, an upbeat joker who likes hanging in our room. My busted-jaw roommate especially likes him. He's the only nurse who laughs with him and tells him jokes. The nurse's eyes widen and he gives me a look of *What the Hell Are You Doing?* I start jogging and give him a wave.

I head across Le Conte Avenue. I go into a convenience store and buy a bag of corn chips, a bottle of tonic water, a lime, and a bottle of gin. I stand in line with an IV line dangling from my left forearm, a hospital ID bracelet on my wrist.

When I walk out of the elevator back into the stroke ward, my night nurse sees me and walks quickly after me. I pick up my step and beat him back to my room. He comes in and quickly closes the door.

"What are you doing?" he demands. "You're not supposed to leave the hospital! You can't just walk away like that!"

I tell him my wife is going to be arriving soon, and I had to get a little welcoming package. I sneak him a peek of the gin and tonic. "You want some?" I ask. He rolls his eyes. "You're not supposed to do that in the hospital either!" Then he sighs. "I don't want to know about this."

He leaves, closing the door behind him, and I mix up some drinks in a pair of plastic cups. I open the bag of chips, fluff up the pillow, and raise my hospital bed. I recline and wait. I am most certainly not going to look like a feeble invalid when my wife arrives.

After a brief wait, there's a polite knock at the door. It's Julie. She comes in, eyes wide. She's not sure what to expect. I'm kicked back, Hawaiian shirt and jeans on, a pair of G&Ts waiting on the counter.

"Welcome to the stroke unit," I say.

7

Nice to Meet You, Donald Sutherland

The next morning the team comes by for morning rounds, and what a
different response from them! Julie has stayed with me overnight—
no kiss and tell about what happened—and the doctors seem surprised when they meet her. For two days, I've been alone, a John
Doe from the Midwest who walked into the emergency room. Now
with Julie by my side, they treat me very differently. Perception is
reality. Julie is a doctor, and she's articulate. Their talk immediately
veers into medical jargon. The attending physician again says my
stroke is a blessing in disguise. Had I not gotten a small stroke as
a warning shot across my bow, he says, I could have been inca-
pacitated or killed later by a bigger stroke. The diagnosis seems
pretty simple: I sat in my truck nearly motionless for forty hours
driving from Minneapolis to Los Angeles. The inactivity could have
allowed small clots to form in my legs. If I did have some blood
clots in my legs, they could have migrated to my brain via a hole in
my heart.

Shortly after they leave, I am wheeled into the hospital basement again. This time I'm not alone. Julie walks beside my wheelchair. I again feel completely ridiculous being pushed around like a vegetable.

Every other test has been completely painless. MRIs and CAT scans are the lazy man's treat: lay on a pad, let a big machine thrum and vibrate around you.

This test, an echocardiogram, is different. I am told I will be swallowing a large tube that will take pictures of my heart through the wall of my stomach lining. "This is not pleasant, not at all," the gabby lab technician warns me. "It would be nice if we could sedate you, but we need you awake."

I appreciate her honesty. It is not pleasant. I don't swallow the tube, but rather the tube is shoved down my throat. My gag reflex kicks into overdrive as soon as the ultrasound probe touches the back of my throat. I immediately begin trying to vomit it out. They keep pushing it farther down my stomach. I keep retching.

For twenty minutes, it goes on this way. I'm retching so hard I sound like a dying water buffalo. There is nothing I can do. My body wants the probe out. Julie holds my hand and keeps me from grabbing the tube.

Even though I'm retching, I'm required to bear down on my gut muscles, as if I'm constipated and I'm trying to expel the remains of some supersize burrito. As I do it, a technician injects air bubbles into my veins through a needle in my arm. The test is supposed to see if those air bubbles cross the wrong side of the heart. I'm puking, gagging, grunting, and being injected with air bubbles, all at the same time.

It's an awesome way to spend a Monday morning.

I'm wheeled again to my room. Now Julie and I wait. I'm getting anxious—my 508 class at USC resumes on Tuesday. I'm desperately hoping I can get back to campus in time for class. I'm already missing my first screenwriting class.

On Tuesday morning, I shower again and am in my street clothes when the stroke unit doctors come by for their morning rounds. And they are smiling.

"Great news. You have a PFO!" says the attending physician. The residents actually line up to high-five me. Everyone seems thrilled at the news. I have a hole in my heart! Celebrate! A moderately sized hole that can let blood leak out and flow to my brain!

I'm not as thrilled as everyone else is. I have a freaking hole in my heart! The attending physician tells me it will be a relatively simple procedure to close the hole surgically, to which I'm reminded that I was supposed to just swallow the ultrasound probe. He suggests waiting until my Christmas break and doing it back in Minneapolis. Until that point, he says, take some baby aspirin every day, take some cholesterol-lowering medicine (my cholesterol wasn't beyond normal range), watch my diet—and get heart surgery in four months. He discharges me.

Julie and I hurry to pack up and get out of the hospital. My first class is at 1 P.M. I walk out of the UCLA Medical Center a free man at 11:30 A.M. and find three parking tickets on the dirty windshield of my Suburban, which is parked in a hospital parking garage next to the emergency department.

I gun our big Suburban down the 405, then eastbound on the 10. Julie tells me to slow down. I glance at her as we race along at eighty-five miles per hour and deadpan: "What, it's not like I could have a stroke."

I hear myself say it and I realize I sound like a complete asshole. *What if I did have another stroke?* I think. I slow down. My first class will start in less than an hour.

T he 508 course is structured like 507. There are fourteen students in seven partnerships, one lead instructor, several assistant instructors, and several student teaching assistants. Pablo is our lead instructor. Our cinematography instructor is Charles, an affable, sunburned Englishman. Our sound instructor is an intense bundle of no-nonsense energy named Frank. It's a fitting name. He's blunt and no-nonsense. Frank. Thankfully, there are no acting classes in 508, but we do have an acting instructor who gives us advice when we watch dailies.

I walk into the class, my hospital ID bracelet still on my wrist. No one seems to notice. No one knows I was in the hospital, not even Dan. I had been admitted to the hospital on Friday evening. I was released Tuesday morning. It's Tuesday afternoon, and now that I'm sitting, I take stock of how I feel.

I feel weird. I feel I'm levitating. I feel I'm rising slightly off the ground. When I speak I choose my words carefully. I don't want to stumble or slur my words. It feels as if big words are difficult to find. Because of that, I speak in short sentences. I rehearse my words in my head. I don't know if it's an aftereffect of the stroke or if I'm just hyperconscious of how my brain works. I do know I'm worried my brain will freeze up again and I'll be unable to talk. And I feel my memory is muddy.

I have three conversations going on simultaneously in my head: one is observing what's going on in class, another is rehearsing what I'm about to say, a third is monitoring the functioning of my brain and body. I'm constantly doing a pilot's checklist of my physical functions: feet moving, check; fingers balanced, check; eyebrows moving in unison, check; face not drooping, check.

It's an exhausting task, and I know my own mind is running at a hundred miles per hour when everyone else's in the room is probably idling. My mind also feels like it's mushy. I've got the gas pedal floored—I don't think I can go any faster or do any more than what I'm doing, which is next to nothing. I'm sitting in a chair in a classroom at USC, listening to an instructor. If someone were to look into the room, they'd see polite boredom. But my interior conversations are vivid and disquieting. I briefly take my pulse. It normally runs in the low fifties. My heartbeat is now more than eighty beats per minute.

It's the first day of class. We're going over ground rules, expectations, planning. It's all pretty boring stuff. Pablo is a quiet speaker, and he's friendly and kind in class. I'd dealt with him when I quit, and I smile at how things have worked out. He's now my instructor.

I survey the class. I know from my 507 class that these thirteen other people will shape the tone and tenor of the next four months. I will spend hundreds of hours with these people.

The class has five women, again. And again we are a melting pot of races and accents. The partnerships are intriguing. It's interesting to see how the mating dance from the previous semester played out. There's a tall black guy with a soft southern accent partnered with a stocky Romanian guy who's got the same ever-present five o'clock shadow as the late John Belushi. Two fashion-forward black women from the same South Side Chicago neighborhood are another partnership—one of them went to elementary school across the street from where Julie and I lived in Hyde Park. Another two women are paired up—a white Los Angeleno, a true Valley Girl, is partnered with a tall exotic-looking Asian-Anglo whose name is Kat. They're both groovy-girl club kids, and they seem as perfectly matched as the women from Chicago. The fifth woman in the class is from the Philippines; her long jet-black hair is lustrous, her accent sweet, and she's paired with a guy from South Florida whose parents fled Castro's Cuba. There's an exceptionally tall Mexican guy with a huge haystack of hair—he's quiet as a mouse—paired with a grinning and chatty Chilean. Two square-jawed athletic white guys—they both seem to be out of a Polo catalog—are paired together.

Then there's Dan and me. We're the oddest couple by appearance. Dan is slight and boyish. He's twenty three and could pass for nineteen. He's got a mop of reddish blond hair, freckles, and exceptionally fair skin. I'm in my forties and I could pass for a guy . . . in his forties. And even after spending time in the hospital, I'm still deeply tan. My skin shows the decades I've spent outdoors. A few months earlier, I commented to my kooky barber that I wanted my hair a bit shorter—"Like Daniel Craig had in the last James Bond flick," I said. She thought of someone else with a shaved head and immediately gave me a buzz-cut. With no hair, I look fierce, with a touch of Travis Bickle. I'd since kept the boot-camp hairdo. Dan and I have already been confused for being father and son, and we quickly learn to add *filming* partners when we tell outsiders we're partners.

Our class is exceptional in one way: the men are all handsome, the women all pretty. Compared to my first go-round, the class looks older, more mature, and more poised. I expected the reverse, since I am two years older, and the undergraduates on campus certainly look younger. But as we introduce each other and spend the first day in class, I realize all the men in the class are straight and, well, *manly*. Four of the women are straight, and the one lesbian, the Valley Girl, is straight out of the imagination of Howard Stern. Everyone seems confident and upbeat, in school to work. It's as if our class sidestepped the usual film school clichés I've already witnessed at USC—the slacker, a cigarette dangling, who yammers on about avant-garde French cinematographers; the Lexus-driving Marxist, who drones on about the total unfairness of the world economic system; the wandering rich kid, who uses film school as some sort of extended personal therapy session.

Everyone in my 508 class seems interested in making films, not posing, not complaining, not searching. It's only the first day, of course. And I wonder how much of my observations are shaded because of the simple fact I'm just out of the hospital. Four nights in a stroke ward makes everything look good. I notice the air smells good. The sun shines brightly. USC looks beautiful. It *is* beautiful. It's August. The days are long. The sun is hot. It feels like the Southern California the Beach Boys sang about.

After class, I tell Dan I spent the weekend in the hospital and he seems to brush it off—*okay, cool, how do ya feel?* I don't want to dwell on the details, and I make my patient time sound pretty minor. If he's worried, he's hiding it well. I introduce him to Julie and they hit it off. We joke that we are going to take our son out for dinner, which we do.

O n this first day back, the San Fernando Valley hits 102 degrees. It's in the nineties at USC, which is down in the L.A. Basin. When Julie and I return to Carl and Irene's house, we find my room is heavily damaged. The broken pipe sprayed enough water to soak all the carpets, which in turn soaked the walls, which in turn damaged the sheetrock. The carpet is pulled from four rooms, and a handful of large industrial fans are drying the mess. The air-conditioning is off. It's hot, humid, and loud, as the fans blast 24/7. We spend a sleepless night, my first out of the hospital.

Julie needs to return to Minneapolis, and I drive her to the airport at 5 A.M. It's still eighty degrees outside. I return to USC, park, and leave my engine running and AC blasting. I try to take a nap in the back of the Suburban. I can't sleep. I'm now six days into my return to grad school and I've had a mild stroke, I discover I have a hole in my heart, and I find that my home-away-from home has been damaged in a way that seems a mocking echo of my own body. As I lie there, the Suburban engine sucking gas, the sunlight filtering in the window, my head still aching slightly, I realize the broken water pipe is so spot-on for a metaphor that it wouldn't work in a fictional script. I hear the critique already: "Too on-the-nose, Steve. Try something a little more subtle."

I feel very alone. Julie is gone. Classes are starting, and I don't know a soul on campus other than Dan. I made him promise not to tell others about what happened to me. I know film school is a gossip chamber, and I don't want misinformation to spread.

Luckily, film school semesters at USC start with a slow ramp-up: in 507 and in 508, I'm not expected to do much in the first few days of class. I haven't missed a thing, nor fallen behind. The first long weekend is meant, apparently, for students to socialize and get settled before the real work begins.

As I lie in my truck's backseat, I think: *What am I doing here? Why am I doing this? Am I an idiot?* My mind spins toward the macabre. I foresee a news story:

From The Associated Press: A forty-two-year-old Minnesota man was found dead in his vehicle on the campus of the University of Southern California yesterday afternoon, apparently from natural causes. The man was enrolled in the university's School of Cinematic Arts, officials said, and was pursuing a master's degree in film production. Police and USC officials refused to release the name of the man until relatives could be notified.

A classmate said the man apparently had been hospitalized earlier in the week for a stroke. The classmate, who only identified himself as Dan, said the death of the Minnesota man "was kind of a bummer."

"He didn't seem a bad guy, but he was a pretty old dude to be going to school," Dan said. "This is sure going to f'-up my semester." Police were unable to determine exactly how long the man was in the vehicle, but officials noted that his 2002 Chevrolet Suburban appeared to have been idling until it ran out of gas. "Judging by the smell, he'd been in there a while," said one officer, who asked not to be identified. Police ruled out

foul play. No other details are available at this time. An autopsy
is pending.

I realize the thoughts I'm having are self-defeating. Feeling sorry for myself and being scared aren't going to help. I didn't come back to USC to fail, and I'm not going to quit again. It's time to pull myself up by my sorry-ass bootstraps.

Though it is early, I call my pal Pete Krause.

Pete and I met at Gustavus. We lived in the same dorm and had an English class together and that was that: we became friends. We had a grown-up, thoughtful friendship.

For example, when we were in college, we spent the evening before our graduation visiting a few bars in little St. Peter, Minnesota. Then we went visiting the apartments of various friends. It's a small town, St. Peter. I'm a little hazy on the details, but I recall shoving carrots into a powerful room fan and laughing hysterically as carrot shrapnel sprayed about the room. I remember challenging some locals in their muscle cars to a race, with me on foot. I recall us carrying glass syrup dispensers filled with whiskey, dispensers we had borrowed from a local pancake restaurant. We figured the cops would be hoodwinked by our clever trick. When we drained our "syrup," we began conducting liberation raids into campus housing looking for more drinks. Sometime before dawn, we found ourselves at the entrance of the college, where a four-foot-high stone sign announces GUSTAVUS ADOLPHUS COLLEGE. Spread out in front of the sign was a beautiful tulip garden, perfectly manicured and loamy in the warm May night. Pete and I both climbed up on top of the sign, and we leapt off and did belly flops in the soft, muddy earth. Then we did it again. And again. And again. It was like landing in water, the ground was so soft.

Over the years, our friendship grew and actually matured a little bit. He went to NYU to study acting after college. I gave him an old leather motorcycle jacket I owned, figuring he would look like a New York toughie with it.

I moved to southern Minnesota and worked as a reporter. I'd visit his family over the holidays. He'd come down to Rochester and hang out. Somewhere in the archives of Minnesota Public Radio, there is a story featuring Pete. I did a comic spoof talking to Santa Claus. Pete was Santa.

Pete was a good actor in college, and it was clear he had that special *something* onstage. Right out of NYU he was hired by Carol Burnett to perform on her short-lived reboot of a comedy show. It wasn't a fluke hire. He worked steadily in Hollywood and kept climbing the ladder. When Julie and I visited California so she could interview at Oxnard, we stayed at his house. Pete had been a lead on SPORTS NIGHT, Aaron Sorkin's dramedy, but the show had been canceled, and he was looking at other gigs. One morning during our stay, he pulled me aside and said he just got word he was cast in a new series. It was called SIX FEET UNDER. It would be on HBO.

Julie and I had just moved to California with our girls when they had the red carpet premiere for SIX FEET UNDER. Julie and I sat next to him as his face filled the screen of the Egyptian Theater in Hollywood. It was very cool and somewhat surreal to see your college buddy's mug on the big screen—or on any screen.

During the three years Julie and I lived in Ventura County, Pete's place became a getaway pad. Sometimes I'd take the whole family, sometimes I'd visit myself. We couldn't have been less ENTOU-RAGE-like. Pete and I played a lot of ping-pong in his awesomely huge living room. Swam in his pool. Went for runs. Talked. Went out for pancakes or Mexican food or sushi.

That was it. We never went clubbing. Pete is a private guy, and he got where he is by working hard, and the last thing he wants is to find his face in the publicity beast that feeds on Hollywood mischief. When I was staying home with the girls and going a little stir-crazy, Pete came up and hung with the kids and me. After Annette died, I was feeling very low. Pete told me he'd take me out and "do anything I wanted."

He drove up to Camarillo and took me bowling and we had some beers. Then we went to In-and-Out Burger.

Pete became a star. He was nominated three times for a best dramatic actor Emmy for his work on SIX FEET UNDER. He's worked with a Who's Who of talented people.

In 507 I had been too busy to see him much. We touched base a bit. I didn't want to look like I was trading on his celebrity. Now, I don't give a rat's ass. I just want to see my old pal. We meet for lunch that day. He approaches me with wide eyes. I tease him by giving him a jerky, Frankenstein-like hug. It's defensiveness on my part, really. I don't want to admit I'm scared. So I joke about it. Joking about mortality is a lot better than crying about it.

I assure him I'm feeling good, that everything is back to normal, that I'm going to have heart surgery, and that I'll be right back in the game. He treats me as if I'm going to break if he drops a napkin on me. I assure him I'm fine. He's skeptical and worried, but we agree to spend a day on the set of his latest TV show, DIRTY SEXY MONEY.

When I get back to USC, my bravado dwindles. I decide to move into a hotel near campus. Carl and Irene's house is a disaster zone. The walls need to be torn out, and we're in a heat wave.

That night, I'm sleeping in my hotel room when I wake after a nightmare. I'm unsure where I am. My heart is pounding. I keep thinking I'm going to lose my ability to talk again, to read, to understand. The next morning I give myself another of my little pep talks—*get going, Steve, and quit feeling sorry for yourself.* I lace up my running shoes for the first time since I've been released from

the hospital. I attempt to run around the USC campus. I can't go
more than a few blocks before I slow to a walk. My legs feel awful.
They're heavy as stones and painful. I knew from my ultrasounds
that I had no large clots in my legs. My doctors said it is possible,
however, that I have microclots in the tiny capillaries of my legs. If
so, I'm going to jog them out.

My workload at USC is amazingly light in this first week. Dan is
directing the first film of our 508 partnership. Other partnerships are already doing preproduction, but Dan hasn't finalized his
script. So until that happens, I do nothing. I've got a screenwriting
class, too, but that's getting off to a slow start.

On Friday I meet Pete at the DIRTY SEXY MONEY set. It's
in the Paramount lot, a massive complex located in the heart of
Los Angeles in a neighborhood that has seen better days. Driving
through the gates of Paramount is to go back in time. Inside, it's a
beautiful place, with carefully trimmed shrubbery and employees
zipping around in electric carts. Pete's show is taping several
scenes, one featuring a limousine dropping off two of the characters and another in an office featuring Pete and Donald Sutherland, another of the lead actors on the show.

It's a good day to visit because Pete has a fair amount of down-
time between scenes. When I arrive, he gives me a tour and introduces me to various crew and the director and several of the
actors—William Baldwin among them. Pete is eager to show me
off. "This is my friend Steve," he says to Baldwin. "Do you know he
just had a stroke?" Baldwin, like others, seems to think he's joking.
I'm standing there looking fit as a fiddle. "I'm not kidding, he *really*
did," Pete adds, thus launching us into a little session where I
explain what the heck had happened. It is a funny little shtick, and
the mood on the set is upbeat and happy. The show is just a few

days from premiering and there is obviously a lot of enthusiasm by everyone in the cast and crew.

Pete has his own trailer—a high-end camping trailer like you'd find at a nice RV park. We sit and talk in the velour chairs while the AC blows cold air and the crew preps the next scene. Pete is relaxed yet focused. He explains that part of his appeal to producers has been his work ethic. He says his reputation is of someone showing up on time and knowing the script and not being a drama king on the set. He says he takes pride in almost never needing a prompt on his lines. Today his scene is being reworked, and Pete's not worried. He says he'll memorize the material quickly, then focus on the acting. He's unfailingly polite to everyone on the crew. He holds a door open for some crew members when we tour the set.

We step out and grab a snack from the food cart, when Sutherland appears. I'm not a guy who gets very excited about meeting stars. I was lucky enough to interview a good number of VIPs as a reporter, including presidential candidates making the rounds in Iowa. But . . . when I meet Sutherland, I can't help but be a bit starstruck. I try not to stammer as we shake hands. *Whoa, this is cool!* I think. *This is the guy I watched in soooo many great films.*

Pete introduces me, again, as the guy who had a stroke. I wave Pete off, but Sutherland is interested in talking medical issues. We discuss various ailments, and we engage in a bit of medical ailment one-upmanship. He tells me about nearly dying of an infection in Europe decades ago. I counter about the time I had my ferocious bike accident that broke most of the blood vessels in my pecker. Pete stands back and grins. Sutherland is an intriguing conversationalist, and I'm glad to hold my own. For the last few days, I've been feeling my brain is slow and I'm not on my A game, but this afternoon the words flow freely and I'm relaxed and happy. We talk for quite a while, standing by the food cart. It's clear by the behavior of the crew that Sutherland is treated like royalty, and I'm catching a few curious glances. I have to suppress a smile. They don't know I'm merely a second-semester film student.

A production assistant approaches and tells Pete and Sutherland they're wanted in a meeting. They disappear. I walk onto the set and find the director, James Frawley, and ask him if I can observe. He motions to an empty chair next to him. "Sit there. You can watch all you want." Frawley is a gentle bear. He's extremely clock-conscious but relaxed. He's been directing television shows since he got his start helming THE MONKEES back in the 1960s. He's been working in the business for more than forty years! I watched reruns of THE MONKEES when I was a little kid.

We're joined by the script supervisor, and the three of us sit in front of the video monitors as Frawley directs Baldwin and an actress in the exterior night limo scene (even though everything is staged inside the soundstage).

Baldwin flubs a line. He apologizes, then gets it right. The scene wraps. I'm surprised to find the "video village," the spot where Frawley is, isn't within eyesight of the set. Frawley communicates by intercom to the actors. I was expecting the director to be hovering close to the action, but time is money, and the soundstage has several sets, and moving the video village would obviously take time.

After my extended conversation with Sutherland, I'm stoked. And I'm finding Frawley is a gentleman. He says he sometimes teaches at USC, and he offers me some pointers on camera placement. He also talks about the importance of keeping the energy up on the scene and not wasting time. I'm taken aback because here's a guy who's been on the job for forty years, and if he's faking his enthusiasm for teaching me, he's a good actor.

I'm also enjoying this entry into the real world. My chief complaint with film school students is the interminable delays in decisionmaking. No such problem with Frawley. He's wham-bam-thank-you-ma'am. The only people he doesn't rush are the actors.

The next scene is set in DIRTY SEXY MONEY's office set—a gorgeous sprawling office that "overlooks" New York City, thanks to a large hanging scrim of the Manhattan skyline. It's a long scene with Sutherland and Pete. Sutherland plays the patriarch of a wealthy New York family. Pete plays an earnest young lawyer who is hired to mind the family's business. Frawley rehearses the two for a few minutes. The scene revolves around Sutherland hiding information. When the rehearsal is done, the crew rushes in and marks locations and readies the lighting. The entire crew works like honeybees for a few moments, then the set is ready. It's already approaching 7 P.M. on a Friday night. Pete and Sutherland take their places. Frawley says "action," and through the monitors I'm watching a wide shot of my pal engage in a long dialogue with the great Donald Sutherland. Sutherland seems flat in the first wide shot, and the second. There's a technical issue—a microphone boom drops into the shot. Frawley sets up reverses to be used in editing. Then Frawley goes in for close-ups of each. These are the money shots for both actors. Pete is Mr. Steady, and his performances are intense. Sutherland looks tired and somewhat irritable. Then Frawley focuses on Sutherland. Frawley shoots several takes, none of them memorable. The shooting started later than scheduled because of the rewrite and now Sutherland makes it known that he would like to be done for the day. There's a sense of nervousness on the set. Pete looks fresh and isn't fading at all. Another take is stymied because the sound boom drops into the shot again. Frawley quietly asks Sutherland for another go. Sutherland agrees and rather theatrically announces that this will be his last take. Then as we film, Sutherland lets loose. His flatness disappears. He's suddenly—just like that!—commanding the scene. His blindingly white teeth grin and snap like a wolf's fangs. He circles and looks ready to pounce. There's so much more energy in this take. I sense Pete upping his game, too. The scene is one of conflict barely disguised, and I can feel the energy behind the video monitors. The quality of the take is head and shoulders above any of the others. It's as if Sutherland is showing off: *This is how it's done, boys and girls.* When Frawley yells "Cut!" there's excitement on the set. But Frawley and the script supervisor quickly confer. They're worried. Did the boom drop into the shot again? They look at me. I'd been watching the upper frame of the monitors like a hawk, just waiting for that boom to edge into the frame. "No boom," I say confidently. Frawley smiles. "Check the gate," he tells the camera operator. When he reports back that the camera gate is clean of debris, Frawley yells out: "Moving on!" The scene is done. The crew applauds. Sutherland heads for the exit.

When I drive out of the Paramount lot, I'm riding high. The professionalism and speed were exhilarating. I got to watch one of the all-time great American actors engage in a verbal battle with my friend, another great American actor, and ride shotgun with a director who has four decades of experience on a set.

For the whole day I forgot about worrying about anything. I didn't search for words or have any doubts about my mental acuity. I didn't doubt my brain. At one point, Sutherland came and spoke to Frawley and invited him and his wife to brunch. After Sutherland walked away, Frawley beamed and said to the script supervisor and me, "Not bad! I just got invited to brunch with Donald Sutherland!" I paused a moment, then noted patronizingly, "Yeah, well, he already asked me, but I couldn't make it."

It was obviously an insubordinate comment coming from a mere grad student, but the timing and cheekiness appealed to Frawley greatly. He roared with laughter.

It was one week since I checked into UCLA. I felt blessed.

D an is still wrestling with his script. His ideas change by the day. His stories involve a whiskey-drinking young man wooing a young woman, and (often) an overbearing asshole father. The story changes dramatically from day to day. Dan keeps reassuring me everything will be fine. He has to have a script ready to start shooting in two weeks, which means finding actors, a location, props, etc. We're both producing the film, but with no idea of what our film is, there's no producing to do. Most of the other partnerships are already casting actors and scouting locations and preparing shooting sites.

We meet with Pablo in the second week. Pablo is concerned we are falling behind. He urges Dan to finalize his script. After the meeting, I sit with Dan on a park bench on one of the shady lawns near the film school and ask him to "talk the story out." I offer to transcribe it if that will help. He doesn't accept the offer.

Dan doesn't share what he's thinking. Every day we're another day further behind. Dan keeps saying, "Don't worry, it will all be fine."

The saving grace of the week is that we get our cameras. They're well-worn sixteen-millimeter German-made Arriflex cameras. When the equipment is handed out, everyone in class is excited, and we're all a bit intimidated. I've never used a film motion picture camera. It's a throwback to the prevideo age. We learn how to thread film through the camera, how to make certain there is just enough slack in the film loop so as not to bind in the internal mechanism. I enjoy taking apart our camera. The Arriflex dates back decades—it's older than I am—and it still keeps working, albeit not without constant tinkering by an elderly Russian repairman USC keeps on staff, who cusses and bemoans our general lack of any common sense.

We are strictly limited in the amount of film we can shoot. Our sixteen-millimeter cameras use one hundred-foot rolls, which gives us about two-and-a-half minutes of shooting per roll.

For each film in 508, we are allowed eleven rolls of film, or eleven hundred feet of film. That's only about thirty minutes.

We have three weekends to shoot. The maximum length of the finished film is 5:40.

This is the genius of 508. Because we're no longer shooting video and we're allocated a limited amount of film, we can no longer use the camera like we're spraying water from a hose. We have a roughly five-to-one ratio of rough footage to finished product. This means we must budget our shooting time. The 507 days of shooting a scene over and over and over are long gone. Now we must plan carefully and shoot carefully.

Many of my classmates are worried about the restriction. I like it, knowing it will keep us on a budget. Everyone, including me, is worried about getting an image back on film. Using film requires a leap of faith. Unlike video, there's no way to check quickly if a shot worked. With film, we shoot it, then send it to a developer and get the dailies back a few days later. If anything is amiss—if the exposure is off, if the film wasn't loaded properly, if there's a hair or dirt in the camera, if the film got exposed to daylight while loading it, if the focus is off, if the framing is off, if the camera gets jostled, if there's something in the background that's distracting, if the actor has a booger in his nose—it all gets discovered days after the filming is done.

And our cameras don't cover for us. There's nothing automatic with them. Everything must be measured before pushing the trigger. To shoot film, we need to determine the amount of light on a set using a light meter. Dan and I bought a good light meter for about $300, and we'll find out how adept we are at using it. We must set the film speed, the f-stop, the focus manually.

We're shooting sixteen-millimeter, a smaller and cheaper film stock than thirty-five-millimeter, which is used in most feature films. The sixteen-millimeter film is sixteen millimeters wide, thirty-five-millimeter film is thirty-five millimeters wide, or about one-and-three-eighths inches. All film is projected at twenty-four frames per second. Our sixteen-millimeter stock has forty frames per foot of film.

It costs about $110 to buy and develop a one hundred-foot roll of sixteen-millimeter film. For that, we get less than three minutes of images. No sound, of course. That we'll record later.

The cost of the film and processing is covered by our tuition. If we wanted to shoot our 508 films by ourselves, without the support of the school, each of our short films would cost more than a thousand bucks just in film and developing costs.

Sixteen-millimeter film is used in film schools because it's cheaper than thirty-five-millimeter and the cameras are much smaller and vastly more affordable. However, sixteen-millimeter picture quality isn't as good as thirty-five-millimeter. The image is much smaller, which means there's correspondingly less information projected onto a screen. That's why sixteen-millimeter is used primarily in television and in some documentaries—and in only a handful of feature films. The Oscar-winning film THE HURT LOCKER was shot on sixteen-millimeter to keep costs down. The filmmakers used multiple cameras for every shot and shot a whopping *million* feet of film for a 131-minute feature. Put another way, they shot more than seventy six hundred feet of film for every minute of screen time. We're allowed two hundred feet of film for a minute of screen time.

It shows just how carefully we have to plan our shooting. It feels like we're going on a survivalist's hiking trip and we have the bare minimum of supplies.

In 508, we'll each shoot over three weekends. The first weekend we'll shoot three hundred feet; the next two weekends we'll get four hundred feet each.

We get our equipment, and our camera comes with a heavy-duty tripod and a battery pack that looks like a scuba-diving weight belt. Dan and I also check out lights and electrical cables and flags (which block light) and filters and T-stands (which hold flags and filters). It's a lot of equipment. It's nice to have my Suburban. All the gear won't fit in Dan's smaller sedan.

While we're getting our camera, I spend a little time with the ogre-like Russian who works in the camera department. He's in his seventies and was a cameraman in the Soviet Union way back in the day, and his reputation is akin to the Hunchback of Notre Dame's. He scares many of the students because he often yells at them and mutters obscenities beneath his breath.

His favorite word is *bullshit*—it sounds like *bullsheet*. He smokes constantly, he complains about USC endlessly, he mocks students mercilessly.

When I meet him, I compliment him on some photos of radio-controlled boats he has hanging in his repair shop. He sizes me up and squints. He wants to know if I am *bullsheeting* him. They're his hobby, and he isn't about to be mocked. When he sees I'm not making fun of him, he warms up. He's pleased when I tell him I have three daughters.

Despite his gruff and un-PC exterior, I find him, like Quasimodo, to have a gentle heart. He takes me through his repair area and shows me his collection of film cameras. They're in display cases. It's a little museum. He's got cameras owned by old-timey Hollywood stars, and hand-cranked cameras used by American GIs. He explains to me that sixteen-millimeter film gained widespread usage in World War II because of its smaller size. He points out the technology-loving Americans equipped their fighter planes with sixteen-millimeter cameras that operated whenever the pilot fired the wing guns.

"The Russians didn't do that. Russian pilots come back and say 'I shoot down five, six, seven planes.' That was bullsheet! *You Americans couldn't do that. The film does not lie," he explains in his heavily*

accented English. More important, he notes, the Americans studied the films and used what they learned to teach new pilots. "That's why the Americans were so good at shooting down other planes! They used film! They were smart! The Russians didn't do that! They thought it was bullsheet!"

His job is to keep the dozens of film cameras at USC running. He's like a Havana mechanic working on 1950s Chevys. The Arriflexes are old. The digital future is coming, and he knows it. USC is planning to build a massive new film school with millions donated by Spielberg and Lucas. "I won't have job soon. They don't want me around. Soon it will be all deegital. It is *bullsheet!*"

I tell him I'll visit him again. He doesn't smile, but his shrug tells me I won't get yelled at.

When we get the Arriflex, I take it home and practice loading film into it. I'll be doing all the camera work on our first film. The last thing I want is to expose a roll of film or have an operator error. I load a dummy roll into the camera over and over. I practice it in the dark. I feel kinship with the camera, an old German machine that purrs loudly when it runs.

Before our first shooting weekends, we have a test weekend. It's a chance to shoot a hundred feet of film and check our lighting and focusing and exposures. Because Dan still doesn't have a story nailed down, we elect to shoot at his studio apartment. We need an actor, so I call my nineteen-year-old nephew, Mikey, who is living on a small sailboat in the San Pedro harbor. Mikey is glad to help.

Dan still doesn't have a script. He's still toying with a whiskey-loving boy meets girl, but the asshole father has gone through major modifications. Pablo is nervous. I'm nervous. Dan keeps reassuring us. "Relax," he says.

On Friday late afternoon, I'm out for a jog. My legs feel a little better, but they're still heavy. I've been out of the hospital for nine days. I'm still living out of the hotel near campus. Our test shoot is coming up within twenty four hours, and I'm looking forward to it. Then my phone rings. It's a number from Minneapolis.

"Steve. This is Scott Flaata. What's going on?"

He's not calling for a friendly chat. He sounds upset.

"Uh, hi, Dr. Flaata. I seem to have had a little stroke."

Dr. Flaata is my doctor back home. I've seen him in the past for basic checkup stuff. We've become friends and compare notes about waterskiing during my annual checkups.

"I see that, Steve. That's what I'm calling about. I got all your paperwork from UCLA today. What's going on? Why didn't you tell me? What kind of medicine are you on?"

Actually, he sounds *very* upset. I tell him I'm taking a baby aspirin a day, some cholesterol-lowering meds, and that's it.

"That's all you're taking?"

Now he sounds really upset. I assure him that's what I'm taking.

"I got your lab tests today. Did UCLA ever talk to you about them?"

I assure him they found everything was normal.

"No, everything is *not* normal. There are some labs that came back later. They show you have an elevated risk for clotting. I don't know why they didn't contact you about this."

I feel my anxiety rising. What is he talking about?

"Steve, this is serious. You had two positive results on your lab tests. Both are indicators for clotting. They *really* didn't contact you?"

I assure him they didn't. I did try to call one of the doctors a few days afterward about my concern over my heavy legs, but he was on vacation. Obviously, someone dropped the ball at UCLA. Dr. Flaata got a copy because I put him down as my primary care physician, and he was mailed my charts as part of normal protocol.

Flaata said he was reading my charts on Friday evening and came across the two red flags.

"Steve. I don't know what is going on there. But I want you back here ASAP. Like, *yesterday*. I want to do more tests on you and have you talk to a hematologist and a cardiologist. I want to find out what the hell is going on with you. Can you get back to see me Monday morning?"

Now my heart is pounding. Crap! "I also want you on blood thinners. I'm going to write you a prescription for heparin. Do you feel comfortable injecting yourself with a syringe?"

As he says this, my adrenaline level creeps ever higher. What the hell is wrong with me? My adventure-seeking hometown doctor, a guy who goes downhill skiing in Colorado with a video camera attached to his helmet, is worried enough about me that he wants me back in Minnesota immediately for additional testing? Yikes!

"I don't like what's going on," he says. "If you need surgery, I want to get it done right away. There's no reason to wait four months. Not with these lab results."

I ride the elevator to my hotel room expecting to keel over from another stroke any minute. I'm seriously freaked. I find out where he can send a prescription for heparin, a common blood thinner. And I check flights. I can fly out Saturday at midnight on the red-eye.

I spend my Friday evening going from pharmacy to pharmacy, looking for heparin. When I finally get the medicine, I sit in the front seat of the Suburban, turn on the interior lights, and jab myself in the thigh with the disposable syringe. It doesn't hurt; the needle is tiny. I imagine the heparin flowing through my vessels and dissolving a monster clot just seconds before it hits my brain. I sit back and relax and hope no one is watching me. I'm sure I look like a junkie. I feel like a junkie.

On test-shoot day, I once again walk a fine line with Dan. I try to downplay the seriousness of what's going on. "Say, Dan, I need to dart out of here for a couple days. My doc wants to run a few tests for me back in Minnesota."

Dan, to his everlasting credit, doesn't freak out. He shrugs and says, "Okay. Do what you need to do, I guess." I can't read him. Either he doesn't care or he's good at concealing his fears.

We shoot test footage, and it's very fun. Mikey, my six-foot-four nephew, shows up. He's my oldest brother's son, and he's living the dream at nineteen: he works on sailboats, lives on his own tiny sailboat, and gets around on a beater motorcycle.

We are somewhat sloppy with our tests. Our lighting is only some floodlights we set up against a wall. We shoot a few seconds of Mikey sitting. Standing. Posing. Flexing. Then we do some double images, running the camera backward and reshooting over the same footage. We're just messing around. I'm preoccupied with getting home. Dan is preoccupied with his script. Mikey is preoccupied with the free meal I promised him for showing up.

We have a few seconds of film left in the camera, so I draw a heart on my chest with a Sharpie. I put a hole in the heart. Dan films me. I figure if I keel over in the coming weeks my kids will have at least a tiny reminder that I was indeed at film school.

We eat dinner together and joke a lot. Being busy is the best cure for anxiety. Then I drive to LAX and wait. My flight doesn't leave 'til midnight. I pace.

On the plane, I continue to pace in the aisle. I've been warned not to sit too long, and I take it to heart. I'm standing for as much of the flight as I can. The plane is full of sleeping people, except for me. We land in Minneapolis at 6 A.M.

On Monday morning, I'm not thinking about Dan at all. I'm not thinking about USC. I'm only thinking about what is wrong with my body. I'm seeing Dr. Flaata, who explains I tested positive for lupus anticoagulant and anticardiolipin antibodies. Both are markers for an autoimmune disorder that causes clotting. He tells me a lot of depressing stuff. He tries to keep it in layman's terms, but I soon get the gist.

It's called *antiphospholipid syndrome*, a condition that can cause clotting of your arteries or veins. If those clots form in your legs, it's known as deep vein thrombosis. But the clots can also form in your kidneys, lungs, and other organs. A clot in your brain can cause a stroke. The amount of damage to your system depends on where the clot forms and how extensive it is.

Apparently, my tongue-twister syndrome triggers my immune system to mistakenly produce antibodies that attack certain proteins in my blood. Normally, antibodies attacking is a good thing because they go after viruses and bacteria. But now they're targeting friends not foes.

Then Dr. Flaata really gets my attention. In very rare cases, *antiphospholipid syndrome* can be life-threatening, he tells me. And there's no cure. Luckily, there are medications that can reduce the blood-clot risk.

Swell. I've got a hole in my heart and an autoimmune disorder that causes me to clot. It's doubly depressing.

Dr. Flaata has made appointments for me with Minneapolis' gold-plated specialists. I immediately see a hematologist. Then I see a cardiologist, who explains to me that because of my blood disorder, he can't operate on my heart. He says if there was no disorder, he'd operate in a, well, heartbeat. But he says there's no clear proof that the hole in my heart was the cause of the stroke—and he adds that the FDA won't allow him to install a device that seals a PFO in people with my clotting factors.

To me, it seems stupid. I've got a hole in my heart, and I have prone-to-clot blood. It seems all the more imperative to close the hole.

But the cardiologist explains there's no proof that surgery has any better outcome than taking blood thinners. He goes on: if my stroke was caused by a blood clot that *didn't* sneak through my heart hole but instead developed in my head or neck, closing the hole might give false comfort. He says that instead of fixing the hole, I'll be treating my blood to make it less likely to clot. He explains I'll likely be on blood thinners for the rest of my life.

I don't like hearing this at all. I read up some more on *antiphospholipid syndrome* and learn that because I'm taking blood thinners, I've got to be especially careful not to injure myself and to avoid bleeding.

The medical literature all says I'm supposed to give up all contact sports and other dangerous activities that could result in a fall. I should use a softer bristle toothbrush and waxed floss, not unwaxed. I should shave with an electric razor, no blades. Also, I've got to be careful when using any sharp instrument—knives, scissors, corkscrews, ice picks, glass cutters, thumb tacks, awls, chainsaws—it's a long list.

My whole life has been one long contradiction. I love playing touch football and soccer. I ride a mountain bike. I water-ski. Snow ski. Sometimes I ride motorcycles. I've got a four-foot-high Craftsman roller-chest full of sharp tools. And my toothbrush is extra-firm. I'm screwed. The next stop on the Dr. Flaata magical mystery tour is a neurologist. First, I'll get another MRI of my brain. They inject me with a liquid they say will help them see within my gray matter better. The liquid makes me feel like I need to take a pee, and afterward it makes me dizzy and nauseated. It's like beer—without any of the benefits.

Then the neurologist tells me I definitely had a small stroke, but the good news is it has healed up so well he can hardly see the scarring on this most recent brain scan, taken less than three weeks after the first scans at UCLA. He says there's bad news. He sees several other places in my brain that were likely either damaged slightly by previous concussions or from previous tiny strokes.

Now I really feel glum.

A onetime stroke is a fluke. More than one? I don't want to think about it.

I have a choice to make. I'm sitting on the back steps of our house. It's a beautiful September day in Minnesota. The three kids are at school. Julie is at work.

Dan and I are scheduled to shoot in two days. I don't know what we're supposed to shoot. He still hasn't come up with a script as far as I know.

I mull over my medical news. It sucks, basically. My condition seems much worse than I knew about just a few days earlier. I talk with my oldest brother, the surgeon. Even though the decades have grayed us, he remains the caring and protective big brother. He also knows much more about medicine than I do. He thinks the smart idea is to stop going to USC. He points out that I'm alone in California, away from family, away from support, away from my doctor. It's a wise recommendation. I agree with him that it's a pretty stupid thing for a middle-aged guy in my condition to go back to film school.

The next morning I get on an airplane heading to Los Angeles. I'm going back to USC. I simply don't want to live my life in fear. If I quit, it would be because I'm afraid of being debilitated or dying. I don't want to miss a single day with my kids, yet I want to teach them the importance of working hard at something they believe in. I need to plan on living a long life. To do anything else would be cowardice.

Fundamentally, I want to ignore my PFO, my antiphospholipid syndrome, my stupid little stroke. I don't want them to define me. I don't want them to limit me.

I'm scared and sad as I fly back, that's for certain, but I'm strangely relaxed. I know what I'm facing. I think of troops fighting in Iraq and Afghanistan—they have it tough. I think of my sister and mother-in-law—they had an awful deal. My stuff is minor compared to that. So I say a prayer to the Big Man upstairs and try to let my worries go.

I return to Carl and Irene's house. The heat wave is over; everything is dry in my bedroom; four rooms and a hallway have had the sheetrock partially removed. The carpeting is gone, so the floor is concrete. They're delighted to have me back, and Irene fires up her kitchen to prepare me a welcome-home dinner.

I meet Dan, and he seems calm. He's come up with a script. No more boy and girl and dad. Now it's a story about a boy who lives by himself in a little run-down house by a railroad track. And he teaches himself how to play a guitar by watching TV. And it's going to be a symphony of all the items in the house that make noise: dripping water pipes, boiling water, a ticking clock—plus the guitar.

I *think* I understand the story. At this point, I don't care what his story is, just so we get something on film. When I left, we were weeks behind the other partnerships.

Dan wants to shoot the entire project in his studio apartment. He has pushed his bed and personal items into one end of the studio. We have a tiny amount of space to work with—about seven feet by fifteen feet—and part of that is a kitchenette. We have perhaps the smallest film studio in all of Los Angeles.

It's tiny, but I like it. We have complete control over shooting. We don't have to contend with bad weather, darkness, sunlight, nosy neighbors, police, thieves, or noise.

The studio has a damaged ceiling. Dan had his own pipe leak, and there's a section of the ceiling that features exposed rusty pipes and missing plaster. Dan doesn't tell his landlord because he likes the effect, and because he doesn't want his landlord snooping around while we transform his apartment into a shooting stage.

We spend all day Friday prepping his apartment. We tape aluminum foil on all the windows to block light. I buy an old nineteen-inch TV at Goodwill for $35. The only props we have are a couch, the TV, a guitar, a pot, and a few cinder blocks. We move lights into the studio. The camera and tripod. Some T-stands and flags. Some more lights.

We spend Saturday shooting. We have no actor, so we shoot leaky water pipes. A pot of boiling water. A TV with static. I use my own video camera to shoot Dan's hands playing a guitar, in close-up. We hook the video camera into the old television and play the tape, then shoot film of the TV showing Dan's hands playing the guitar. His hands move from chord to chord. It looks pretty cool.

At night, we move some lights to the outside of the building and cut a hole in the aluminum foil on the window. We shoot a beam of light into the room. I film a wall as Dan "chops" the light with his hand.

That's it. That's all we have.

As we shoot, we notice the apartment gets extremely warm with just the two of us. There's no air-conditioning, and all the windows are closed and blocked. During the shooting, Dan can be a pain in the ass, and I wish he'd relax a bit. He's probably wishing I wasn't disappearing all the time. Dan doesn't talk much. He's very intense. We have only a few boxes of crackers and some diet soda. I get very hungry.

I'm operating the camera, and on every shot I carefully meter the light and adjust the lens aperture to the proper setting. We use a high-intensity Maglite flashlight to focus instead of measuring distance. We unscrew the cap from the flashlight, leaving the bulb exposed. Then Dan holds the lighted bulb precisely where we want to be focused. Through the eyepiece of the camera, it's easy to focus on the bulb. If I'm a little off focus in either direction, the bulb appears to be fuzzy. It allows us to have the focal plane *exactly* where we want it to be. During our test shoot, I used a tape measure, and many of our images suffered from soft focus. We hope the Maglite bulb works better.

Every time I'm finished setting the focus, I tell Dan I'm ready. Invariably, he answers, "Are you sure?" Often, he walks over to check my calculations. After him saying "Are you sure?" a dozen times, I shoot back somewhat testily, "That's what 'I'm ready' means. It means *I'm ready.*"

The apartment is hot. My patience gets shorter by the hour. I get hungrier. My irritability is magnified by the fact that Dan hardly eats a thing. I tell him I'm going to stretch my legs no matter what, every hour. I don't want more blood clots. He sighs when I announce it. We spend a very long day shooting just two hundred feet of film. We save the additional hundred feet for the next week, simply because we don't have anything more to shoot.

On Tuesday, we watch the dailies. Everyone in class is nervous. No one knows if their film turned out. We will find out in class, together. It's exceptionally exciting, as if we're all waiting to open a mysterious gift.

The other groups show their footage. Everyone else shoots three hundred feet—about nine minutes of footage. They all have actors. Everyone else's footage is okay, for the most part, although some of the shooters are having trouble with focus. The old German Arriflexes are a much different animal than modern video cameras.

Then we show our footage. It lasts only about five minutes. We have a dripping pipe. A pot of boiling water. A TV playing static. A TV with hands strumming a guitar. A wall with flickering lights.

Some of the images are slightly underexposed, but the focus is much better than our testshoot with Mikey. The Maglite system works. Technically, it's all okay. There is, however, absolutely no story. It's just cutaways from the inside of an apartment.

The class is silent. Dan and I are silent. Pablo looks at us like we're treating the class as a joke.

Pablo later talks to us privately. "I'm very concerned about you two," he says while folding his hands. Dan says our actor will be available the coming weekend. Then Pablo talks to me alone. I've kept him abreast of my medical issues over the past few weeks. He knows I've been gone for nine days now early in the semester.

"Do you think this is a good idea for you to be here?" he asks me. "You've had some very significant things happen to you."

I tell him yes, it is a good thing for me to be back. He shakes his head. "I'm worried about you."

I force a smile. "I'm worried about me, too. I just don't want to dwell on the negative."

Pablo sighs. "You certainly seem persistent," he says.

I leave. I feel bad for Pablo. First, I quit under his watch, now I'm back and I have a feeling he wishes I had never come back.

Immediately after the screening of the dailies, I'm responsible for putting together a rough cut of our dailies for Thursday's class. Because we have merely a small collection of stationary objects, there's not much there.

I edit our footage into a tiny directionless film. On Thursday, we show the rough cut to the class. It meets the same response as our dailies: a deafening silence. Dan and I are new to the class, and we're not doing much to earn the admiration of our classmates.

Here's the bottom line, the dirty truth about film school: film school is a constant competition. People respect the winners and avoid the losers. It's a simple Darwinian response. Although some may find it unpleasant to admit, it's the way life is at USC. The entertainment world has thousands upon thousands of wannabes. The odds of success are so long that people instinctively gravitate toward those they think might better their odds.

In the first few semesters, we students feel like we're floating in an ocean. There's land somewhere, we hear, but no one knows exactly where. We're treading water and instinctively making our way to those who seem to know how to swim the best. Everyone is hoping to find something or someone to hold onto and float. Everybody tries to avoid weak swimmers for fear they'll drag them down. In my first semester at USC, I found myself swimming alone.

After my time away from USC, I thought a lot about my experiences. I realized that instead of thrashing and drifting in the water, we'd have been much better off by banding together and keeping each other afloat. After all, every year, fewer than a hundred people like me are admitted to the production program at USC. We're just a tiny fraction of those trying to make it in the moving picture business. In 507, I felt more animosity toward my fellow students than was warranted. I loved the competition, but I began to think the SURVIVOR-like behavior fostered at USC is counterproductive in the long run.

Before I rejoined 508, I wrote an email to all fifty students who were then in 507. It was when I was looking for a partner. This was part of my email:

> *I suffer from being irreverent most times and I'm a contrarian at heart, but I have been a dad for 11 years now, and that changes a fella. I stop and look both ways very carefully at intersections now. I don't care if you're male, female (my original 508 partner was female), what kind of people you like, who you voted for, and what you eat as long as you can reciprocate the feelings. I view film school as a chance to build partnerships and relationships with all sorts of types. If USC had a problem, at least in my semester, it was that the school seemed*

to foster a spirit of pitting student against student. I saw it differently.
The real wolf at the door isn't another student—it's the world outside
of USC. The more people can work together in film school, the better
chance they have of succeeding outside those iron gates.

When I meet people planning to go to film school, I tell them
this: be generous, and try to work as a team because you never
know how the future will turn out. Today's irritant may be your
ally tomorrow. I tell them to help other students as much as possible, and to be a giver instead of a taker whenever possible. In
507, I was a taker. Now I want to be a giver. Granted, it's vastly
easier with my family two thousand miles away. I simply don't have
family conflicts and responsibilities. The USC production program
takes up nearly all of my time. I work seven days a week, and I'm
almost always out the door at 7 A.M. I'm not done until 9 P.M. at
the earliest.

With Dan's film barely moving forward, I should be losing sleep.
I'm not. Dan's smart, and I like him, and though he's silent as a
Sphinx when it comes to future plans, with all that is going on in
my life, the fate of a 508 short film doesn't rank that high.

I'm continuing to pursue screenwriting this semester. I missed
my first class because I was in the hospital, but nothing much
happened. So many students drop or join electives that the first
week of school is almost always a lesson in hurry-up-and-wait.
I join the class the second week and find myself moving at full
speed with the others—and there are only a half-dozen of us in
this class.

In the production division, students can choose which specialty
to pursue. There's directing, editing, producing, sound, and screenwriting. Screenwriting seems to be the oddball branch. Not many

production students pursue it, perhaps because USC offers a two-year degree focused entirely on screenwriting. Those who only want to write gravitate toward that degree. The number of us in the production division who want to write is small.

I consider us the true filmmakers, of course. Along with these other students, I believe everything starts with the word. Dan is also pursuing screenwriting, and so is a student named John Thompson, whose brilliant 508 film SONGBIRD wowed Sundance just a year earlier.

The instructor is a former television writer. She's formal and precise in her bearing, and I'm excited to have her as a teacher. I've learned quickly that the adjunct instructors at USC are normally excellent teachers. A great many classes are taught by these adjuncts, nearly all of whom have extensive experience working in the trenches of Hollywood. It's one of the great advantages of going to USC.

The adjunct instructors have a different attitude than many of the full-time faculty. I never find any sense of academic elitism from them. They're generally more fun; they're impossible to pigeonhole. Their politics range from right to left, their income ranges from barely-making-it to wealthy. They're engaged in The Industry, with all its sleaziness and bile, and they're not ashamed of it. My adjunct writing instructor wrote for THE A-TEAM, one of the great campy TV masterpieces of the 1980s. She's proud of the work she did on the show—and her stories of writing entire episodes on extremely tight deadlines are exciting and inspiring.

The full-time faculty in the production division has a fairly unified outlook. Dan and I call them The Aging Hippies, which fits much of the student body as well because many USC students are avid readers of the *Daily Kos* and firm believers in the wisdom of Che.

One day, Dan and I are walking across campus when he makes a comment that sums up the zeitgeist found at USC: "You know what the perfect trifecta for a USC film is?" Dan asks. "It's a pair of lesbians who run an abortion clinic on an Indian reservation."

I laugh. He's hit the nail on the head. There's a lot of emphasis within the school to be "serious" and to do important work. Yet so many times what we watch from other students is just an easy PC cliché. We both agree we don't want to do cliché films. In screen-writing, nobody is writing a cliché.

Dan is working on an awesome comedy that involves a man who wants his wife kidnapped so he can rescue her and add some zing to their marriage.

I'm writing about an accident-prone water-ski jumper who takes a summer job at a going-out-of business Wisconsin resort . . . and who hires the mentally ill to fill some openings in his water-ski show. I title my story CRAZYHOUSE ON SKIS.

The next shooting weekend arrives and so does our actor. He's a cute kid, about the same age as my middle child, and he's escorted by his mother. She's a single mom who looks to have fallen on hard times. She wants her child to succeed as an actor. We also have a studio teacher, an annoying older lady who reads a novel the entire time and doesn't care what we do with the child actor.

The five of us are in Dan's tiny apartment. It was hot with two of us, now there are five, and the weather is hotter, and we've brought more lights into the apartment. It's a sweatbox. I'm the camera operator, and I often have my back up against a wall. I'm on my knees constantly because we're shooting from a very low position. Luckily, I have the same knee guards I used in my 507 acting class.

Dan has given me the script, but it changes so often I'm still not entirely certain what we're doing. I tell Dan I'm his hired monkey and to just tell me what shots he wants. I know I'm supposed to be aware of what the story is and give cinematic feedback based on that, but I don't know what the story is about. Maybe it's my muddy brain, maybe it's Dan being tight-lipped. Dan rarely eats, and he seems very uptight. He's nervous, I reason. I suggest he eat something. He refuses. I shrug and eat.

We film the child actor strumming a guitar, making macaroni and cheese, watching TV. We push the camera very close to him, in some cases within just a couple feet, sometimes even closer. I've got the camera aperture opened as large as it will go to let as much light as possible into the film. I'm being extremely careful in focusing.

Dan is getting on my nerves, however. It starts when I'm changing a roll of film. I'm doing it in the dark, behind a folding door. I'm being careful not to expose the film to any light. I hear Dan's voice: "Aren't you done yet?" His voice is a mixture of irritation and condescension. "No," I answer, "I'm *not* done yet."

I hear him sigh. "Well, how long is it going to take you?" he asks. At this point, I've practiced changing rolls of dummy film so many times I can do it with my eyes closed. In cinematography class, I've become the go-to guy for film loading. And now Dan is harping on my film-loading speed?

Every hour, it gets hotter in the apartment even though it's raining outside. On the first evening, the power cuts out. We're in the dark, and we think we blew a fuse in the apartment. Then we realize the entire neighborhood is out. An hour later, the power comes on again, and we're in business.

It takes all weekend to shoot our three hundred feet. Dan is highly focused during the shoot, but he's in his own world.

On Tuesday, we see the dailies again. The preteen actor looks good on film. The set looks decent, too. Dan deliberately wants as little color as possible in the set—everything is black and white; the kid is dressed in black; and he's got pale white skin. The only color in the set comes from the screen of the TV.

Our only problems are action and focus. There's still no action. The kid isn't doing anything. Some of the shots are slightly out of focus. The face of the boy is fuzzy in some takes. I'm really upset—I spent so much time trying to nail it. I'm embarrassed in front of my classmates, but I'm hardly alone. Many of the cinematographers in the class are having trouble with focus and exposure. This is the first time most of us are shooting film, and it shows.

I'm also irritated I'm giving Dan ammunition to keep harping on me and watching over my shoulder.

After class, Dan and I are both upset. I'm upset with him because there's nothing in the film so far but static images. I'm still in the dark what the story is. He's upset with me because of focus issues. Every other partnership is showing footage that tells some kind of story. We have random images with no conflict and one child actor. It seems worse than any of my 507 films. We leave class hardly talking.

I take the Arriflex the next day to the old Russian to have it checked out. There must be something wrong with it. Some of the images "breathe" a bit, that is, the focus slowly goes in and out. The old Russian pulls it apart. Shrugs. "Nothing wrong," he says. "You are the problem."

I talk to my cinematography instructor. I'm hoping he can help. As I diagram my shots, he interrupts me. "Steve, you have only a tiny area that can be in focus with the way you're shooting." He opens a book on focusing charts. He shows me that with a wide-open aperture, low light, and the camera just a few feet from the actor, I have in many cases only an inch of depth where I'm getting clear focus.

He says no wonder I'm having trouble focusing. If the actor moves a tiny bit, I lose focus. He advises me to bring in much more lighting so I can close down the aperture and increase the depth of field. He also suggests I study the depth of field charts in the back of our cinematography textbooks. For the next four days, I do just that.

Part of the problem in film school is we often learn stuff after the fact. The learning curve is steep, and it always seems we discover something important—like depth of field and lighting—a day after we need it. It is why school projects should be viewed by outsiders as works-in-progress. The whole point of these films is to teach, and to give us students a place to make mistakes. It's like waterskiing: if you're not crashing, you're not pushing it.

I edit the footage for Thursday's class. There's still almost nothing to stitch together. I put together a quick compilation of the boy playing a guitar, making macaroni and cheese, boiling it over. It's really dull. Dan reviews it and hates it. "No! That's *way* too short," he says. He scribbles out the exact shot list he wants. I make it longer. Dan isn't happy about the result, but at least he's not as unhappy as he was.

When we show the cut, it is the worst of the class, by far. We've gone through two shooting weekends, with only one to go.

With class done, Dan and I head outside to the school's courtyard. We're both pissed. Other students take a wide berth around us but watch us out of the corner of their eyes. It's a Film School Argument. I'm really frank with Dan and tell him he has to have some action in the film. The actor has to do *something*. Dan tells me I've *got* to figure out the focus issues. He's also pissed at me for using the term *hired monkey* on the set. He says it sets a bad example for the actor, that I'm making fun of my job. And he hated my edit.

We vent for long minutes. Finally, we calm down. We sit on a bench, poke our feet in the ground. We have one more weekend left. We both understand we're in deep trouble. In 507, I was a mild outcast for having so-so films. Now we're both treated like pariahs in class. No one knows us. Our stuff is completely, absolutely un-understandable. Dan and I are seen as the newbies who suck. We've hardly interacted with the other students in class because I've been gone or we've been locked up in Dan's apartment.

We sit in silence, stewing. We're both screwed if we fail. Here I am, disregarding advice to quit film school, and I'm in a stifling apartment shooting film of a prepubescent actor sitting on a couch holding a guitar while his stage mother hovers nearby. Here Dan is, paired with an old guy who keeps disappearing for days with medical issues, and who can't keep the shot in focus.

It feels like we're in a football huddle and we're losing 28-0 in the fourth quarter. Our relationship has been less than perfect, but we can either give up and go home defeated, or we can do something about it.

Dan and I look at each other and agree we have to do something—anything. We come to an agreement. This is D-day, and we're not going to lose. We're going to go forward, together. We have a lot to do—we have to shoot the majority of the film in one weekend. We agree to get off our arses and get to work. We have nothing to lose. We shake hands and go our separate ways.

Pablo sees me leaving our huddle and calls me into his office. He asks if everything is all right. I assure him everything is. He doesn't seem to believe me. Every week, everyone in class sends Pablo an overview of how things are going on their shoots. It's something only he sees. I've been bitching about Dan in my weekly emails, and I can guess Dan is doing the same about me. I assure Pablo, "Really, things are going to work out." He looks melancholy.

On Friday, Dan and I run around Los Angeles like cats on catnip. I head to Kino Flo in Burbank. They make and rent low-wattage lighting equipment. Low wattage means we can pump more light into the apartment without blowing the apartment building's electrical circuits. Normal incandescent film lights gobble up a tremendous amount of energy. A single "little" 1K light uses a thousand watts. Compare that to a standard interior lightbulb, which uses sixty to one hundred watts. We need a lot of extra lighting in the tiny apartment so we can close down the camera aperture and thus increase our depth of field. That's part of the reason we put aluminum foil over the windows in the first place. We don't want Dan's landlord to see an ungodly amount of light pouring from the windows at night.

Now we understand why professional film shoots use large generator trucks to light a set. Filming uses an enormous amount of electricity, but we can use less with the Kino Flo lights. The Kino Flo lights are also cooler. Less wattage = less heat.

We're buying this, we're buying that. We hit a Home Depot, a Target, thrift shops. Late Friday afternoon, Dan calls. We need to find a music box the kid can hold. I race to antiques stores and find nothing. Dan also finds nothing. The next morning on the way to his apartment, I stop at Los Angeles' antiques row. Most of the stores aren't open yet. I'm out of luck.

But Dan has procured a pair of small snow globes. One has a winder on it. The other looks very pretty.

We go over the script: the boy enters a dirty, dingy apartment. He starts cooking a pot of mac and cheese. A freight train passes, shaking the apartment. The boy peers out at the train. He sits down, turns on a TV. There's an instructional show that teaches guitar. The boy picks up a guitar and plays along with the TV. The drips of a pipe create a beat. The music builds. Then magic happens. Flashback to a beautiful apartment. A mom. A dad. Colors. Beauty. But the pot of water is boiling. More music, more beauty. Smoke curls to the ceiling. A smoke alarm goes off, the boy jumps up and smacks it to turn it off, a train passes again, the TV goes dead. The boy is alone once more, and there's no more color in the world and no more magic, but then the TV comes on, and the guitar lesson continues.

There's much more action in the film than before. The kid won't just sit there now—he'll emote a bit, interact.

Dan and I have to shoot the lion's share of the movie in two days.

We set up the Kino Flo lights. We pray the actor and his mother show up. They do. The weather is mild and sunny. We cross our fingers against blackouts. We put more light into the whole apartment, and I stop the aperture down. Dan agrees to push the camera back a bit. Not every shot has to push right into the kid's nostrils. We still have very shallow depth of field, but it's not impossibly shallow. I now have a several inches of sharp focus in a shot instead of an inch or less.

The kid actor keeps going all day. There's no speaking, so it's like he's a fashion model much of the time. Dan and I are running and gunning all day, aware that we can't use the actor more than the SAG union rules allow.

All day long, we shoot, shoot, shoot. We have five hundred feet in my camera bag because we undershot the first weekend. The kid holds the snow globe in the air in one scene and ponders the flakes falling. The lighting is gorgeous. I'm looking through the eyepiece of the camera and holding my breath so as not to make any movement.

At the end of the day, we're pushing past the SAG guidelines, but the kid is game and so is his mother. The studio teacher shrugs. She doesn't care. She hasn't looked up from her book all day. I think of the school rules requiring a studio teacher. This old hag knows she's gaming the system—she's getting $20 an hour to read a book while a kid's mother is three feet away. And now, when technically she needs to speak up and say, "I'm sorry, this young lad has worked his ten hours," she's mute. It's good for us, of course. We want to finish, and we're not abusing the kid. He plays video games between shots, and it seems he's used to just hanging around.

Finally, we finish shooting for the day. The kid is tired. So is his mom. The studio teacher leaves before they do.

They walk to their car with both of us congratulating them and, between the lines, inferring that it's super-duper important they return the next day. Our film depends on them coming back. I now realize Dan's film is a high-stakes gamble. Having one child actor means we're putting all of our eggs in one very fragile basket.

After the kid and his mom leave, Dan and I transform his apartment. We hang orange Christmas lights everywhere, hang curtains, and rework the little set into a dramatically different stage. It goes from white and muted to orange and bright.

On Sunday, the actor and his mom are shocked at the transformation. We start shooting the *magic* scenes. Dan gets a neighbor woman to pose as the kid's silhouette mother. Dan is the kid's silhouette father. The studio teacher doesn't want to come today, so for a small bribe, she signs off on the form that she was there.

The actor is fading as the day goes on. We urge the little fellow to keep his energy up. We ply him with food and praise. I feel guilty—we're working this little guy like he's a mule, and I'm using every trick I know as a parent and soccer coach to keep him in the game. This kid holds the key to our film. If he has a temper tantrum or gets a sore throat and wants to leave, we're pooched. So we pull out the stops to make him feel wonderful. Toward the end of our shoot, we're high-fiving the kid and *"hoo-hooing"* him when he strums the right chord on the guitar. Welcome to Hollywood. It's a gorgeous weekend, and this kid is sitting in a hot, stinky apartment with two sweating film students who tell him he's the greatest thing in the world. Finally, we wrap up in the late afternoon. The kid and his mom go home. When the door closes, Dan and I slump. I'm glad they're gone.

We shoot a few more scenes for cutaways and finally run out of film. It's dark. We're tired. Dan suggests going out for a steak. It sounds good, and I would like to eat a big bloody piece of meat, but I'm too tired. I just want to go home. We spent three straight days working with as much intensity as we could, from early morning to late at night. We'll find out Tuesday what our fate is.

Monday, I write all day on CRAZYHOUSE ON SKIS. It's such pleasure to shift back to a private task. The yin and yang of production and writing is very attractive.

On Tuesday Dan and I assume our usual chairs in the back of the screening room, just next to the door. Our 508 class has moved up in the world, and we no longer have class in distant Zemeckis. Now we meet in a small classroom in the heart of the film school. Today, we'll be watching the dailies. Everyone is nervous as hell. Everyone in the room has a tremendous amount riding on the dailies. Everybody needs their final weekend of shooting to turn out.

Dan and I have the most to lose, by far. Judging by the dailies of the other partnerships, it should be possible for them to cut together at least a mediocre film somehow. Dan and I have so far shown nothing. Just static images.

The screenings are in no particular order.

Dan and I are both silent as we watch the dailies of other partnerships. The anticipation is killing us. There are seven series of dailies to watch, and we comment after each of them, a bit like we did in 507. This time, the commentary from Pablo and the students is very gentle. We all know when we mess up; we don't need people to point it out with a heavy hand.

Unlike 507, when all films were screened with a thick layer of music larded onto them, in 508 we are watching silent film dailies. It's so quiet we can hear sighs and groans from the filmmakers. It's an amazingly intimate process.

Dan and I have now watched five of the other dailies. We still haven't said a word to each other. I'm so worried we'll have a technical issue.

Then our film appears on the screen. It's perfect. It's not just perfect, it's fantastic. Every image is as sharp as a tack. We're using our actor's eyes as the focal point, and on some scenes he fills the screen, his face perfectly lighted, perfectly focused. Dan and I still don't say a word.

Then the scene with the snow globe comes in. Even though we're shooting in color, our set and actor are so muted that nearly every previous shot looks as if it was in black and white. But the snow globe is a burst of color, and the orb reflects a perfect circle of light onto the actor's young face. We can see his pupils following the falling snow in the globe. Our cinematography instructor can't help himself. "That's *gorgeous*," he says out loud. Suddenly, we see our magic footage and it's bursting with orange. Every reel is perfect.

We're saved.

The lights come up. The other students clap and cheer. The instructors—who had lamented our earlier awful work—now trip over themselves with praise. Pablo says the footage was "extraordinary."

Dan jots down a comment on my notebook: *Saved by the snow globe.*

I grin. I write back a simple one-word answer. *Yes.*

We're like squabbling teenagers who have decided to be friends again.

When class ends, Dan and I are euphoric. We high-five and yell. It's as excited as I've been in film school. I want to high-five everyone I meet on the sidewalk.

8

BMOC, WTF

Dan's film is fantastic. When we display it to an audience of several hundred people in the Norris Theater, the crowd roars. We have the best film of the class, and, we think, the best film of the semester so far of all the 508 groups. After we finish shooting, Dan adds some terrific stop-action animation he shot with a thirty-five-millimeter still camera. The film is just magical. The music score is beautiful. It's a great short film.

Our reputation is now secure. Just like that, we're now *Dan and Steve*, those cool guys in film school. The 508 screenings are where reputations are made or lost. Much of the film school turns out to watch the screenings, and it's a great evening. Dan has named his film THE ORPHAN.

This is not to say the editing and sound mixing are a piece of cake. *Noooooo*. There is a time during editing when I'm ready to take Dan's thin neck and squeeze it between my hands. I have thoughts of homicide. He moves his hands a bit and says a few words and expects me to understand. He's exceptionally impatient with my slow editing. I remind him that I'm a quick writer, and it took him until shooting started to write a five-page script, but it doesn't have any effect on him. He sits in an editing lab and watches my cuts. "No no no no! I don't want *that*," he says. He desperately wants to grab the keyboard from my hands—a no-no according to the class rules. I ask him what he *does* want. He wiggles his hands in the air. "I want . . . it's gotta be different," he says. "Don't you get it?"

I come home late and tell Carl and Irene of my day's tribulations. They have pity on me and take my side in every story. I appreciate it because I'm really getting sick of Dan. Yes, sometimes I can imagine being Dan and watching me, his fat-handed film partner, slowly plonking on AVID. As much as I try to walk in his shoes, I still feel hostility toward him.

I'm also upset at Dan because he leaves my name off the producer credits. In 508, film partners typically share producer credits on both films. But Dan, on the final cut, shows his graphics. He lists himself as director, producer, sound designer, and animator. I'm listed as editor and cinematographer.

We have another after-class discussion. I ask him why the hell I'm not given a producer credit. "Well, you were gone a lot in the beginning. I had to do everything then," he says. True, I add, but since then we'd been working together on everything. I remind him who bought the TV, the stepladder, various do-dads, rented the low-wattage lights, supplied the video camera, bought the food, used the Suburban. It has no effect.

Pablo intercedes and recommends Dan share the producer credit. But Pablo explains that Dan has the final word, as it is his film. Dan goes with a solo producing credit.

With Dan dropping my producer credit, I vow I will return the favor. But in my case, I will expect Dan to do absolutely no producing whatsoever. His job will be to shoot and edit the film, that's it.

Revenge is an excellent motivator.

When I had my stroke, I thought a lot about mortality and my place on this earth. I thought about my relationships with other people and my own legacy. I felt ready to live each day as my last. I thought about Dan, who I often wanted to throttle. Did it mean I was going to forgive Dan? Did it mean I was going to be a *nicer* person, warmer and more generous and kinder?

In my honest moments, I realized I didn't know.

For my 508, I wanted to do a film about redemption, about spirituality, about desire and greed and human nature. I started with some simple premises. What would happen if wood from the Ark of the Covenant turned up in modern times? And what would happen if it did indeed have the power to allow people to see God? What would those people do?

I then took it a step further. In the Bible, the Son of God is born in a cold and dirty animal stall to a woman so poor and without status she isn't even accorded space at an old-timey motel, even though she is extremely pregnant.

So what would happen in our modern age if the vessel that allowed humans a glimpse of God was similarly low in stature? What would happen if that wood from the Ark had been trans-formed into a roll of toilet paper?

When I pitch my idea to Pablo, he grimaces. "Are you sure?" he says.

I think about it. Yes, I am sure. I tell him I want to incorporate the tale into a modern retelling of the Three Wise Men. And I want to use a porta-potty.

Pablo is still skeptical. "But porta-potties are so . . . ugly. I mean, outhouses can have some real beauty. I know, I've built them. But a porta-potty? They're so—industrial. There's no beauty in them at all," he says.

That's my point, I add. If a lowly place on earth two thousand years ago was a cold and dirty animal pen, then certainly one of the lowliest places on earth now is a porta-potty on an industrial job site. Pablo isn't convinced.

I kept honing my idea while running around the USC track. With my work on Dan's film done (he was mixing sound into THE ORPHAN at this point), I have time to exercise again. I head out to the USC track every day at midday and run three miles. At first, I am slow, but I keep upping the pace. Soon I am running my three miles in twenty-four minutes. Then twenty-three minutes. Finally, I'm at twenty-two minutes for my three-mile jog. At that point, I have my script figured out. The porta-potty is gone, but everything else remains.

I talk to my parents on my cell one day while cooling off after a run and tell them my film idea. I'm soaked with sweat, shirtless, walking around the USC track. They like my idea. They're both devout Lutherans, and I'm surprised they're receptive to it.

Here's the story: We see an empty desert landscape. Morning sunlight. The middle of nowhere. Then we see a truck. It's got a sign on the side: ARIZONA SURVEYING. Inside are three surveyors. They stop, get out, stretch, take a piss, have some chewing tobacco, and wordlessly get to work. They load up their gear and head into the wilderness, where they begin laying a line with their tripod-mounted surveying gear. We don't know exactly where they are, but it may be close to the Mexican border because a brown-skinned woman darts through the brush unseen by the surveyors.

During a lunch break in the shade, the three men take a nap. From out of the empty blue sky sails a roll of toilet paper, its tail flowing. It hits the smallest surveyor. He looks around, sees no one. He uses the toilet paper for a pillow.

As soon as he puts his head on the roll, he's transported. Our dirty, sunburned surveyor is suddenly a doctor, examining a patient in a busy hospital. But then his reverie is interrupted when he's toed in the ribs by his boss.

The boss tramps off into the wilderness, but the little surveyor is in awe. He doesn't follow. Instead, he shows the roll to his coworker. When the coworker touches the roll, he, too, is transported to a dramatically different place—he's a pianist, playing a concert.

When we see them again, the two have built a little temple to the toilet paper out of rocks. They both kneel before it, touching it gently.

The boss enters, angry, and pushes them out of the way and grabs the toilet paper. Before he can throw it away, however, he, too, is struck. Suddenly the pissing, spitting boss is standing in an ornate, candle-lit cathedral.

But then he blinks, and he's back in the desert. He looks at the roll, and he understands.

He runs, carrying the roll with him. The other two take chase, and now there's a footrace through the desert. The boss is intercepted in a narrow draw by his second-in-command, who holds the sharpened survey pole like a spear. The roll changes hands. The second-in-command is then chased across the landscape by the third-in-command and is finally caught at the top of a cliff, where the two engage in a fistfight on the very edge of the precipice. With a mighty swing, the tiny third-in-command surveyor punches his coworker in the chin, sending the toilet paper roll flying from his hand down the cliff . . . right into the hands of the boss. The boss laughs, gets into the truck, and guns it. He's free and clear, looking at the other two suckers in his rearview mirror when . . . *Wham!* He hits the brown-skinned woman with the truck and runs her over.

She's sprawled in the dirt, bleeding, dying. The three surveyors gather around the woman. Then, the smallest surveyor pulls toilet paper from the roll and applies it to her bloody wounds. His coworker takes some of the paper and applies it to her head.

The boss, the guy who started the fighting, finally takes the last of the toilet paper and puts it under her head. Then the woman opens her eyes.

The film ends.

My script has everything my 507 fiction films lacked: conflict, action, adventure, humor, surprise, suspense, and depth. It also has a bigger cast—this little film features four characters—and it tackles a bigger issue. The central theme is what might happen to people when they see God or when they *think* they see God. My script is also ambiguous. It doesn't try to tie up every loose end. It doesn't answer questions. I want people to keep thinking about this little film when it ends.

When writing the script, I feel a freedom I didn't in my first semester. Then my stories were simple little affairs. Short hits to the infield. Now I'm swinging for the fences. I work as if there may be no tomorrow, and there's a lot of freedom in that. Before I had my stroke, I'd joke I would die at 105 after being shot in the back by a jealous husband. Now I don't know what the future holds.

The script is easy. Now comes the hard part. I need a location, three surveyors, a truck, survey equipment, a Mexican woman, and about twenty-four rolls of toilet paper.

I put a notice on Nowcasting.com, the online matchmaking site for actors and producers. I write I'm a USC grad student shooting on sixteen-millimeter color film who needs actors who can work in extreme heat or cold out of doors for six days over three weekends, in difficult terrain. I warn there will be no dialogue—so no speaking parts. I note that the shoot will take place somewhere outside of Los Angeles, rain or shine, dawn to dusk. There is no pay, just free food. It sounds like that famous advertisement for the Pony Express: *Must be expert riders, willing to risk death daily. Orphans preferred.*

I now need to find a location, which is complicated by yet another fire season that's being called one of the worst in memory. I've now been in California five years, and every fire season, the locals seem to have short memories. Every year is bad, one of the worst, according to the locals. This year is no different. As a result, all National Forest Service lands are closed to all filming. That means almost every bit of public land in Southern California is off-limits. I call Film LA for help. They never return a call. As usual, they're worthless. I go online and find nothing.

After several days researching via the computer and working the phones, I go back, fill up the Suburban with gas, and start driving. I'm looking for private land. I stop at horse farms, ranches, shooting ranges. I drive up canyons, get out and ask.

No one I talk to wants to have a crew of USC film students on their property for six days. Despite my assurances, the owners worry about fire risk and liability. It crosses my mind they think I might be a thief—I'm sure I sound preposterous when I say I'm a film student—or that I'm looking for a location to shoot porn or do something else illicit. I go to a paintball range, quarries. No luck.

I'm driving late in the afternoon, and I've been on the road for eight hours. I'm in northern Los Angeles County on Highway 14 when I see a promising road off the highway. I turn onto it and see a sign advertising a *Film Shooting Ranch*. I follow the sign.

The place is closed. But off in the distance, I see some very cool rock outcroppings, and there's a sign for Vasquez Rocks County Park. I drive in right before closing time and find an unbelievable location. There's a weird slanted rock outcropping and uninterrupted vistas to the east. It's a small park, less than a thousand acres, but it seems eerily perfect.

I go to the ranger's office and knock. When I step inside, I realize I'm not the first person to find the area unique for filming. On the wall are photos of movies and TV shows the park has hosted: STAR TREK, THE FLINTSTONES, BONANZA, and THE LONE RANGER to name just a few.

A grandmotherly park ranger greets me. I tell her I'm looking to shoot a student film, and she asks me which film school I attend. I say USC, and she says, "Oh, that's good. You give us the least amount of trouble." I ask her to clarify and she says she's had some bad luck with other Los Angeles–based film schools. She shrugs and won't explain any further. She pulls out her scheduling book, and I see how many other production companies are slated to use the park in the coming two months. She says the set for the next STAR TREK film is under construction, so we can't use the park Monday through Fridays. She looks down her ledger and announces we could shoot weekends later in the month. "You'd be the last group I can take. There's already an AFI crew coming those weekends." AFI is another film school—American Film Institute. She needs me to fill out permits and a site map where we'll be shooting and lots of insurance paperwork. And, I'll need a filming permit from Film LA.

She's friendly and upbeat. I can't believe my good luck.

I've never heard of Vasquez Rocks. USC has a rule that 508 films must be shot within a fifty-mile radius of campus. Vasquez Rocks is within that radius. It's perfect.

The next day, I drive to the park and tromp through the wilderness and onto the fantastic rock outcroppings in my Red Wing boots. I'm glad to have them because this is snake country. Yet it's a mystical place where it's possible to lose perspective. I see why

Hollywood has loved shooting here since the 1930s. It's sunny and gorgeous, and I can't imagine a better place to film.

The next things I need are costumes and props. The big film studios will rent an amazing variety of equipment to film students—if you're willing to pay the price. I can't afford to spend much, so I try to rent some dated equipment from survey supply stories. I can't. Then I call a half-dozen surveyors. Nothing. Call another handful. Zip.

Then I get a call back from a surveyor in Glendale, Robert Hennon. At first, he's wary, but he becomes friendly the longer we talk on the phone. He invites me to meet him at his office later in the week.

When I walk into Hennon's office, I find he's made his decision already. There's a stack of surveying equipment in the corner. Poles, surveying telescope, backpacks, orange safety vests . . . the whole nine yards. He says he and his wife thought it was a pretty cool idea for a film. "Surveyors are never in films. And if they are, they're always bad guys," Hennon says. He entertains me with surveyor lore and shares a tremendous amount of information about his profession. "Do you know that a licensed surveyor is the only person who can legally trespass through private property without a warrant?"

"No, I did not," I answer.

"What do you think is the first man-made thing on earth a visitor from space sees?" Hennon asks.

"Um, the Great Wall of China?" I answer.

"No!" he explains, triumphant. "It's the original survey grid of America!" He points to a photo of the earth taken from space. Sure enough, there's a patchwork of squares of farmland in the Midwest. The entire American West is defined by one perfectly straight snap-line, an idea thought up, he says, by Thomas Jefferson, a surveyor by training.

We talk more and discover I live just a few blocks from his house. That seals it. Now I'm really a good guy.

I ask him how much he wants to charge for his equipment. "Ah, nothing. Just don't lose it. The equipment's still useable and it would cost me a lot to replace it."

I gulp. "Thanks. You sure?"

He's sure.

We load the equipment into my truck and shake hands. "Bring it back whenever you're done," he says. "Maybe I'll come out and give you a hand when you shoot, if you want."

I drive away, having ticked another item off my list. I'm feeling really lucky. Dan is still toiling day after day on the sound for THE ORPHAN, and I've got a location, costumes, and props.

An hour later, my phone rings. It's Hennon. "Hey, Steve, I was just talking to my wife about you. We both thought it would be great if you wanted to use our old surveying vehicle. I'm buying a new pickup truck, and we won't need our old truck when you're making your movie."

I'm wondering if he's pulling my leg. He's not.

"It's a really great-looking truck," he goes on. "I mean, it's old and battered and it's full of surveying gear. My guys beat the crap out of it. It's really great."

I remind him I'd need a vehicle for three long weekends, and I'd be putting hundreds of miles on it. "Oh, I don't care," he says. "We've had that truck for twenty years, and it means a lot to us. My wife and I would love to have it be in a movie. Then we can watch it and remember it. We started our business with that truck."

Okaaay, I say.

I've now got a free vehicle.

I'm still missing the most important thing I need for my 508 film. I check NowCasting.com. I posted for three roles on the site: Boss, who needs to be physically imposing; Matt, who needs to be medium-sized; and Lil' John.

The list of those who responded to my posting and submitted their information is a bit short.

So I call and email everyone who submitted and invite them to an audition on the USC campus. I'm aware from conversations with classmates that only a fraction of actors will respond. The audition serves two purposes. One, it obviously gives me a chance to meet actors face-to-face. Two, and perhaps the most important thing, it makes actors jump through some hoops. If they really want a role, they'll fight through traffic and make a pilgrimage to the intersection of Hoover and Jefferson.

I get a call back from a dozen actors who say they'll come to my audition. I set it up for a Saturday. I reserve a classroom. Make signs giving directions. Buy lots of donuts.

USC asks that all students holding auditions do so in pairs at a minimum. It's to protect the actors and avoid casting-couch temptations—or the allegations thereof—and to protect the students because they are inviting strangers into a closed room. Because I'm producing this by myself, I don't have the luxury. I'll be doing the audition solo. I'm not worried. I'm casting men. I can take care of myself.

The day of the audition, I've got my afternoon blocked off from 1 P.M. to 3 P.M. It's an open call—show up when you can. At 1 P.M., a neatly dressed man named Robert enters. We talk, he gives me his headshot. He's a likable guy, we talk, he leaves. For the next hour, no one else comes. I'm bored, so I move out into the hallway and take a seat on some of the chairs I've lined up. I grab a donut and eat it. I eat another one. There are a lot of donuts left. I eat another one.

As I'm eating, a guy walks down the hall and sees the number on my audition room door. He's an outdoorsy looking guy, hiking boots and a thick stubble.

"Here for the audition?" I ask.

"Yeah. You?"

"Yup," I say. I pause a moment, and continue: "I don't really know if I wanna go through this. I've been listening through the door. The director sounds like a king-sized ass."

"Really?"

"Yeah. A few minutes ago, another guy left. The director was yelling at him."

"Wow."

"Yeah," I say. "It's really too bad. We come all the way down here to USC and get treated like this."

The guy doesn't want to agree with me. He just shrugs.

I keep piling it on: "These film school directors suck."

He's silent.

I stick my hand out. "I'm the director."

He breaks into a big smile. "I'm Jeffrey Miles." We shake.

We spend a few minutes talking about the role and his acting background. We never leave the hallway. I like this Jeffrey Miles. He leaves.

Fifteen minutes later, I get a call on my cell. Another actor. He wants to know if I'm going to be there. I am, I assure him. He'll be there in ten, he says.

Fifteen minutes later, a small, fine-featured man runs down the hallway. He apologizes for being late. I've made sure to write down a long list of names on my legal pad. When he gives me his head-shot, I add it to a folder that I'd prestacked with other headshots. I want to give the impression that all of Los Angeles is vying for a spot in my film. The actor says his name is Dream. He's bubbling with energy. He says he really wants to work on this film.

He leaves, and I'm left with a half box of uneaten donuts. Three hours. Three actors.

They don't know it, but they all have a role in my film.

Lots of people in Los Angeles say they want to act. But when the rubber meets the road, few seem willing to spend the time and effort to get a role. For me, what starts with thirty-eight applicants ends up with three willing actors.

I wait a day to call the three back. And this being the training ground for Hollywood, I feed them some bullcrap.

Me: "Hey Robert/Jeffrey/Dream: I really liked you. I think you'd be awesome for the part."

Robert/Jeffrey/Dream: "That's great!"

Me: "Now, there's a lot of interest for this part. I think you're the best, but I need to know for certain that you can make it every single weekend. This is six days of shooting. I simply can't have anyone dropping out. If you have any doubts, let me know and I'll go with someone else."

Robert/Jeffery/Dream all insist they will be there, every single weekend.

Everything is turning up roses for my 508 film. Location, props, costumes, actors, script. I call up my nephew Mikey and ask him if he's game to be an assistant during the shoot. We'll be in the desert, and I need as many hands as possible. He's excited. He's got more energy than a Lab puppy. He'll drive his motorcycle up from San Pedro, a ninety-minute haul.

Robert the surveyor says he will indeed come out to the set, if I don't mind. He'll show me the ropes, he says, and stay out of the way. He gives me the keys to his old truck.

Irene tells me she's going to cater every meal for the cast and crew. She refuses to be talked out of it. "I can make some really nice roast beef sandwiches and a coleslaw salad and some fruit. Do you think they would like that? I'll put some cookies in there, too."

She and Carl want to come and watch, too. Is that a problem? they ask. Of course not, I tell them.

I've had a sign maker create a pair of metallic door signs for the truck: ARIZONA SURVEYING

The only thing I can't find is a pair of Arizona license plates. I spend a morning at auto salvage yards in the far reaches of the San Fernando Valley looking for an old Arizona plate. It is time badly spent: a junkman tells me California law prohibits selling old license plates.

We have eight vehicles between cast and crew and an hour drive. It's becoming a real production.

The week before shooting I'm watching two films over and over before I go to bed: THE SEVENTH SEAL, directed by Ingmar Bergman, and LAWRENCE OF ARABIA, directed by David Lean. I use them both as inspiration.

The day before the shoot, I walk the desert. I've got a list of shots I want sketched out on storyboards. I spend the day tramping around, running up rock faces, standing atop the huge outcroppings that make Vasquez so unique. In the still desert air, I feel my blood pump in my ears. It's so quiet. It's so beautiful. I just hope everyone shows up.

I've now preproduced the entire film. I've never so much as texted Dan asking him for help.

The first day of the shoot is scheduled for Vasquez Rocks, 8 A.M. Saturday. The park gates open then, and close precisely at 5 P.M. We have our work cut out for us.

On Saturday, I leave before 7 A.M. in the old surveying truck. It creaks and groans like an old ship, and the leaky windows create a roar inside that makes the radio pretty useless. The surveyor had warned me about the brakes—they were bad, he said—and he was right. I push the brake pedal on the Highway 14 off-ramp and the truck slows slightly. I grunt down with both feet, and the truck loses speed with only a little more alacrity. The truck has character, however, and it looks perfect.

I've long felt that the right props and the right location don't make a movie, but they sure can kill it. When I watch a film, I obsess over the little things, and I look and listen for errors. If I find them, they take me out of the film. Good films and television shows are good for a reason, and attention to detail is a big part of it. On this film, I feel I've got all the details right . . . except the darn license plates.

I'm at the entrance to the park by 7:30 A.M. Today will be the acid test. Will the actors be on time? Will they find the park? Will they show up at all?

By 7:50 A.M., I have my answer. Everyone has arrived. We're lined up on the road outside the park gate, and I'm grinning like a fool and high-fiving the actors. It's an auspicious start.

We start shooting the first scene by 9 A.M., and I find something strange with my relationship with Dan. I'm not irritated at him. The first order of business is to load the camera. Dan disappears into his car and covers himself with a blanket to block light from getting onto the film. He's gone a *lonnnnng* time. He comes back, looking a bit sheepish. He was impatient with my loading skills during his shoot. Now he seems chastened. I don't rub it in. "Loading a camera in the dark is fun," I say in commiseration.

As we set up shots, Dan is helpful and enthusiastic. He knows more than I do about camera work, and I'm very happy to have him on the set. From hour one, the relationship is much more cohesive and upbeat. I think it has to do with security and insecurity. I'm twenty years older than Dan. I'm old enough to know that I know very few things in this world, and I'm not ashamed to admit this to Dan. Dan has the cocky assurance of youth, someone who knows everything and is loath to admit ignorance. I was the same way when I was twenty-three. When Dan was director, he seemed uptight and nervous. Now that I'm the director, he's loose and relaxed.

We have a great deal of back and forth. I'm happy to have his input.

Dan also seems impressed that the shoot is running like clockwork. The producing duties are largely done, and we've got a great cast, nice props, and an awesome location. He's had a nice break to focus on his other classes. Any doubts he had about my organizing skills are put to rest.

We shoot that morning and dine on a feast for lunch on a shade-covered picnic table. Irene's spread is delicious. Surveyor Robert Hennon has indeed come to give technical advice, and he's a gent. He shows the actors how to use the surveying gear.

The next day we meet again and shoot again. It goes swimmingly well. Mikey is there to be a gofer—we cover a lot of ground and he gladly hauls camera equipment and props.

By the end of the weekend, Dan and I are sunburned and tired. My feet are blistered because we've walked so much. We got every scene on my shot list. We're on budget, and everything is looking good.

When we look at the dailies on Tuesday, I'm not nervous. I've spent enough time shooting that I know our exposures are right, and I trust Dan's camera work. I trust him enough that when he recommended we slightly overexpose the film by one half-stop, so as to give everything a hyperbright, slightly washed-out look, I agree to it. (We later learn we could have done the same thing in postproduction, but, alas, another thing learned too late.)

I simply know we're going to have knockout dailies.

And we do. As soon as the first frame fills the screen, it's gorgeous. Dan and I have now established our reputation in class thanks to THE ORPHAN. And with the first day of dailies, we cement that reputation. The scenery is just outstanding. The slight overexposure means we're pushing a tremendous amount of light onto the screen, and the slightly washed-out look adds to the grittiness of the location. The actors look good, the truck looks great, and every scene we've shot is just dandy.

We shot one scene of the three surveyors hiking up a razorback ridge. They look tired, just one day of work in a thousand. They're in silhouette against the intensely bright sky. I had composed the shot like a scene from THE SEVENTH SEAL, and as the scene plays out, Pablo comments, "That looks like something from a Bergman film." I punch Dan in the leg I'm so gleeful.

Pablo loves everything. The cinematography instructor has nothing but positives. The class wants to know where we shot.

Dan and I are euphoric.

There's a simple observation in literature that a devil makes better drama than an angel. On the first week and the second, there's no drama in the making of this film. In fact, the second week goes even better than the first. Pablo is only concerned that my story is too big for a five-minute-and-forty-second film and that we won't get the needed number of shots with our eleven hundred feet. I'm conscious of conserving our precious film, and so is Dan. We shoot very little on the front of each roll. Our footage of color charts and ID boards—there for the photo processors—is very brief. We're aware that we're probably pissing off the FotoKem lab techs who are processing our film, but we know it allows us to squeeze another few feet from a reel. We also keep close tabs on the film counter on the camera. When we're running low on film, I deliberately shoot a scene that is short, so we don't run out of film in the middle of a take and thus waste it.

Most important, I limit reshoots on a take. If a take looks good, I'll shoot only a second take at most. On several occasions, I shoot just one take and move on. We'll shoot the same scene but from a different angle in order to give us something to work with in editing. But always, I am trying to conserve film. It's like squeezing every last drop out of a tank of gas. It's something I did a lot when I rode a motorcycle, and we're getting a lot more out of each roll than some of the other partnerships.

In the first half of 508, while we were working on THE ORPHAN, one of the other partnerships completed its first weekend shot list with plenty of film left. Instead of saving the remaining film or shooting additional scenes, they simply squandered the film by firing off the camera on a long take of silly behavior. Dan and I looked at that and shook our heads. It was foolish, like pouring precious water on the ground during a cross-desert hike.

The second round of dailies comes, and our footage is again gorgeous. In fact, this time it's even better. We look at the footage of our flying toilet paper—we ran the camera at maximum speed. The more a camera is overcranked, the more an image appears to be going in slow motion when played at the usual twenty-four frames per second. We are lucky to have received a camera with a slightly oversized motor (the old Arriflexes are not totally standardized), and we can film at sixty frames per second. Because we're shooting in lots of light, we don't have to worry about underexposing the film. We simply open up the aperture the necessary amount. The result is that our toilet paper roll flying through the desert sky looks completely magnificent, regal even. The tail slowly waves in the breeze at the slow-mo speed. It reminds me of royal banners with their long silk tails.

"I stand corrected about the toilet paper," Pablo says in class.

"It's really rather remarkable how good that looks." Pablo is a dozen years older than I am, and he's been teaching for much of his career. That he's impressed by our footage is exceptionally encouraging.

We have so much footage from so many scenes that for our second week of rough cuts we have a fairly lengthy film already. Like all the partnerships, we still need to get the all-important third week.

As I lie awake at night, I go over why this film is so much more enjoyable for me than THE ORPHAN:

We're using adult actors. We're not having to pamper or cajole them or flatter their mother. I can joke with them, be direct with them, treat them like adults.

We're outside. We're shooting a Western, essentially, and we all comment how downright pleasant it is to be out of Los Angeles. It's sunny and warm, and we're all getting tan. I feel a tiny bit like John Ford must have felt when he directed one of his sweeping Westerns. We're lucky because it's gorgeous fall weather.

The script is fun. There's a lot of action and a range of behavior, from sleeping to fighting, from boredom to high anxiety.

Our food. It's quantum leaps better. We mostly ate one meal of Subway sandwiches in Dan's apartment during our long days of shooting there, and one time we ate leftovers on a Sunday. We never broke for dinner until it was late. I was always hungry. Now we're eating huge lunches of top-quality food prepared by Irene and Carl. I know our meals are as good as those served on any film set anywhere. When the cast and crew are dining on huge piles of Carl's smoked beef ribs and fresh-baked buns and Irene's home-made potato salad and tossed spinach salad and a peach cobbler, topped off by lots of lemonade and soda and Gatorade, it's a happy cast and crew.

Plus, we eat family style, all of us lined up at a big picnic table, and we gel as a group. The actors and Dan and Mikey and I all share jokes and stories. We are joined one time by Robert the surveyor. Another time by Carl and Irene. We become a tight-knit group during our weekends in the desert, and the meals help create an environment that makes everyone want to drive a hundred miles roundtrip and work for free. We eat like it's our best meal of the week. And maybe it is. If an army travels on its stomach, a film set lives or dies with good catering. The largest item in my budget is food, and it is worth every penny.

But the biggest reason I'm having so much more fun is this: I'm in charge. Being a director is simply liberating. No joke, the view is much better for the lead dog than the second dog.

The final shooting weekend is approaching. Before that, we meet our actors individually at a doctor's office, a recital room at USC, and the same Catholic church where I shot my second 507 film. It's a busy week. Dan and I are getting along famously. There's no tension. It's as if the acrimony from the first half of the semester happened another lifetime ago. We're having such a good time together we start getting . . . smug. Another classmate tells of his troubles with his filming partner, and later Dan and I shake our heads. *Tsk tsk tsk, they really ought to work things out.*

Dan and I now realize we're going to have two excellent films in 508. With THE ORPHAN, we rose from the dead in the final days. With my film, we're rolling from day one. To extend the earlier football analogy, we're again in the fourth quarter, but this time we're ahead 49-0. We both feel we've got our mojo working, both of us, seamlessly together. Dan is confident about his camera work. I'm comfortable with my story. We confer about camera placement, future editing options, pace. It's a great learning experience. I treat every shot like an unsolved riddle: Where would be the best place to put the camera? What should the actor spacing be? How are the actors performing? How much film can we spend on this scene?

It's so much more fun and challenging than 507. Then I was alone. When floundering, there wasn't anyone to ask for help, for advice, for feedback. Now with Dan (and Mikey, who provides a running stream of entertaining, unsolicited commentary), I can bounce ideas off someone. In filmmaking, two heads are better than one. Lots of people feel filmmaking is a province of the auteur— the lone genius who rules supreme. I couldn't have made my film without Dan's help, simple as that. Sometimes I disregarded his suggestions, more times than not I incorporated them. It's not democracy, of course. Being a director means I *direct* and get to have the final word. It's a great deal of fun.

On Friday, I get ready for the weekend shooting. I again drive to Vasquez Rocks by myself to scout the location. I've been doing it before every weekend shoot. After all these days in the park, I'm getting to know the topography well, and I find some dramatic locations to stage the final action sequences.

I drive back to Carl and Irene's and spend the night going over shot lists and storyboards. At about 9 P.M., my obsessive-compulsive bug bites me and I check over our equipment one more time. I've got the camera case even though Dan is supposed to be in charge of it. In a strange twist of fate, Dan's apartment is now the uninhabit-able one. His landlord is spraying for termites, and Dan is staying at a hotel in Hollywood. Because he'd be in a hotel, I agreed to take the camera and tripod.

That night, I open the camera case and plug in the power outlet. I turn on the motor, and the old Arriflex purrs like a kitten as usual. I spin the motor to top speed to test it and before I can turn the knob all the way to the right, the motor emits a quick *ffffffzt* and goes dead. A little smoke curls out of the camera. Oh crap.

For thirty minutes, I fiddle with the camera, trying to find the problem. It clearly seems to be the motor. I smell burned wiring. I'm hoping I can find a short but no luck.

I call Dan. He's not picking up his cell. He's probably in bed already. I call my cinematography instructor. He's at home, and at first he sounds surprised I'm calling him so late at night. He's not a repairman, and he suggests finding another camera. He suggests calling his teaching assistant. I do, and he sounds like I just woke him up. I did. He's just gotten back from a weeklong shoot and is exhausted. He groggily tells me there should be a backup camera available. He tells me whom to contact. I call them, but they're gone. I leave a message.

It's now getting to be 11 P.M. on a Friday night and our camera is dead. No camera, no shooting. We have a call at 8 A.M. at Vasquez Rocks. We have a full day of shooting, and it will be our last full day because several of the actors can't make it Sunday.

If I don't have a camera, I am completely and totally screwed. I feel a big blast of that old 507 anxiety. I'm wondering if the early good luck I had shooting for 508 was just a cruel joke. Nothing has gone wrong until now. It seems insane. I've been hypervigilant with our actors, with Dan, with everything. And now a supposedly super-reliable mechanical camera goes belly-up right before we shoot.

I'd call the Russian repairman, even if it meant waking him up, but no one has his number and he's not hired as an on-call technician. I don't even know his last name, so I can't search for his address. Finally, I get a return call from the person with whom I'd left the message. She wasn't on call, she says, another guy was. I feel I'm getting the royal runaround. Then she says the other guy's name. Anthony Kuntz.

I ask: *The* Anthony Kuntz, the tall, bespectacled writer of outlandish sci-fi spectaculars who's in my screenwriting class? The one only, she says. I call Anthony and he groggily answers the phone. He's asleep, too. Aren't film students supposed to be night owls? So much for Friday-night partying. He yawns and tells me I woke him up, but, yeah, he's got an extra camera. I tell him I live in La Cañada. "No problem," he says. "I've got to be at USC at 6 A.M. for a shoot so I'll drive it to your place before that."

I want to hug my pillow when I go to bed. My body is so drenched with adrenaline it takes several hours to fall asleep. Then I sleep fitfully, hoping Anthony doesn't oversleep.

He doesn't. At 5:30 A.M., exactly when he said he would, Anthony pulls up in his car. He's got another Arriflex in his trunk. It's like a handoff between spies on a dark street. I kiss him on the cheek, which I don't think he appreciates.

I'm so relieved, so thrilled; I have a big breakfast and get ready for the last full day of shooting.

When we gather outside the gates of Vasquez Rocks, I hand Dan the replacement camera. He inspects it. It's even more scratched and worn than our previous one. We hope the thing works.

One by one, the actors arrive. The actress is late, but that's no problem. We only need her for a few hours. We continue shooting, and when she arrives, we move to the accident scene. The park officials have been gracious enough to let us drive onto parts of the park where no other vehicles are allowed. It's great because we are able to shoot in a secluded area, directly under a high cliff. The cliff will be where a fight takes place. It's also a natural location to shoot down on the truck. The camera angles will look as if we're using a boom to elevate the camera.

The last day's shoot goes perfectly once more. We go through scenes one by one. The actors are so receptive to directorial instruction. Their characters all have their arcs, with the boss' being the most pronounced. At first, he's a taciturn old salt. Then he shows his greedy side; when he's stealing the roll of toilet paper, he's wild-eyed. Finally, after the accident, he's contrite. Jeffrey, who's playing the boss, is in his thirties, a recent transfer from Texas, where he worked first as an engineer, then as a professional guitar player and music teacher. Now he's in Los Angles to act, and he's got a small nest egg he earned in Houston that allows him to pursue his dream in La-La Land. He's had a few small TV roles so far.

It's a blast directing a real actor. I realize what I missed in 507 by leaning too heavily on friends and family. I missed out on working with professionals.

On the set, we learn a lot about each other. Dream says his father was a Thai national kickbox champion. He demonstrates his own kicks, and we all see he could break my jaw in an eye blink. Dream pays his bills by waiting tables, but he wants bigger things. Robert is a schoolteacher who wants to be a professional actor. Jeffrey is the musician who wants to act. And then there's Dan, who wants to be a director. And Mikey, who wants to sail around the world. And me, who wants to support a family.

We all have our dreams.

The final day of shooting is sublime. We're just having so much fun, it seems we shouldn't be doing this for school. The cliff-top fighting stunts and truck spinouts work so well. My big jar of red-dyed corn syrup is insanely sticky, but it looks like blood—kind of, sort of. The actress flirts incessantly with Dream. I'm constantly—constantly—yelling for the actors to stop laughing so we can resume filming.

I'm also the bearer of an old Arizona license plate that Carl and Irene found for me by networking with their friends. It seems the perfect cherry on the sundae. I attach it to the truck, and we reshoot the opening scenes. We also reshoot a scene in which Jeffrey takes a piss. I give him a big squirt bottle of watered-down lemon Gatorade. He creates a big arcing stream of perfect yellow urine and scratches his rear as we shoot. We don't see he's holding the squirt bottle. We only see the liquid arc. It's very funny.

When we watch dailies, Dan and I are nervous about one thing only: Did the replacement camera work? As soon as we see the first images of our footage, we relax. It's all there. The footage looks simply great. Chris Caraballo whispers over to me when he sees the Arizona plates on the truck. "*Nice*," he says. It's the details that count.

I realize in filmmaking there is no big lead—no 49-0 score. We almost lost everything, and in retrospect, we were lucky our camera broke on Friday night. Had it fritzed on Saturday at Vasquez Rocks, we'd have been out of luck. We'd have lost so much time getting a replacement that the day would have been squandered, with no way to replace it.

The Russian repairman later inspects our camera motor and demands to know what I did to break it. Then he pulls the motor apart and grunts: "Ah, this went bad!" He's pointing at a rheostat that controls the speed. "It just . . . pffft . . . Nothing you could do. These sometimes just die. They are bullsheet."

Now Dan starts the final edit. Pablo says our only worry is getting it down to the maximum length of 5:40. "You could have a nine-minute film there," he says.

Another 508 class component is our sound class. In 507, sound was mostly a theoretical class under Holman, but now it's all practical, under an intense drill sergeant named Frank. Frank's a sound editor with impressive credits: he worked on THE FUGITIVE, THIS IS SPINAL TAP, WHITE MEN CAN'T JUMP, and many others.

His classroom behavior is just a notch less intense than the manic drill sergeant in FULL METAL JACKET. Frank struts. He cajoles. He teases. He gives everyone a nickname. (I'm "TV star Steve." Why? I have no idea.) He closes the door precisely at the start of class and starts lecturing. If someone dares look at their laptop or Blackberry or phone during class, he walks behind them and quietly snatches it and continues lecturing without missing a beat. He puts the offending electronic device on his podium and tells the guilty student he or she can collect it after class.

Dan and I both love Frank. Frank is so refreshingly candid, blunt, and amped-up that he makes every class a Red Bull–drenched excursion into sound design. Our 508 films have no sound recorded on set. We're only shooting images. None of the characters say a word on-screen.

Now we must build the sound for the entire film, piece by piece by piece. Under Frank's tutelage, we learn how.

In screenwriting class, my comedy CRAZYHOUSE ON SKIS is taking shape. Mondays are always writing days, and I spend the entire day on my laptop, with a quick run in the middle of the day and, as usual, an evening phone call to Julie and the kids back in Minnesota—something I do every day at school.

The next-to-the-last edit of my film is a dandy. It's all there, so much so that there's too much there. With every scene in place, the film is three minutes too long. Dan isn't worried. While I sit behind him, he trims the film until we're at exactly 5:40. I recommend we take a few more seconds off for safety, and we do. Bingo. The visuals are striking, and the story is compelling.

"It's a real shame you can't use this as your thesis film, Steve. It's very compelling," Pablo says in class. Dan and I add graphics, which in this case are only titles and credits. Dan doesn't flinch when I put only myself as producer. I do feel petty. I consider adding him as a coproducer, but he didn't question my decision, and he didn't produce anything. So he stays off. An eye for an eye.

We color-correct the images so each scene fits the other—adding a bit of brightness here, deducting a bit there, to smooth out any rough transitions. It's like using fine-grit sandpaper on hardwood.

Just the last tweaks, and the title. I had a working title of PAPER, but it seems entirely too dull. Now, without anyone but Dan and me knowing, I name it WTF. Dan thinks it's a very funny title. I know I can tell my young children the title means "With Tender Feelings." Everyone else will know what it really means.

Finally, we picture-lock. The images are set. Nothing will change until we screen it. The final picture lock is completed late at night.

Now I'll spend two very long weeks putting sound under the film, which means recording sounds with a tape recorder and mixing them into a timeline that corresponds with the picture. Door slams, spits, grunts, footsteps, bird cries, wind noise, fluttering, engine revs, wheel spins . . . they all need to be recorded. We get a short session in the USC Foley lab—a little soundstage where we can record while watching the film. It's perfect for matching footsteps, throat-clearing, and the like. The Foley lab looks like any other recording studio: two rooms separated by soundproof glass, with a microphone in one room and electronic mixing equipment in the other. The only difference is the room with the microphone has all sorts of flooring and a sandbox (for different footsteps) and boxes full of things that make noise. I recruit Jeffrey to record sounds. He's sick with a chest cold, which is perfect for some massive throat-clearing noises, but when he tries to match the running footsteps of the characters by jogging in place, he starts coughing. But we get it right eventually.

The sound design of my film is straightforward but incredibly time-consuming. Frank is a taskmaster, too. He looks at the layers of sound on my film and always wants more. We're only working in stereo—no 5.1 surround sound mix here—but my sound track has layer after layer of sound. It takes nearly as much time to add sound to my short film as it does to shoot it in the first place.

I have a musical score, too. Early in the semester, I attended a meet-and-greet with USC student composers. I pitched my story and was approached after class by a grinning kid who looked twelve years old. He wanted to compose for me. I grabbed his name and ignored him for days. I wanted a good score. I didn't want some comic-book-reading teenager working on it. He called me twice, wondering if we could meet. Finally, when I needed to have a composer on board (all 508 music must be original—nothing can be previously copyrighted), I called the kid. I figured I'd let him have a crack at it before I contacted someone else. I told him what I wanted and showed him a rough cut of my film. He grinned, and said he'd love to "whip something together."

I'm not expecting anything. Zero. Three days later, the kid, Niall-Conor Garcia, brings me a score he recorded. I put my headphones on and listen. My jaw slowly ratchets down. The score is stunning.

I ask Niall, *Who are you?* He says he's an undergraduate. A sophomore. He says he really wants to work as a film composer. He keeps grinning.

The day after that, I bump into the head of USC's conducting program on a sidewalk. He asks me how my project is going. He's got a twinkle in his eye. I tell him Niall is amazing. "Yes," he says. "I've heard he's better than most of our graduate students. He's something of a genius."

Niall has created a score for a string quartet, a trumpet, a piano, and percussion. I set up a recording session in a USC soundstage, and he sets up the musicians. Niall works for free, but no one else does. On the night of the recording session, I bring a thick roll of $20 bills to pay the mixer and the musicians. And the score is simply phenomenal. It sounds like music from a Hollywood blockbuster. I'm in awe listening to the group play. A couple of the musicians are from USC, a couple of others are professionals—they're moonlighting at USC to make a few bucks. In an hour, we have Niall's score down pat. It is synched to the film, and it drives the action.

I know everything so far on the film is strong. Now I aim to do one more thing to put it over the top.

From early on in 508, something is different: we all get along. There are no cliques and almost no negative comments. Maybe I'm viewing the world through rose-colored glasses after being released from the hospital, but I think there's more to it than that. When I returned from Minnesota after learning all about my blood issues, I came clean in front of the class. As we sat in our classroom, I explained what had happened to me. I asked all of them to call 911 if they ever saw me acting strangely or having difficulty speaking. The class was silent and respectful. I don't think anyone thought they'd be hearing such a story from a fellow student.

At the time, I didn't know most of them well. At a break, a few of them came up to talk. Rene, the tall Mexican, and Manny, the stocky Romanian, offered to help if they could, as did a few others. It was a very serious moment in our class, and for a few weeks, I noticed my fellow classmates were watching me closely. As the days went by and I *didn't* turn into a drooling mumbler, they relaxed. After that I'm teased, slightly at first, and then with more vigor as the weeks go by. Rene, who I start calling the World's Tallest Mexican, teases me by doing an over-the-top stroke-face whenever we meet. "How'ya doing, old man," he says, mouth drooping. It's funny and a good sign. Everyone in class, men and women, treats me as one of the tribe's favorite chimps. And our tribe is very tight.

One day I'm speaking alone with Pablo and he brings the issue up. "This is an exceptionally cohesive group," he says to me, and adds that he thinks my talking about my stroke had something to do with it. Perhaps it's all because we're a bit more aware of mortality, and like survivors on a desert island, we're willing to go the extra mile to be supportive.

It also helps that we're helping each other. Dan and I are often in our own world, as are the other partnerships, but there are moments of shared hardship. Manny, the burly Romanian, asks me if I can help tow Jason's car to a repair shop. Manny and Jason are

508 partners. Jason's car was mashed in an accident and is undrivable. My Suburban with its ample space and trailer hitch is a coveted vehicle on campus. I say, "Sure."

It turns out his car is in an underground garage in Hollywood, and the repair shop is in an awful area of Compton, some twenty-five miles away. The quick little tow takes more than five hours total, but Manny and Jason are appreciative, and the trip is an adventure. Manny is in his car and Jason rides with me, and as we wind through the gang-infested streets of Compton trying to locate a bargain-basement repair facility, I tell Jason, who is black, that I'm glad he's riding with me, the white guy. Jason is from a small Mississippi town and seems as wary as I am in Compton. After we get the car delivered and return to Hollywood, we've all learned a lot more about each other—and it has nothing to do with filmmaking.

Pablo, too, has a gentle way about him. He's forgetful sometimes and always—always—faithfully upholds the banner of peace-loving hippie-dom, which is amusing to students who are only in their twenties. I've learned already that plenty of film students are either rich kids slumming for a while, delaying their entry into the working world, or they're rich wannabe revolutionaries driving their Lexuses or Audis while bitching about The Man. In our class, we have none of that as far as I can tell. Everyone wants to make films. Everyone wants to make a career out of the business somehow. We don't fit many of the film school clichés. We're almost all of middle-class or lower background. Caraballo is a staunch Reaganite and is fluent in Cuban-inflected Spanish. Brent and Justin are both superjocks. Brent played hockey through college. Justin works as a weightlifting trainer. Manny is a Romanian immigrant with nine siblings and a knack for knowing something about everything under the sun, from car repair to camera operation to cold fusion, and he worked for a spell as a TV cameraman.

Jason comes from a tiny dot on the map in the Deep South. Rene, the World's Tallest Mexican, was raised on the Tex-Mex border and was on a basketball team that won a Texas high school championship. Alan is from Chile and always seems to have a surprised smile on his face. Lea is from the Philippines and lied to her parents about why she was coming to the United States. She told them she was coming to medical school, not film school. Jeanette and Resheida grew up in the same South Side Chicago neighborhood and both have the Michelle Obama thing going as far as height and fashion. Both have supportive, generous families. Michelle is a glam lesbian Valley Girl, and her film partner is Kat, a wanderer and raver who told us a frightening story about getting lost hiking with her boyfriend in a snowy Pakistani valley.

There are fourteen of us in the class. Just as in 507, we spend hundreds of hours together. Outside of the partnerships—where conflict is inevitable—I rarely hear an argument. As the semester goes on, we talk about how much we look forward to getting together, and how there is such a feeling of support. Although in 507 I'd sometimes drag myself to class, wondering what hardship awaited us, in 508, I invariably bound up the stairs to our classroom, eager to start our day's adventure. One felt like a mandatory office gathering, the other like a really good party.

On our last day of 508 class, Pablo has us gather in a circle. He turns down the lights and asks us to meditate together. At first, the class nervously giggles. *Oh, it's Pablo doing his granola thing again.*

I groan, too. This gather-in-a-circle stuff seems so contrived and, well, phony. But I go along with it. We breathe in. We breathe out. The giggles subside. In the darkness, I reflect back on the semester. It started with me in a hospital bed. Now I'm focusing on meditating with a graying hippie and thirteen other people who have come to know me very well. I breathe in and out. I hear the others breathing in and out. We keep meditating and focusing on what the past four months have meant to us all. We go on for quite some time in the darkness, and eventually I hear a woman softly crying. Everyone is into the moment, including me.

The lights come up. Everyone looks chastened, and maybe a bit embarrassed. Pablo quietly asks us to talk a bit about what the semester meant to each of us. We are all serious, touchingly so. When it comes my time to talk, I feel my throat tighten. I breathe deep again. I tell the class I appreciate them all, and I appreciated them being supportive of me and upbeat with me despite all my medical crud. I thank Dan for his talent and for putting up with my constant need for food. I feel my voice catch—it is really a bit emotional—and I explain how my second time at USC has been so much more satisfying, so much more collaborative, and so much more rewarding in ways I can't put a finger on. I say I've changed for the better. I stop because my voice won't go any further. I look around and I feel real friendship with the others in the class, and I know I'll be going through the rest of my time in school with these same thirteen people. I am grateful.

When we have finished going around the circle, Pablo speaks. "This class has been the most exceptional class I've ever had in my years of teaching," he says quietly. "There were cases where some of your partnerships looked in dire straits"—he can't help but glancing at Dan and me—"but you turned it around and had truly phenomenal results. The films in this class are very strong. I'm very pleased, and I'd like to thank you all for what has been a really exceptional experience."

9

Limes Regiones Rerum

I mentioned in the introduction that I know two Hollywood actors, both college pals. One is Pete Krause of SIX FEET UNDER and DIRTY SEXY MONEY (and currently PARENTHOOD) fame. The other is Pete Breitmayer, another Gustavian who has made a career in Hollywood. Breitmayer is a comic song-and-dance character actor, and he's been in films by Clint Eastwood and the Coen brothers and a lot of TV shows and a bazillion TV commercials. If you see a rubber-faced guy on TV who makes you laugh, there's a chance it's Breitmayer.

For WTF, my 508 masterpiece, I want to add a voice-over. I want it comic, I want it serious. I want it to be in the first person. The Boss will be telling the story, giving his side of what happened, as if he's reminiscing from a smoky bar. I call Breitmayer and ask him to voice it. He's glad to, and he meets me at USC one morning right before we sound-lock the picture. Breitmayer is wearing a porkpie hat, and we catch up on family talk—his wife and son are doing well, thank you. I'd given him the script the night before, and when we enter a soundproof room to record, he asks me if he can ad-lib a bit. I tell him to ad-lib as much as he wants. I turn on a microphone, get a sound level. Then I open my laptop and project a silent copy of WTF so he can time his voice-over to the action. Then I leave the room. An hour later he's done. We have lunch, and he drives off to an audition.

That afternoon I listen to the tape. It's freakin' perfect. His ad-libs are simply right on.

I cut together the best of his voice-over and lay it onto the soundtrack. It's the last piece of the puzzle. Shortly after that, I do my final sound mix. A professional sound technician does the mixing of the score, the sound effects, and the voice-over—it's the one concession to keeping the schedule moving. My technician listens to the musical score with Frank, the sound teacher, hovering nearby. She listens to Breitmayer's voice-over. She listens to my background sound effects track. She shakes her head. "These are all really good," she says.

I shrug and give Frank a wink. "I know," I say.

Julie arrives in California the day before the screening of WTF. I'm so nervous about the screening I take her swimming at the USC pool to stay active, and I walk into the pool with my cell phone in my swim trunks.

Hundreds of students and crew and cast members turn out to watch these 508 films. I throw a party beforehand, right outside the auditorium, for the cast and crew and significant others. We eat Irene's cookies and quickly drain a mini-keg of beer. Then we tramp inside and sit together. There are sixteen of us. When the film comes on, the crowd laughs hard at the movie and gasps when the woman is hit by the truck. At the end, the applause is loud.

Really loud.

I walk to a podium with Dan after the film to make a short speech. It's the USC way after screening. I call up everyone who was part of the film, and soon Robert and Dream and Jeffrey and Mikey and the surveyor and the surveyor's wife and Niall-Conor and Breitmayer gather around us. It's like every awards show you've ever seen, and it probably looks just as hokey to an outsider. On the inside, though, it's a good moment. I point out that this is truly how many people it takes to do one small student film, and how they all worked for not a penny, and how, without them, there really wouldn't be a film. And then I point to Julie, who is sitting in the crowd next to Carl and Irene, and I thank her.

T he screening is a smash, I feel great, and my briefcase is stolen. After the bigger USC student screenings at the Norris, there's a wine and cheese soirée outside the theater. During this gathering, I put my briefcase down against a wall so I'm not lugging it around while I socialize. When I return, it's gone.

My phone is kaput from the dip in the pool. My briefcase—a very cool and distinctive red bicycle messenger bag that I got as a gift from Julie—is stolen. After Julie flies home, I have to remain on campus several more days. I check the campus police department. Nothing. Luckily, I did not have my laptop in the briefcase . . . and whoever stole it got nothing more than a lot of personal notes and a version of CRAZYHOUSE ON SKIS. I keep my eyes peeled on campus, hoping to find someone carrying my bag.

When it comes time to fly back to Minneapolis, I'm in a quandary. I can leave the Suburban at long-term parking at LAX for a month (for more than $200) or take a cab from La Cañada to LAX (more than $200 round-trip). Then Manny tells me that USC has a shuttle program to the airport. I can leave my truck in a campus parking lot for free and catch a free student shuttle to the airport. Sweet! I look up the shuttle timetables and one matches my flight perfectly.

A hard, cold December rain is pounding Los Angeles the day I'm flying out, and I realize my free shuttle trip means lots of hoofing it from the campus parking garage to the shuttle stop in the pouring rain. I'm soaked waiting for the airport bus, and surrounding me are thirty undergraduates. I feel so old, so out of place. The bus pulls up and the driver gets out holding a clipboard; she asks the students to check their names off the list as they get on the bus. A list? I didn't know anything about any list! I thought space on the bus was on a first-come, first-served basis. The bus is huge, and the crowd isn't going to fill it, but we're supposed to have a reservation. It's pouring. I wonder how long it would take to get a cab in the rain.

I make my decision: students are having trouble getting their suitcases into the bus. I'm carrying a light carry-on bag. I see a young woman struggling to get her suitcase up the stairs, and I skirt around the bus driver and help her, Mr. Chivalrous. The driver never sees me. Then I take a seat at the rear of the bus. I keep my soaked head down.

Now I feel really old, and a bit like one of those weird, smelly outcasts who sit all day at the free computers at the public library, gazing at who-knows-what for hours at a time. I'm surrounded by dozens of young bubbly undergrads who are going home to Mom and Dad for winter break. I'm sneaking my way aboard so I can go visit my wife and kids. They giggle and chat. When we get to LAX and stop at Terminal 2, I make my way for the door. As I pass the bus driver, she glances up at me with surprise on her face: *Where did you come from?* I give her a smile. "Thanks for the ride, ma'am," I say as I exit.

My winter break is good but tempered by more mediocre medical news. Dr. Flaata tells me additional tests show my autoimmune disease seems to be worsening. The numbers are inching in the wrong direction. I'm also having problems keeping my blood thinner doses regulated. I'm getting my blood tested every other week, and sometimes my blood is too thin, other times it clots too quickly. I regulate my diet: limited greenery and no more grapefruits. Those foods interfere with the warfarin I take daily. Every time I get bad medical news, it's a kick in the shins.

I tell Dr. Flaata I'm also suffering from extremely sore feet and knees. I'm barely able to do my daily three-mile runs, and I keep several different kinds of shoes in the Suburban so I can switch them during the day. I read a great deal about my ailment—and it seems my body is attacking my joints. Despite my issues, everyone who sees me is relieved to find I'm healthy-looking and tan. My brain also seems to work just fine—no problems there, except for the nagging worry that my stupid little mistakes—submerging my phone, leaving my briefcase unattended, not noticing that the USC shuttle bus needed reservations—were due to some deficiency in my memory bank.

The good news is the kids and Julie are doing well . . . and have survived four long months of my absence. They've all become swimmers and train at nights at the local YMCA pool. It feels so peaceful to be home. My feet and knees are so sore I begin swimming with them at the Y. The water feels good. Christmas comes and goes, and then New Year's, and the days until my return to USC count down. Julie works a ton, and she's saved lots of her on-call weekends for when I'm around, so she's gone more than usual. There's a long list of home repair projects; it's hardly a leisurely vacation, but I take Julie and the girls out cross-country skiing as often as possible. Skating is out for me—I'm wary of whacking my head on the ice while my blood is slow to clot with warfarin. But skiing is gentle or so I tell myself.

Leaving for L.A. is never easy. The kids hug me and cry. Julie hugs me and bites her lip. There's always a strong pull to abort the trip, to spin on my heel at the airport security checkpoint and return home.

This time, this semester, no one is depending on me. I'm not doing any major film projects. If I hadn't done so well in 508, I don't know what I would have done. Perhaps I would have listened to the voice that said, *Enough, this is stupid.* But I did do well. My reputation on campus has risen greatly, and I feel so much more connected with my classmates than I did after 507.

So I walk through security and get on the airliner flying to L.A.

When I land, it's a copy of the day I left: hard, cold rain. I land near midnight, and I have a cab drive me to USC, and I feel like an adult as I pay the cabbie instead of like a sneaky freeloader on a campus bus. On the upper floor of a USC parking garage, I find my Suburban. The garage is almost completely empty, and my boots click on the cement. It's a lonely place, and I cross my fingers that the Suburban will start after sitting for a month. It does, and I arrive at Carl and Irene's house early in the morning of my first day of classes. In my carry-on is a fresh supply of blood thinners, a new cell phone, a new briefcase, and a new pair of swimming goggles.

I'm not making any major films this semester. I'm going to focus on course work and fulfilling required classes. Many of my 508 classmates are crewing on fiction films or documentaries, but a handful of us are spending the semester focusing on specialized areas of filmmaking. This semester, for me, is all about focusing on writing and cinematography.

When I get back to USC, construction crews are digging a giant hole, the site of an upgraded film school building. We students had earlier seen a mock-up of the new facility, and none of us paid much attention to it. But the growing hole in the ground gives us an indication of how big the structure will be.

The building is being funded by George Lucas, who donated a cool $175 million. The gift from Lucas is the biggest ever to any film school anywhere. It's also the largest donation to USC in its history. Industry heavyweights such as 20th Century Fox, Warner Bros., and The Walt Disney Company kicked in another $50 million.

The interior of the new building will total a hundred and thirty seven thousand square feet, or more than twice the space of two football fields, end zones included. Judging by the scale model on display, it will have a Mediterranean vibe and a grand entryway.

Lucas later tells *The New York Times*: "The only way you are going to get respect on a college campus, or a university campus, is to build something that is important . . . Schools and universities mainly understand money."

The new facility looks like it will be stunningly different from our current building, which is an ugly, cramped, and abysmally designed structure less than a third the size.

Our space is woefully overcrowded. Counting all majors and specialties, graduate and undergraduate, there are more than fifteen hundred film students at USC. As a result, many of my classes are held at a distance from the film school proper. I have classes in the school's education department building, in a general classroom building, in the Norris Theater, in the Zemeckis building. Before the new construction got under way, I'd never paid much attention to the fact that the USC School of Cinematic Arts spills over into the surrounding USC campus like a well-fed amoeba.

When we move into the new building, our current digs will be demolished. Already film students are grumbling and waxing nostalgic about our classrooms. I think: *Are they smoking crack?* I know it's a common human tendency to think the Golden Age is the one that's just passing, but I scratch my head when I hear the complaints about the new project. The reality is our current building stinks; the classrooms are small, badly ventilated, and mostly windowless. The elevator is miserably slow. Many students, myself included, just hoof it up the stairs, one set of which is an exterior fire escape and a favorite place for students to smoke. The building's few classrooms always seem to be occupied—so holding auditions in them is all but impossible. And I always study somewhere else—there's simply no room to plug in a laptop and work.

In addition to being cramped, our current film complex, built in the early 1980s, must have been designed by rabbits on acid because it's a surreal warren. Getting from classroom A to classroom B can mean following a zigzag of walkways and stairways and even a mini-bridge. There are sidewalks that go nowhere if doors are locked. Mysterious corridors. Everyone gets lost when they first visit. Everyone gets wet when it rains. There's hardly any space to study. I had been in school nearly a year when I was invited one day into the animation department, which was hidden in a corner of the warren where we production students rarely venture. There, like Santa's elves, dozens of animation students toiled on fantastic projects.

Our complex features a sunken garden that I suppose looked good on paper, a place where the architect apparently thought students would congregate and share in Socratic dialogue with their instructors. In reality, hardly anyone uses the garden. It's damp and chilly most of the year. And because elevated walkways surround the sunken garden, being there is like being an animal on display at a zoo. The few times I'm been down there, I expected students on the walkways to throw me peanuts. I avoid the garden, as do most others.

The favorite student gathering place is an old picnic table that sits on the film school's concrete loading dock. The table looks as if was hauled to the dock and just left there by accident. Accident or not, it's our home. Here, film students gather and gossip and eat and smoke and ignore the passing tourists and other USC students.

When I come back for this new semester and pass the picnic table, I see my friends. They smile, I smile, and I come over to talk. There's Manny the Romanian and Rene the World's Tallest Mexican and Justin the weightlifter. We do bro hugs (a soul-shake handshake with right hand, half-embrace/hug with left arm). The bro-hug is just a trendy version of the Back Slap Hug, a favorite of Midwestern men who don't want to get *too* close.

It's good to see them all. We talk about what classes we're taking. Several of them are sidestepping major filming for the semester—I'm not the only one. I share a couple of classes with Rene, one with Manny, one with Dan, but none with the others. A handful of us agree to grab some lunch at the Jocketeria, the dining hall that serves student-athletes. The Jocketeria is notable for serving huge portions of meat. It attracts those of us film students who want to gorge on protein at least once a day. When we visit the Jocketeria, we stand in line with various future NFL prospects such as Clay Matthews, Mark Sanchez, and others. We eat and compare notes and laugh. It feels good.

At USC, our first year is mostly predetermined. But in year two, we students get to pick and choose which classes we'll take. And USC, bless its heart, requires us to register for classes in the time-honored system of standing in line. It's first-come, first-served. And it works perfectly. Those who really want classes are rewarded for their efforts. Those who snooze, lose.

When I registered for my third semester, I knew about this system, but I hadn't experienced it. Registration day for us came on a day in December. A rainy, cold day. The registration office is located in the sunken garden courtyard. The door wouldn't open until 10 A.M.

To make sure I would get the classes I wanted, I got up earlier than normal that morning and drove to USC at 6 A.M. I figured I'd get one of the first few spots in line.

When I got to the courtyard, I found a crowd of students already waiting. In the rain. Most had been there all night, some having come straight here when the bars closed. There was a pile of blankets and sleeping bags in a small alcove that provided the only shelter from a steady forty-eight-degree rain. My classmates were tired and giddy and hung over and cold and hungry. A few were still drunk. I was seventeenth in line. For the next three-plus hours, we stomped and paced to keep warm and cowered like a herd of cattle. We laughed and talked and compared notes on what classes we were signing up for. Because I was in the first twenty students, I was all but guaranteed any course I wanted.

As the morning went on, we watched as other students, their eyes big, would come down the stairs and see our huddled mass. A list went around posting our order so there would be no disputes. Those who had been there all night were in no mood to let late-comers crash the party. When the registration office doors finally opened, we went in one by one and picked our classes. When I walked out, I saw more than twenty students still waiting to register. I raised my arms. "They closed directing!" I yelled. "You can all go home now." A big groan went through the crowd. Many of those waiting wanted to get into the directing track. Quickly, I added: "Kidding, kidding. Plenty of space left." A wave of relieved laughter went through the crowd.

I had registered for directing, for a cinematography course, for a screenwriting class (the next step in getting a major in screenwriting), for another Drew Casper critical studies course on the musical (the only palatable critical studies offering), and at the last minute, a class called Preparing for the Documentary. One of my classmates assured me that by taking the Doc class we could potentially direct one without crewing on a film first. I thought: awesome. So I had my semester set. Although it's an overloaded twelve-credit schedule, it's one that put me a step closer to my goal of a double major in writing and directing.

T he motto of USC's School of Cinematic Arts is *Limes Regiones Rerum* or, loosely translated, "Reality Ends Here." It's all true. We learn the black arts behind filmmaking: how to manipulate sound and image and story to affect other people. In my second year, I'm no longer watching film or television for entertainment. I'm constantly watching and listening to see how they're made. It takes some of the escapism out of it, but there's still plenty of fun left—it's just a different sort of fun.

I take the motto to heart. My time at USC is in so many ways a departure from my reality that I vow to throw myself into the program with as much openness and energy as I can muster. How it will treat me, I don't know. In my first semester, I never fully embraced the whole notion of film school. Now, after two semesters, I'm willing to play the game at USC. Reality is outside the gates, where my student loans are growing and my kids are growing up without their dad for long weeks at a time. Inside, it's a make-believe world of films and screenwriting, and I'm throwing caution to the wind and trusting that the path I'm on will be a good one.

One morning after registering, I'm sitting on one of my favorite study places, a USC computer lab located near the gym. Most of the students using the dozens of computer workstations are foreign engineering students, and the lab affords me a quiet place to write on my laptop and check emails on the faster campus computers.

On this day, I've got two computers open and I notice an email pop onto a screen.

The message announces that a course offered by the film school's writing division has a couple of openings for any interested production students. The special projects course is called Pitching 101: How to Sell Your Story and Yourself, taught by one Trey Callaway. The email explains that he's a writer/producer on CSI: NY and will be teaching how to pitch projects to Hollywood. The email says interested students will be accepted on a first-come, first-served basis.

I blink twice, then shove my laptop and papers into my briefcase as fast as I can and run for the exit. I take steps two at a time down to the sidewalk and start running for the film school. It's a long block away, and I gallop down the sidewalk in my cowboy boots, my heavy briefcase thumping against my side. People step aside when they seem me coming. I'm running either away from something very bad or toward something very good. When I get to the film school building, I dispense with the elevator and power my way up the stairs to the third floor, where the writing division offices are.

I enter the writing offices breathing too hard to talk. I collect my breath. "Is there space in the pitch class?" I ask. "You just sent an email about it."

The secretary pulls out a folder, scans down the list. "Yes, there are two spots open." The class is an elective and won't count toward my majors. It will cost $3,000, money that will come from student loans, a reality that gives me deep heartburn. My children are less than a decade from college themselves.

Before I came back to USC the second time, lots of people asked me why I didn't go to film school in Minnesota. My answer was always the same: "USC has instructors you just can't find elsewhere." Here in the writing division office, I take a deep breath and sign up for the class. I can't help but smile. I'm gonna take a class from a guy who writes one of the top dramas on television.

A few minutes after I sign up, Chris Caraballo, the free-market loving, Castro-hating Cubano-Americano runs into the writing offices. He gets the final spot. The class is full.

With the semester starting, I'm feeling comfortable my schedule is going to be predictable. I'll do my class work and projects during the day and evening and work out over the lunch hour. It feels like I've got a job to do. The manic ups and downs of the first year are history.

On the second day back, I grab my swim goggles and head for USC's outdoor pool complex. I leap into the water. It's warm. It's January, and I'm swimming outside. My achy knees and feet appreciate the water and I begin swimming laps, slowly.

Cinematography class begins, and it's clear it's going to be a fun course. The instructor is an upbeat, energetic soul with a Hollywood résumé that goes back decades. We meet in one of the school's soundstages and for three hours set up lights and a camera and discuss how to shoot a variety of scenes. Rene is in my class and we sit next to each other. "Hey, old man," he says as a greeting. He looks at me and says, "You growing your hair out?" Rene has a huge mushroom cloud of hair. "I'm just trying to keep up with you," I say.

I am. My shaved head is in the past. I'd cut my hair just once in months. I'm going to grow it out. It's graying, but at least I have a lot of it left. My blood thinners cause my hair to fall out more easily and make my fingernails crack. I can't do anything about my nails, but I might as well add to the volume of my hairdo if I'm going to be shedding like a dog. I'm even drizzling some cheap hair color into my locks. When Julie sees it she frowns. "I'm going Hollywood, baby," I say, as I run my fingers through my increasingly long, suspiciously dark mane.

The screenwriting class takes up where the last ended: I'm putting the finishing touches on CRAZYHOUSE ON SKIS. The instructor is new. She's another woman, this time one who wrote some made-for-TV movie scripts. The number of us pursuing screenwriting continues to dwindle: just me and Dan and four other students in the class. Over the semester, we're supposed to put our polishing touches on our scripts.

On my first day in Preparing for the Documentary, the instructor sets me right about what I heard in the soggy mess of registration. The class is not a golden ticket to allow us to pass straight to directing, she tells me. I'd still have to crew first if I wanted to direct. I debate dropping the class. I'm woefully overscheduled for the semester— I'm taking fourteen credits instead of the usual eight to ten. My directing class is next, the one dozens of us stood in the cold rain for. Shortly before the class begins, I learn a different instructor will be teaching the class. In the dark gloom of a Zemeckis soundstage, the new instructor tells us we'll be working on our relationship with actors all semester. He's got a heavy Russian accent. He sounds just like the repairman, Mr. Bullsheet. I don't want to spend my semester talking about Uta Hagen again, so I decide to drop this class and keep the Doc class. The USC documentary division has several Academy Award winners on staff and I want to sample their wares. I'd done lots of documentary-like projects in my radio days, so it feels like I'm returning to familiar ground.

Now the mystery class: Pitching.

This class takes place once a week, Thursday evenings. We meet in one of the overflow classrooms not far from the film school, in a nondescript building that looks like a suburban high school. When I walk in, I wonder if I'm going to hear the echo of cheerleader practice coming from down the hall.

LIMES REGIONES RERUM ■ 261

We take our seats—I sit next to Caraballo. Other than him, I don't know any of the dozen other students in class. They're all writing students, and because this is a 400-level class, there are undergraduate writing students here, too. Caraballo and I are the only two from the production division. In a way, we're crashing this writing party. But that's the least of it. Once again, I'm the old guy. Being fortyish with some of my production pals who are in their late twenties is one thing. But being with *barely* twenty-year-olds makes me feel protective, almost like a father figure.

We're sitting down when Trey Callaway starts the class with a bang. He enters and with almost no introduction launches into a story about growing up in Oklahoma and being caught in a terrible storm. The story and the storm gather in intensity as Callaway is telling us how he's running for the storm shelter and hoping a coming tornado doesn't sweep him away. He's got a lot of energy, and he's a big, fleshy guy with almost no hair. And he seems to be exactly my age. I see him playing linebacker for an Oklahoma high school a few decades earlier. I hear a slight Oklahoma twang in his voice—my uncle and aunt moved to that state when I was a kid and my cousin picked up that red-clay drawl in about three seconds flat. But Callaway also has the *I'm so stoked, Dude!* thing in his speech that so many white Angelenos have. No matter what Callaway sounds like, he's compelling.

Callaway tells us he came to USC as a college student to study writing in the film school, but no one ever taught him how to pitch his material. "In Hollywood, as a working writer, you're going to spend probably more time pitching than you will actually writing," he says. He graduated from USC in the late '80s. In the mid-'90s, he wrote the horror flick I STILL KNOW WHAT YOU DID LAST SUMMER and jumped into writing for television. He wrote for MERCY POINT, wrote for Disney's animated W.I.T.C.H., and then landed a gig on CSI: NY. He also sold a handful of pitches to the network. He tells us pitching is key to his professional life: pitching episode ideas for CSI: NY, pitching original ideas to the networks, pitching, pitching, pitching.

The Hollywood writers' strike has been going on for two months, and one of the union tactics is that writers will "put their pencils down"—no writing. So Callaway, who is on strike, says he thought it would be a dandy time to return to his alma mater and share some of what he has learned. "I actually pitched the idea for this class to Jack Epps," he says, referring to the head of the writing division and the scribe of TOP GUN and other films.

Callaway tells us our final assignment will be to pitch to a panel of industry heavyweights. He doesn't throw out any names, so I'm not certain if he's stretching the truth about heavyweights.

Still, the thought that real Hollywood types might listen to us sends a murmur of excitement through the class. It certainly gets my motor running. I can't wait to learn what Callaway has to teach. I've been a pitching machine for years, albeit on a different level. I'd worked in newsrooms where most of the story generation took place at the reporter level. I'd create a fresh list of story suggestions—mini-pitches—every week and mostly work off that list. I learned that the better my pitches were, the greater the chance I'd get to do something that interested me . . . instead of being assigned a story by the bosses. I successfully pitched stories about how people find hired killers and where the happiest orphanage in America is and why a rifle-wielding character came to be part of a Christmas display at a major mall. Plus, *GeezerJock* was essentially one big pitch that landed two successive investors and space on the Barnes & Noble magazine rack. All of these pitches, however, put very little money in the family bank account.

Now I want to pitch at a different level, where the stakes are higher and the rewards are greater. One television script sells for as much as I made in a year as a newspaper reporter. The thought of it makes my mouth water. I feel like a dog smelling meat.

Callaway lays out the ground rules for the semester: each of us will pitch two projects. One will be a television pitch, the other a film idea. We will spend two months on one project, then two months on the other. It doesn't matter which one we choose to do first, only that we create pitches for both a television series and a feature film. Callaway also explains that we'll build our pitches from small to large. We will start with the elevator pitch: a quick sixty-second news brief. Then we'll graduate to a midlevel pitch: five minutes, no more, no less. Then we'll do a twenty-minute pitch. He says he'll be timing us. If it's too short, we'll be expected to fill the time. Too long and he'll cut us off.

Callaway also warns us that he'll sometimes act like a studio executive by interrupting or fiddling with his phone or looking out the window. He says he wants us all to be able to walk into a meeting and pitch our ideas, no matter how much time we're given and no matter the situation to which we must adapt.

And, he adds, we can't use any notes. Everything must be memorized.

I look around me. A few students are biting their lips or looking discomfited. It's asking a lot, and it seems the class will be as much about theater as about writing.

I'm having trouble not squirming in my seat with excitement. I'm loving it. I love every bit of what I've heard about pitching a story, relying on a clock, being theatrical. It sounds like a bit of heaven, and I have experience in all of them.

At my first job, I was pressed into duty as a morning news anchor at Minnesota Public Radio. I was dreadful at it at first. The Morning Edition program I anchored had specific local cutaways, always timed exactly to the second. If there was dead air, I was expected to talk about the upcoming programs or give a weather update or tell people what a swell group they were for listening to Minnesota *Public* Radio. The first few times I attempted to fill dead air I bumbled nervously and sounded like the village idiot. I learned quickly never to start a sentence without knowing how to finish it, as when I announced one very cold day that the wind chill would be dangerously low and then, desperate to kill some time, figured I'd explain what *wind chill* meant. "The wind chill is," I solemnly announced in my deepest public radio voice, "when the wind . . . uh . . . when the wind . . . well . . . um." Long seconds ticked by. I started to sweat. I had to finish it up somehow. "Well, it's when the wind meets the chill." A minute later, the studio phone lit up. It was a friend. She was laughing hysterically.

Callaway gives us one last bit of instruction: we can pitch any idea we want. We don't have to have written a full feature script or a television pilot script. Because all of us fancy ourselves writers, we all have a pet project to pitch. I'm going to pitch my feature script, CRAZYHOUSE ON SKIS. That will be the first part of the semester. For the second half, I'll have to dream up a television series. I'll worry about that later.

10

Trey, the Pitch Master

As the semester gets rolling, I'm experiencing a level of calm I've never had in film school. I've got no pressing issues—no impending potential catastrophes, no partnership conflict, no bad medical news. Instead, I've got five classes that I need to tend like little growing flowers. If I keep watering each one on a regular basis, I should be fine.

Walking into Drew Casper's first lecture is déjà vu all over again. This time, I sit quietly near the rear of the Norris Theater and keep my head down. I don't want to become one of his foils. I'll let someone else do that. He doesn't see me, so my first lecture on the history of the musical film is a quiet affair.

In screenwriting class, we follow a now-familiar routine. We exchange scripts, read them, and in class, we listen to the instructor make suggestions—especially on any new material. Then we students will give feedback, advice, and criticism. It's a format that is impossible to do well with more than a half-dozen students.

With too many students, the classes become watered down. This semester, our class size is ideal, as is the makeup of class. Dan's in it, and he's expanding his PG-13 marriage comedy; Thompson, who had his 508 accepted at Sundance, is writing an R-rated supernatural horror film; another guy, an older student in his thirties, is writing a PG-rated historical adventure drama. There's a woman who is writing a PG-13 story about Indian grave robbers. There's a baby-faced former child-actor who is writing a dark and violent thriller, a definite hard-R-rated film. And me, with my small-town summertime resort comedy/drama, a definite PG film.

We're all writing good stuff. After the first class, we leave and stand on the sidewalk and comment how we have a full multiplex of films among us. And we're all writing something that could sell. We've got an epic adventure tale, maybe with Russell Crowe in the lead. A violent thriller, maybe with a leather-clad Angelina Jolie in the lead. A marriage comedy with two cute young rising actors in the lead. A serious historical drama with a social message, a film begging for Philip Seymour Hoffman. A horror film that feels like a David Lynch film. And my comedy, an ideal role for Adam Sandler strapped into water skis. We laugh and note that all we need is a G-rated animated film to round out our multiplex. And, we add, we first have to *sell* our scripts.

In class and afterward, I revel in the discussions. I've stepped up the ladder of screenwriting at USC, and the quality of the storytelling in this class is head-and-shoulders above the screenwriting in my first semester. Then, most of the stories were disjointed, flimsy things. Now every story in our class has heft and quality.

I plot out my future. It's becoming clearer that my path is the right one for me. I'm going to push my writing and learn enough directing to helm my own films. Along the way, I'll also study cinematography and sound and editing. Every month in school I'm more confident in my abilities. When I started, I was distracted by the little things and I thought small. Now I'm realizing there's no reason to bunt or sit in the dugout. I see I'm good at this film-making thing.

It's the perfect strategy: I'll use Callaway's class to develop a pitch for CRAZYHOUSE ON SKIS, hone the script in screenwriting, and develop a documentary idea for possible later use in film school. In an upcoming semester, I'll have to crew on student films, but I'll also have a good chance of shooting one. Failing that, I'll produce. I drive home late that night to Carl and Irene's house and grab a Big Mac just before the drive-thru shuts down. I get in the door after 11 P.M. They're both asleep. Carl has installed new floors to replace the damaged carpeting, and I pad quietly to my bedroom so I don't wake them.

The next morning I'm up at six thirty and off to campus at seven. My days soon become as orderly as an obsessive-compulsive's pencil box. At USC by seven thirty, check emails, correspond. Then from eight 'til one, coursework. Then I head to the gym, for a swim or weightlifting. If my knees and feet aren't too achy, I'll run on the track. On a couple of days, I have a 1 P.M. class, so I'll run earlier and grab a quick bite beforehand. If I don't have a class, I'll hit the Jocketeria, then walk to the Doheny Library to study and write. My evening classes don't start 'til 7 P.M. and run until at least ten. Then I drive home and try to beat the local drive-thru's 11 P.M. closing time. Then I'll grab a beer, hit the sack, and start all over again.

I've got five classes this semester, so I only spend about fif-teen hours in a classroom, far less than in my first two semes-ters, when classroom commitments and rehearsals and meetings could eat up twenty-five hours or more a week. This semester I've got very little weekend filming, and that's only for a short demo tape for the documentary class. I feel guilty for having such flexibility. It's a remarkable change from my 508 semester. Then, every weekend was booked solid with filming or editing. I now have enough time to explore Los Angeles, at least a little bit. I can get out more.

One morning, I have a long breakfast with Breitmayer at a quirky cafeteria in a run-down block of downtown Los Angeles. He just wrapped shooting a role for Clint Eastwood's CHANGELING, and he's waiting to see if he snares a part in the Coen brothers' A SERIOUS MAN, set in our home state of Minnesota (he does). Breitmayer moved to Los Angeles about a decade earlier. He'd been a full-time actor in Minneapolis doing comedy clubs and theater before moving west one freezing winter day. He's made enough to buy a house in Los Angeles and a condo in St. Paul, and to support his wife and son. I ask how long it took him to get traction in Los Angeles. He stabs his big brisket of beef and answers: "I get asked that question so much from actors back home. They want to know how I do it. I tell them I treat auditioning as a full-time job. If I'm not putting in forty hours a week doing auditions, preparing for auditions, meeting my agent, doing readings, then I'm not working." He stops to take a bite. As he chews, he goes on. "So many people think to act in this town you're gonna just suddenly 'make it.' Then they don't, and they quit. My attitude is just constantly to be auditioning." Breitmayer is a stout fellow with a rubber face. He's terrifically funny, a great character actor. His stock keeps rising in Hollywood, and he's getting bigger roles year by year. His career arc is different from our mutual friend Krause, who was cast as a regular on a network television show in his twenties and has been a leading man ever since. But both have the same Midwestern work ethic as the corn farmers who plowed the fields adjacent to Gustavus Adolphus College. Both took risks that seemed very un-Midwesternly by going into acting. During the times I question my decision to attend USC, I look to them for a bit of inspiration.

When I was researching my TEACHER'S PET paper at the Academy's library, I spoke at length with a woman who was in

TREY, THE PITCH MASTER ■ 269

her seventh semester. She was taking the Casper class to fulfill a missing elective, and she had grown bitter about USC.

"They promise you all this great stuff, but they don't tell you how many people come out of here and actually do anything," she said. "I have so many classmates who are just angry. Everyone comes in with stars in their eyes, and then they leave. And they don't know how to pay off their loans. I don't know how I'm going to pay mine off!"

She looked really frustrated. And scared. She'd been in graduate school for three-and-a-half years; she said she owed more than $120,000 in student loans . . . and she was sitting in a library doing research about a film from the 1950s. Even at a low 6 percent rate, she'll be paying $600 a month just to cover the *interest* on her student loans. No wonder she's freaking out. The money needed for film school is staggering, and when I heard her story, I felt a big voice in my head say, *What the hell are you doing here, Steve?* At times like this, I think of Krause and Breitmayer and take a deep breath and keep moving forward.

A t the next class with Callaway, we start pitching. He had asked us the previous week to create a pitch from an existing film or television show. Mine is MAD MAX, the classic 1979 Australian motorhead revenge saga that made Mel Gibson a star and launched director George Miller into the big-time. We are to pitch as if we have written the script.

Callaway's basic instruction from start to finish for our pitches:

The ramp. We segue into our pitch with a story or anecdote that is personal and timely.
The overview. A concise summation of what the film or series is but including nuts and bolts details.
The structure. A brief summation of what happens.

The characters. A tight and tidy rundown of the main characters.

The plot. Of the series' pilot episode or of the film.

Callaway also says for a television series, we need to have a season arc thought out . . . and be ready to talk about other sample episodes. That way we'll have an answer if an executive says, "Love it, but what would episode six look like?"

Callaway also gives us his Most Important Rule: *Take the bottle of water.*

"When you go do a pitch, you'll almost always be offered a bottle of water. Always take it. Always," Callaway says. "One, you can use something to drink during your pitch. You don't want to get dry mouth when you're talking. That's bad. You can also use a drink of water for dramatic effect or to buy some time if you momentarily lose your train of thought. Then you'll really appreciate having that water bottle in front of you. But the most important reason you'll want to take that bottle of water is because you'll at least get *something* for your pitch. Most pitches won't get you a dime, but when you walk out into the street after a meeting, you can say, 'At least I got a free bottle of water!'"

The class laughs hard at the line. Callaway's candor is refreshing.

He gives another basic piece of advice: keep the attention of the people in the room. If an executive starts looking at her phone or drifting away, do something dramatic. Up the energy level. Clap your hands to emphasize a point. Do whatever it takes *to get the attention back on your pitch.*

Callaway explains he's done dozens upon dozens of pitches for major studios. He tells some horror stories about pitches gone wrong—executives who take calls in the middle of a pitch, executives who spend the pitch reading messages on their smartphones, executives who close their eyes and appear to be asleep during a pitch, an executive who started having a seizure during a pitch.

Callaway warns us that studio executives hear pitches all day long, day after day. He says the sad fact is great material can be overlooked if the pitching is poor. So Callaway wants us to memorize our material and *practice, practice, practice*. He sounds like a 1950s basketball coach. He's all about the fundamentals, about not making simple mistakes. If we're pitching a comedy series featuring animated animals, say right up front: *This is a comedy, an animated comedy series featuring talking animals in the spirit of Bugs Bunny*. Overlook these simple facts, he says, and at the end of a pitch, the executives might be thinking you're pitching a serious animal documentary for the Nature Channel.

His advice is spot-on for film school. I'd already heard classmates' story ideas that lost me from the opening sentence.

To build authenticity, Callaway has the pitcher leave the classroom and then reenter to duplicate the dynamics of a real pitch session, where an executive is already in an office.

When we start pitching, it's sweet and funny. We're performing in front of other writers and, trust me, most writers are not born performers. Many of the students speak too quietly, and Callaway gently reminds them to speak up. Many are visibly flushed and nervous. I wonder what an energetic stand-up comic like Breitmayer would do in a class like this.

Just as we did when we were directors in 507 screenings, we take a hot seat in the middle of the room. This chair faces Callaway. The rest of the class is in a U-shape behind the hot seat. Callaway sits at his desk, his iPhone timer running.

When each of us is finished with our pitch, Callaway gives his feedback, along with any from students who want to talk.

Our first practice pitches are medium in length. When it's my turn to go, I ramp into my pitch with a story I read in that day's *Los Angeles Times* about gang violence in the city, and I talk about how there is a thin line between civilization and anarchy. "My film is about one man's battle to hold that line. It's set in a not-too-distant future when civilization is crumbling. This story is about a young cop who faces a gang that drove over his wife and child and burned his best friend. The name of my film is MAD MAX."

When I mention the name of the film, Callaway smiles and nods. When I finish, I get what may be a backhanded compliment. "You chose a great, great film. It's hard to go wrong with MAD MAX," Callaway says.

I think, *Okay, we like the same film. Does that mean I had a good pitch?* He explains I could use more energy, but all in all, it was a decent job. One of the students pipes in. He says my delivery is too mellow: "It's a little too much like a smooth jazz radio announcer." I rub my forehead when I hear this. I'm going to have to lose my public radio voice for pitching.

The semester seems to accelerate. In an eye blink, we're done with January and into February. The flavor of film school is now so different from my first two semesters. Now I understand why they call the first year the "boot camp" year. In the first year, the learning curve is intensely steep. Everything then was new, and just when I felt comfortable with a skill or technique, I was forced to move forward. Now I'm building on my base.

I also see that film school is like shampoo. We wash, rinse, repeat. Wash, rinse, repeat over and over but with increasing complexity as we go. First semester is solo, second semester is tandem, third and onward is larger groups. But because we've had a chance to do *everything* in the first year, when we return to it again in a more specialized form, it's not nearly as intimidating.

My cinematography class, for example, is a joy. I was a camera ignoramus in 507, barely capable at the start of 508 . . . although much more comfortable with film at the end of 508. Now I'm feeling relaxed and excited about honing my techniques in cinematography. We're shooting with sixteen-millimeter film most weeks, but we get to shoot with a studio-quality high-definition video camera on occasion, and we have a large soundstage to ourselves. Every student in our class is director for a week, and we're to bring a scene and actors and props. Then we rotate roles. It's great fun, and the instructor, Rob K., keeps the energy level high. The weekly class is four hours long, and in that time, we move quickly and can shoot a remarkable amount of material. Our pace is radically faster than the days of inching through group projects in 507. If we dawdle, Rob K. claps his hands and shouts, "Keep it moving. Keep it moving!"

As my confidence grows, my joy does, too. I feel free in the soundstage. It's big enough to park a dozen cars inside or pass a football without hitting anything, and high above the floor there's a wooden catwalk with all sorts of lights suspended in place. During class, I scamper around. On the catwalks I look down at the action on the floor and feel like I did as a little kid when I visited the lumberyard my grandpa worked at. The soundstage also looks remarkably similar to the stages at Paramount where DIRTY SEXY MONEY is being filmed. It's fun in here, where there are no windows and it can be as dark as midnight at high noon. It feels like the real deal.

Rob K. is also a master of creating beautiful scenes with a minimum of lighting and movement. It's all about those two for him. During one of the first classes, we quickly build a simple set: two movable walls put together in an L shape. One wall has a window, the other a door. We light the scene to mimic nighttime. It's very moody and mysterious. Inside our little house is a chair, a table, a lamp, and a few other pieces of furniture. Rob K. picks a student to be the actor.

We shoot from "inside" our little house. The action is as simple as our set. The actor comes home, turns on a light, flips on a TV with a remote. There's a knock at the door, causing him to turn with a startled look.

Now we don't have a TV, but we build a lighting kit to make it appear he's watching a TV offscreen (TVs don't throw much light anyway). We don't have streetlights, but we make it appear they are there. We have lights that will go on when he clicks an imaginary wall switch.

Rob K. then shows us how to follow the action. The camera starts on a shadow walking past the window, then swings to the door just as the actor opens it. The camera follows him as he enters the room and goes about his business. When we shoot the scenes after only a couple hours of setup, we have a gorgeous-looking, very moody image. We shoot several takes using a video camera and then watch it on a monitor. The results are fantastic. We students know how flimsy and minimal our set is, but on the monitor it looks very real and very noir. The scene has a great deal of tension in it, simply from the lighting and the camera movement. The shot builds tension throughout the entire scene. There's no dialogue or even any acting, so it's just camera work, lighting, and staging that gives a sense of drama. When we're done looking at the image, we break down the set and put away all the material and lights and coil the electrical cords and leave the set exactly as we found it—empty.

Rob K. later lectures at a national convention of cinematographers and shows them our scene. He says they're impressed by our work and couldn't believe we did it in three hours from start to finish with fewer than a dozen students.

When it's my turn to direct, I shoot a short scene where a trio of beautiful actresses, dressed to the nines, blow kisses and wink at the camera. When the point of view is reversed, it turns out they're flirting with an unshaven, potbellied film student. I've got an $80,000 studio-quality, high-def camera at my disposal, and my classmates build a long set of dolly tracks so the camera can glide by the women at walking speed. We build a reflector that's as big as a camping tent to bounce additional light on the women. We shoot on a grassy area of campus near the music school, and we attract a host of spectators who are curious to know if we're shooting a commercial. Rob K, as usual, hovers and points out ways to improve my shooting. At one point, I kneel down to add a shim to raise the metal dolly tracks (they're like miniaturized railroad tracks) and he chides me, "You're the director, Steve. Don't spend your time doing that. Get someone else to do it." So I do.

As I go forward in Callaway's pitching class, gain more skills in cinematography, listen to Casper lecture (I continue to keep a very low profile this time around), and learn about the details of creating a documentary, I go backward in one class: screenwriting. My instructor likes to have us rewrite. I've got most of CRAZYHOUSE ON SKIS written, and I'm looking forward to finishing it. My classmates are in the same boat. We're all nearly done with a script we started the semester before. Now, with a new instructor, we start slicing bits and pieces off of our scripts. In the first week, it's minor, just little nicks from our pages. As the weeks go on, our instructor keeps suggesting we cut more, rewrite more, delete more. "I'm a very big believer in rewriting," she says in class. After a month, I'm rewriting my opening pages. When I bring them to class and read them, she shakes her head with a frown. She doesn't like it. She suggests rewriting it again. Dan's comedy gets whittled down. Thompson's horror film gets cut. The historical action film—completed—goes through a dramatic rewrite. The instructor keeps shaking her head. "No. I don't think so. I really think you should take another go at that," she'll say. It doesn't seem to matter to whom she's talking. So we cut and slice and pare. My screenwriting class is a four-credit monster—so it's expensive. Nearly $6,000 for this class alone. I'm taking it because I want to get a screenwriting major, and this is the way to do it, but I'm rather discouraged by what I'm getting out of the class, and so are my fellow students.

Callaway's pitch class is much more satisfying. My short pitches for CRAZYHOUSE ON SKIS have gone well, and now we're building the Big Pitch. My actual script for CRAZYHOUSE, which I'm working on in screenwriting, has shrunk from ninety pages down to forty pages, but my pitch for the story has grown to twenty minutes.

The class, like every class, settles into a rhythm. We know what to expect, who will be animated, who will be earnest. It seems to be as much stage training as writing, and our Thursday-evening class can get very long. It starts at 7 P.M. and sometimes runs almost to eleven. By ten, my eyelids start to droop and no matter how good the pitches are, I find it's hard to keep my energy up. I almost always sit by Caraballo, and we'll occasionally nudge each other if we sense the other falling asleep. I blame my fatigue on getting up at 6 A.M., and the fact that I have two other classes on Thursdays — my doc class and my cinematography class—that run from 9 A.M. to 5 P.M. However, the truth is, it sometimes gets boring listening to the same pitches week after week. Callaway, amazingly, rarely shows signs of fatigue. He's always sitting at his desk, surrounded by a horseshoe of students, with one student in the hot seat. He always seems focused, his eyes alert, like some beefy wingless eagle. I wonder if he ever gets tired. On some evenings, when my eyes are bloodshot and I've been sitting in a classroom for twelve hours, I wish he'd put his head down on his arms and call it quits for the night. But he never does. He listens, he gives advice. He is gentle on the tenderhearted students, more assertive with the tougher students.

During this time, the writers' strike comes to an end. A handful of us students talk in the hallway before class about whether Callaway will stop teaching because of his day job at CSI: NY. When class starts, Callaway says, yes, he may have to be absent for some classes, but he fully intends to work through the rest of the semester. He says he's enjoying teaching. I breathe a sigh of relief. It would be a rotten deal if he left. True, the class can get wearying, but I pin most of that problem on scheduling and my own inability to keep my eyes open late. I never adopt the late-to-bed schedules of my fellow students. Minneapolis is two hours ahead of Los Angeles, and in order to talk to Julie before her day gets crazy, I get up early. Also, when I fly home, it's already almost impossible to get up when my kids get up and my body thinks it's 4:30 A.M. If I stayed up late like most of my classmates, who seem to shut down at 2 or 3 A.M., I'd be completely out of synch with my family.

We launch into our long pitches. Twenty minutes is a long time to hold court. There are absolutely no surprises anymore. I've heard Caraballo's pitch over and over and over now in ever-expanding detail. I've heard everyone's pitch multiple times. Somehow, Callaway keeps his spirits up. He sits for hours, his hands under his chin, focused. Nodding slightly. And then giving feedback with his red-clay/L.A. accent.

There are no major breakthroughs, just steady work by us in class. We all have to sit in the hot seat, and there's a great deal of empathy for students who freeze or flub their pitches. There's a lack of one-upmanship, perhaps because we realize we're not competing against each other. How we do *in class* doesn't matter. How we do *in the real world* does. I enjoy getting to know some of the writers. I rarely intersect with them in film school, and they're in a position I very much could be in. I debated applying to the writing division, and it's the place where I feel most at home. The writing division students, however, view me and Caraballo as odd ducks. We're production students, the guys always carrying cameras and lugging cases of lights. Yes, I'm taking advanced screenwriting classes, but those classes are only for the handful of production students who want to be scribes as well. So far, I've not crossed paths with students from the writing division—until now.

During class breaks, I get questions from the writing students about the production program—they're curious about what we do. They sometimes seem a bit envious. We get to *make* what we write—at least in school. They also suspect that production students have a better shot at getting paid in the near future as editors or sound people or camera assistants. That's precisely why I went into the production division. I also find my production experience has sharpened my writing skills greatly. Writers can envision anything they want. Before I came to USC, I read a scriptwriting book that urged writers not to be constrained by physical reality, to write anything they can imagine.

It's a liberating idea, but I've since learned as a production student the reality of making imagination into a film. When I write now, I think of locations. And I think of actors and casting. How would I shoot this scene in CRAZYHOUSE? I also write scenes with a budget in mind.

Thus, a character can enter a bar and:

- Work his way through a crowd of people and ask the bartender a question.
- Enter a mostly empty place and ask the bartender a question.

The empty place requires fifty fewer extras, which is a whole lot cheaper. If the size of the crowd in the bar doesn't affect the story line, then a big crowd is something that a producer would love to cut. Many of the writing students are pitching films that are very large in scope. If they were made, they'd be $150 million spectaculars. As a production student, I'm focused on how to write a $4 million film—heavy on character and acting, light on special effects. One woman in class is pitching a story about an underworld fantasy world. Very LORD OF THE RINGS-like, and one that sounds delightful, but when she pitches it, I think, "Lord, that would be expensive."

I remind myself that MAD MAX was made for $400,000 (Australian) back in 1979 and was edited in a family bedroom. They had so few cars at their disposal the filmmakers repainted some of them and put them in different scenes. For stuntmen, they relied on Aussie biker gangs. All low budget. All successful.

So I pitch CRAZYHOUSE, and I imagine the scene: a small run-down resort in Wisconsin. A half-dozen major characters. Some of the stunts and skiing would be done by local talent. In my script, I have a broken-down professional water-skier show up at a Wisconsin resort to take a summer job running a low-budget water-ski show. In the Midwest and in parts of the East, water-ski shows are an odd and endearing summertime tradition. The skiers create human pyramids, do tricks, jump off ramps. They wear spangled, revealing outfits, and it's as silly and visually compelling as ballroom dancing. It's more cornball though, and comic. In decades past, it was a much bigger deal. Many theme parks—Cypress Gardens and Sea World among them—featured ski show spectaculars. In recent years, the number of shows has dwindled to a few holdouts in the Midwest and Florida. When I conceived my idea, I was motivated by the success of STRICTLY BALLROOM, director Baz Luhrmann's

1992 ballroom dancing drama. At the time, ballroom dancing was a dying art form, performed mostly by aging Arthur Murray instructors. My own mom had dated an Arthur Murray instructor before she met my father and was an excellent dancer. While growing up, my siblings and I thought ballroom was for squares and fuddy-duddies. Then STRICTLY BALLROOM reignited interest in the art form. Now ballroom dancing is a prime-time television staple. I'm convinced water-ski shows—funny, quirky, sexy, campy, athletic—have the same potential, at least in a film.

In my pitch in Callaway's class, I explain the corollaries. Most of the students nod politely. They don't know what a water-ski show is. Without a visual aide, it's hard to explain what I mean when I say *human pyramids*—a boat tows nine skiers. Five keep their skis on, four kick off theirs and clamber onto the shoulders of the five skiers to build a human pyramid. In my pitch, I can look sideways and see some of the students' eyes start to glaze over. It's hard to explain without seeing it, and as Supreme Court Justice Potter Stewart said about pornography, "I know it when I see it."

My final CRAZYHOUSE pitch goes well enough. I've got the entire pitch memorized, and for my ramp I use the latest ratings for DANCING WITH THE STARS, and segue into Luhrmann's film, then use it to launch into my film, which I call "the next great water-ski comedy."

Callaway laughs at the line. He's one of the few to laugh. He's old enough to get the joke. There never has been a great water-ski comedy, of course, unless you count the corny 1973 Disney flop SUPERDAD, which features a brief scene with Bob Crane on water skis. I go through my characters and detail how the lead character saves the resort and wins the big end-of-summer water-ski competition using a handful of quirky residents from the local half-way house . . . and redeems himself along the way.

I'm satisfied. I'm looking forward to pitching CRAZYHOUSE to the industry panel in two months.

There's still two months, however, and I've got to come up with a television show to pitch for the rest of the class.

My documentary class has become a pitch class in its own right. The final exam for this class will be pitching a documentary project to a faculty panel. This pitch will be mostly a video, with a short verbal section. In the first few weeks, I sifted through other ideas presented in class. Rene and Manny are also in the class. Rene's documentary pitch will be about a type of upper-class traditional Mexican wedding that involves horses, guns, and lots of liquor. Manny is going to pitch a story about creating underwater reefs by sinking old ships. They're both good ideas, but very difficult to do as a film student based in Los Angeles. I want to do something very L.A.-centric, something with some visual pop, and something no more than a few miles from USC. After tossing out some serious ideas (a day in the life of an overworked medical resident, obese kids, a doc about Drew Casper), I settle on having fun. I tell the instructor I want to do a documentary about Los Angeles' drag-racing culture. L.A. was the birthplace of the National Hot Rod Association and the home of early drag racing. Now there's only a handful of drag-racing tracks left, but the city is still a hotbed of racing—it takes place illegally, on the street.

I like my idea, but the size is daunting. I'm busy with Casper's class, cinematography, Callaway's class, screenwriting . . . and finding more than a day or two per week for this project is impossible. So I fall back to an idea I'd done before. I'll pitch a documentary about the same twisty road and the same dare-devil motorcyclists I chronicled in 507. That was an eight-minute documentary. Now I've got to pitch a project that, if made, would be twenty-six minutes. I've got to shoot new footage.

Spring break is coming. A few nights before I plan to fly home, I invite my nephew Mikey to dinner to make sure he eats something. He's nineteen and seems to live on ramen and water on his sailboat. We eat at a Sizzler steakhouse across the street from campus. Our steaks are tough as a saddle, but Mikey downs a huge piece of meat and several side dishes. He never seems to fill up.

The next morning my gut aches. It's centered on my right side. I blame the steak, but by the next day my stomach is not getting any better. It feels like I've got a burning lump under my right rib cage. I'm feeling pretty crappy all around, too. I call Mikey and ask him how he feels. He's great. That afternoon I'm in the USC locker room. I'm gonna try to work out, even though I've now got what feels like a baseball covered with glass shards under my ribs. I'm hunched over on a bench when an older guy getting dressed down the aisle asks me if I'm okay. I say I am, but I don't look all that good in the mirror.

When I fly back to Minneapolis for spring break, I'm a bit better. But I'm holding my side, and it hurts to breathe deeply. I keep waiting for whatever it is to go away, but it doesn't. At the end of the break, I finally call Dr. Flaata. He gets me in immediately. When I see him, he pushes his fingers under my rib cage. I flinch badly. It hurts. He suspects I may have a gallstone. "If you do, we'll have it out in no time and you'll be fine," he says. But some of my symptoms are unusual for gallstone. He orders up a CAT scan and a bunch of lab tests. He says I might have to have a camera-equipped tube shoved down my throat to investigate, and I shudder. The test results won't be ready until the next day, the day I'm supposed to be back at USC, so I delay my flight.

I ask him what the heck is going on with my body. I'd been impervious for decades, and now this, too? "Sometimes stuff just happens,

Steve. It's the way medicine goes. I wouldn't read too much into it," he says. Of course, I have read too much into it. I've read lots and lots on the web, and by the time I'm heading to my CAT scan on Monday morning, I'm convinced they're going to find liver cancer. Or pancreatic cancer. Just like I did when I had my stroke, I wonder what underlying issue is causing this weird breakdown.

Worrying makes the symptoms worse, and by the time I'm lying on the CAT scan table, I'm freaked out. I know the lab technicians aren't supposed to make diagnoses, but I can't help myself. "So, how does it look?" I ask. "That's up to the doctor to discuss with you," the tech says.

I drive home, waiting for the phone to ring. A radiologist is supposed to read my CAT scan and report back. All afternoon, I pounce on the phone every time it rings. Will I need surgery? Do I have pancreatic cancer? What the hell is going on? I'm amazed how many phone calls our house receives in an afternoon—almost all of them telemarketers. Everyone who calls is surprised I'm answering within a tenth of a second of the first ring.

Finally at 4:30 P.M., I can't take it anymore. I call Dr. Flaata's office. Thirty minutes later, right at five, his nurse calls me. She apologizes, says the CAT scan wasn't read by a radiologist until late in the day. And she says everything looks normal. No gallstone. No anything.

I ask her, "So, they look for, you know, things like cancer, right?" She chuckles at my naiveté. "Yes, of course. They don't see anything abnormal in your entire abdominal cavity." I sit down and breathe a huge sigh of relief. This medical roller coaster is too much for me.

Later that evening, Dr. Flaata calls me on his cell. He says some of my lab results were elevated. It appears I have a mild case of pancreatitis. "Caused by what?" I ask. "Hard to say," he says. The bottom line is that I need to eat mild food, stay away from fats, and, he adds, go back to grad school. He's a big supporter of my journey.

That night, I'm eating noodles and saltines for dinner. It helps a bit, and I schedule my return flight to Los Angeles for late that week. By the time I get back, I've missed a week of most of my classes.

Besides catching up with missed class work, my coming weekend has three items on my to-do list: tweak my CRAZYHOUSE script yet again, shoot video footage for my documentary class, come up with a television show for Callaway's pitch class. During break, I'd thought a lot about what I'd do for the TV project. I settled on doing a drama based on my experiences as a transplant coordinator. Just as I'm getting settled into my routine again, I get a call from my pal Tom. He'd like to visit, on very short notice. As in right now. The Minnesota winter has gotten to him and he wants to visit Southern California.

I groan a bit. I love seeing friends, but my schedule is so booked, I'm always working, and now I'm behind because of missing some classes yet again. I don't have much time to be a tour guide. I tell Tom he's welcome to come, but he'll have to accept the fact that I'll be busy much of the time. He books his flight.

I pick Tom up at LAX. He's white as a ghost. He's got that Minnesota winter tan. I tell him my schedule, and he shrugs. He's cool by it. He just wants to be in the warmth for a few days.

The weekend is all good. On Saturday, I recruit Mikey to hold a microphone boom, and the three of us drive up the Angeles Crest and interview motorcyclists for my doc class. At the top of the mountain, there's deep snow lining the side of the road, so we engage in a long snowball-throwing contest that lasts until our arms are shot. On Sunday afternoon, Tom and I play tourists. He wants to see Beverly Hills, so we park just off Beverly Hills Drive and go for a long walk through the heart of zip code 90210. It's a cool, foggy afternoon.

Tom thinks it's interesting . . . and then we walk past a stately home and see an AAA wrecker truck parked in a driveway. Next to the wrecker is a new black Mercedes with a flat tire. The driver of the wrecker is in the process of changing the tire, while the owner of the car (a healthy guy our age) watches, along with his two young kids. Tom and I silently walk by, taking in this Beverly Hills moment. We both can't believe it. Who would call a wrecker just to change a tire in his own perfectly flat driveway on a Sunday afternoon? It's not raining or snowing. We're both small-town Midwestern boys at heart. Changing a tire, especially in front of your kids, is an honored rite of manhood, something to be excited about, like Ralphie's Old Man in A CHRISTMAS STORY. What is this rich guy teaching his kids?

"That's just wrong," I say as we're out of earshot. Tom nods. "I wonder if the guy calls someone to service his wife," he mutters.

The next morning, I'm up early. I tell Tom I'm going to work on my television pitch. Tom's fine with that. The day is dawning sunny and bright. We stay at Carl and Irene's that day and have the place to ourselves because they're out of town. I get my legal pad and sit in the shade and write down ideas. Tom finds a reclining chair in a backyard patio and strips off his shirt, exposing a mass of blindingly white flesh. At noon, he cracks a beer.

Throughout the day, I write in the shade and run my ideas past Tom, who sits a few feet away in the blazing Southern California sunshine. He serves as my muse. He stays in the sun the whole time and sips his beers. He nods when he likes an idea, grunts when he doesn't. I sip water and work on my pitch. My pancreas flare-up means no beer, no coffee, nothing spicy. As the day goes on, Tom nods more than he grunts. He likes the pitch.

By 6 P.M. that day, I've got my pitch done. Tom is beet-red from the sun. He's happy. I'm happy.

That night, I read over my pitch. It seems pretty good. I start performing it, memorizing it, getting ready for the upcoming class. Tom grills some steaks and listens.

When Callaway's pitch class comes on Thursday, I walk in and . . . he's not there. There's another instructor, a sub. Callaway is busy with CSI: NY, we're told. The substitute is a polite blond-haired man in his fifties wearing khakis and new white K-Swiss tennis shoes. I have no idea who he is. I suspect he's one of the many adjunct instructors USC has at its disposal.

Caraballo is glad to see me back. I assure him I'm feeling fine. When it's time to pitch, I walk in with this pitch memorized:

Two weeks ago, I went to the doctor because it felt like I had a baseball stuck under my ribs. A baseball made of jagged crystals.

He told me I appeared to have a case of pancreatitis. My pancreas was inflamed. He said he didn't know why, that they would need to do more tests.

I was not happy. I knew there are really only two organs in your body that are hard to replace: one is your brain; the other is your pancreas.

I knew that because a few years ago I worked as a transplant coordinator at the University of Chicago Hospitals. I was the guy who carried the Igloo cooler with a human liver inside. My job was to oversee all aspects of the transplantation harvest. I was essentially a producer of a traveling road show that flew all over the country to take out human organs in the middle of the night. I gathered the surgical team; I got us to a little hospital in Arkansas, or Brooklyn; and I actually helped to take the livers out—which was the scariest part because I was an English major turned reporter turned transplant coordinator and didn't know jack about surgery. True story—one Christmas Eve, the University of Chicago was doing an experimental surgery where they were taking out a portion of someone's liver and giving it to that person's deathly sick infant. This was very risky stuff at the time. Very cutting edge. But because they were so short on surgical residents at the time—it was Christmas, and we were doing another transplant operation at the same time—the lead surgeon pulled me out of a hallway and I scrubbed in and helped him dissect this little tiny section of liver that was going to be going into the infant. My experiences at that hospital have helped shape what I think is a great one-hour hospital drama.

The working title is: FOR EVERY BEATING HEART . . .

Every episode of this show is a stand-alone drama. In every episode, we follow a heart as it goes from donor to recipient. From someone who was once alive to someone who is about to die, and gets new life. This drama focuses on one main character: Nic Barnes, a new surgeon-in-training whose job is to follow the donor heart on every step of its journey.

This drama takes place right now, at a major American research hospital, where the politics are intense, the city around them is crumbling, the weather is always unpredictable, and any other place in America is a few hours away by jet.

Major Characters:

Nic Barnes, thirty-one years old. The son of a car salesman and a school secretary. He's a surgical fellow: he's gone through medical school and a long residency and now he's almost through with his training. Nic is a guy without airs. He's got the easy social skills of a salesman, a guy who likes to hang out at run-down bowling alleys and the corner basketball court. But he's whip smart—the kind of guy who knows every single JEOPARDY! question in the snap of a finger. He has a problem with authority figures, however, not a good thing when he deals with his attending physicians, some of the biggest egos in medicine. Nic is single. Good-looking. Never found the right girl. Deep down, he's a poet who finds the time to keep a journal. He's also got a secret that tortures him: when he was seventeen, he lost control of his car and slammed into another car, killing a family of three. To this day, he doesn't drive. Not a problem during his medical school and residency in NYC. A big problem in Chicago.

Dr. Schwartz, the head of the transplant program. Exceedingly arrogant, never wrong, and a man who always wants to be number one, no matter what the cost.

Dr. Whiteside III, second in command. Boston Brahmin, all the right schools, a guy who still wears tweed jackets with leather patches and likes to boast about his stunning assortment of bottled sherry. He has a great curse: his father, Dr. Whiteside II, won a Nobel Prize in medicine in the 1960s.

Dr. Susanna Hanson, a final-year surgical resident, one year younger than Nic. Introverted, tough, a real looker. Fantastic rapport with patients, especially children. Already twice divorced. Her second marriage lasted forty-seven days before she filed for divorce.

Wendy Kim, another surgical resident. Cute, a joker, everyone's best friend. Always upbeat, a complete straight arrow. Or so it seems.

Avio Torres, the hospital's other fellow, which makes him an equal with Nic in the hierarchy of the hospital. But . . . Avio is older, late thirties, a cardiac surgeon who is returning to the university for another year of training so he can do transplants. Avio is a heart-throb: GQ looks, a politician's charm, a backstabber par excellence.

Fat Eddy, the candy bar–eating, slobby transplant coordinator. Seems to know nothing, but he always gets the transplant team to the right place at the right time. The kind of guy who can come up with a dogsled team in an hour, even while eating a leftover pizza.

BASIC SETUP:

Every episode features a through-line of a single transplantation. In that way, it's similar to the LAW & ORDER or CSI or other police and legal procedurals. It also allows for a multitiered story line like SIX

FEET UNDER. In each FOR EVERY BEATING HEART episode, there are the stories of the donor and the recipient and the stories of the transplant team. They will overlap and interweave during each episode. And although the medical team will have a changing dynamic through the season, this is not a soap opera. Viewers watching episode five will not need to know what happened in episode four to understand the action. Each episode will stand fully alone.

This format allows a tremendous amount of flexibility in storytelling. For example, although each episode features a harvest operation and a recipient operation, it is entirely possible to spend nearly the entire hour on just the harvest. Same goes with a recipient operation. There will be episodes in which there is no harvest operation because something goes amiss. There will be episodes in which the recipient operation goes afoul. Sometimes the good will die. Sometimes the simple will not work. This is a show built on unpredictability—a tremendous amount of unpredictability—which gives it a huge measure of its drama.

The show also allows viewers to explore the ethics and controversies and dilemmas and miracles of transplant surgery. Think for a moment: the great police and legal procedurals all wrestle with big societal questions. What does GREY'S ANATOMY wrestle with? Who to sleep with? What melancholy ballad to play under the script? This show, FOR EVERY BEATING HEART, will be the next one that people talk about, think about, blog about.

The Pilot:

Nic Barnes has just arrived in Chicago. The movers haven't arrived yet, and he's just arrived at his apartment. It's a Sunday. He's slated to start his fellowship at the Chicago University Hospital on Monday. He tells his girlfriend—she still lives in New York City—that he'll have an easy first couple of days. Paperwork. Orientation. His doorbell rings.

It's Fat Eddy, the transplant coordinator, who somehow found where Nic lives and tells Nic that they're going to Louisiana for a harvest, right now. Nic can't say no, so they're off. Nic, Fat Eddy, the easy-on-the-eyes Susanna Hanson, and a very young medical student named Tyler. They fly in a chartered Lear to a tiny airstrip in the Bayou and take a run-down cab to the local hospital. It's 2 A.M. They arrive to find everyone at the hospital angry and upset. The donor, it turns out, was the staff psychiatrist, who was killed by one of her patients. The patient threw a Molotov cocktail into her office, burning her to death and damaging the hospital. We have seen these scenes interlaced with the scenes of Nic in Chicago. Now, the two stories collide. There's another complication: the psychiatrist's family is split on whether to donate her organs. She's Creole, and some family members don't think it's right. The dispute spills into the operating room as Nic and Susanna are removing the woman's heart. Nic is forced to calm the angry family. When Nic and the others are finally ready to leave, they're stranded temporarily at the hospital because there is no ambulance—and no cab—to take them to the airport. A member of the woman's family, the leader of the anti-transplantation group, volunteers to take them. A family funeral procession slowly winds its way through the lowlands of the Bayou, taking the Chicago transplant team to its waiting plane. As the team enters the plane, the tearful family stands outside, hugging and crying.

Nic is exhausted. The tough-as-iron Susanna tells him: get some sleep, 'cuz we're only halfway done, and the clock is ticking. They have four hours to put the new heart in.

When they arrive in Chicago, it's already after 7 A.M. Traffic is a bitch, but with Fat Eddy driving—his vehicle is a former police cruiser—they run the shoulder and take shortcuts only to arrive at the hospital and find that the recipient who was supposed to get the heart failed his blood tests upon being admitted. The recipient is a *drunk and arrived blotto. Second on the list of recipients is a famous cellist, but he's in liver failure. Third on the list is a felon, imprisoned in Joliet, who beat a murder rap only because no one would testify against him. The felon's lawyer successfully sued the prison system, arguing that his client deserved the same chance at a heart transplant as anyone else. Now the con gets his chance. And Nic gets to operate, under the watchful and very critical eyes of his two bosses. When they finish, successfully, it's not even noon. Nic feels like he's been gone a month. His boss pats him on the back, says nice work, and now get ready to do it all over again.*

When I get done, the nice man with white K-Swiss shoes looks mildly pleased. He advises me to drop any negative references to other shows. For all you know, he says, a producer from GREY'S ANATOMY is listening to the pitch. And what good would that do you? he asks. (It's also a bad idea to castigate a show created by Shonda Rhimes, a fairly recent USC film school student. And who am I to make value judgments? My wife Julie loves GREY'S ANATOMY.) He also doesn't like the name of my show. Too dull, he says. He makes a few other mild suggestions, but that's it.

Caraballo, meanwhile, has a great comedy pitch about a variety of Hispanic day laborers who meet every day outside a Home Depot in Florida. It's very funny, and with his Cubano accent, Caraballo makes the most of the Spanglish he sprinkles throughout the pitch.

At the end of the evening, I'm walking out of the class when the substitute instructor stops me in the hallway. "That was a really good pitch," he says. "What's your name?"

I tell him, and we chat for a minute. I see the other students looking at me out of the corners of their eyes as they exit. I don't know who this instructor is, but he is very enthusiastic about my show idea. When we're done chatting, I catch up with a classmate outside the building on the sidewalk. "Who was that guy teaching tonight?" I ask. My classmate, a writing student, stares at me like I'm an idiot. "That's Jack Epps."

I'm trying to remember where I heard the name before. Didn't Callaway mention it once? "Jack Epps," the other student says with more emphasis. "He's the head of the writing program. Guy wrote TOP GUN and LEGAL EAGLES. And a lot more."

I nod. Ahhhh. *That* Jack Epps.

The next week Callaway is back. I've tweaked my pitch. My ramp is about seeing ambulances and wondering who's inside. I drop any criticisms of other shows. I drop comparisons to SIX FEET UNDER and GREY'S ANATOMY and put it squarely in the camp of procedurals like LAW & ORDER. The new working title is HEART & SOUL. I throw in a line about using Hoagy Carmichael's popular composition of the same name as an opening song. I tighten my pilot.

I have a change from my first version. Nic Barnes is a much darker character. To calm the situation in the operating room, Nic, the lead character, tells the bereaved and reluctant family of the potential donor a touching story that his own brother died in a motorcycle crash. Nic explains that donating his brother's organs helped him through the grief of his death. His heart-wrenching tale convinces the family they should donate the brain-dead psychologist's organs. When Susanna, the other doctor, later tells Nic she's sorry for his loss, he tells her he never had a brother, that it was all just a story.

When I present my idea in class, Callaway leans forward and purses his lips. The longer I go, the more eagle-like he becomes. This is the first time he's heard it, and he doesn't laugh much at any laugh lines. His questions are pointed, aggressive, direct. He asks me if it's really a true procedural—meaning no meaningful character development through a season.

I hedge my bet. "Well, I see it being a little of both. Every episode would be a stand-alone episode, but I see some character development through the series."

My answer sounds weak.

He seems to frown. He suggests changing this, changing that. Humming a few bars of the song "Heart & Soul"? Drop it, he says with a wave of his hand. It's obvious. He wants me to make certain all the characters jump out. And, he says, what's episode four of the first season?

I pause too long.

I'm about to wing it, and Callaway knows it. "Make sure you have the season plotted out. Episodes one, two, three, four. You never know if an exec is going to ask you for that," he says.

I nod and take my seat. It's unclear if Callaway likes my idea. He certainly was tough on me, even as the next student—a sweet undergraduate woman, very nervous—gets treated to smiles and warmth. I look at my watch. Callaway also spent more than the usual time peppering me with questions. That's a good sign, I think.

Even if he hates my pitch, I've suddenly got so much on my plate it doesn't matter much in the big picture. This is just one class of five. I'm back to running-and-gunning seven days a week, and my documentary class is getting my major focus. I've screened my documentary pitch tape of the motorcyclists who ride the Angeles Crest, and my instructor likes it. I'd like to direct it during the upcoming semester, but unfortunately I'm not qualified to direct until I crew on another film. I tell my instructor I'm not likely ever to direct it—when I get done crewing, I'll be working on finishing my studies and not spending the time and money to take an additional six-credit course. Directing the doc just isn't in the cards. Besides, I say, I'd only be able to shoot this documentary in the fall, not the spring, because the mountain roads I focus on are generally closed because of snow in January and February.

Not long after I explain all this, she pulls me aside. "I think you have a really good chance of getting picked. I've talked to some other faculty and if you can find someone qualified to direct, we'd allow you to codirect with them. We've never allowed this before, so this is a real opportunity."

Okay, I say, I'll consider it. It sounds like a double-edged sword. Codirecting. I would check off my required crewing duties by being a director. That would be sweet! The downside is I'd have to work closely with someone else on a project that is so personal. And, I'm leery of sharing directing duties. It seems like having two captains on a ship.

Still, if I don't codirect, I'll be crewing on someone else's film. Neither option is ideal, but the chance to direct a doc is too sweet to pass up. My instructor says I have only a few days to find someone to partner with before the pitching material is presented to the faculty.

I ask around. I make a pitch to a couple of my former 508 class-mates, but they've got other plans. A handful of students who want to direct documentaries are put in touch with me by my instructor, but none of it pans out. Several are facing the cold, hard reality of grad school: classes cost a lot. Directing a 547 doc is a six-credit class at more than $8,000. If you don't absolutely need it (for a thesis film) or want it, it's a luxury. After a few days talking and emailing and interviewing and hitting dead ends, I'm resigned to crew the next semester and forget the idea of directing my motor-cycle street racing idea. I'm running out of time. The application to direct is due Monday morning.

But on Saturday afternoon, I get a friendly text from Brent, the hockey player from my 508 class. He wants to know what I'm up to—just a shout-out. I text back that I'm good, but couldn't find a codirector. He writes back that he's interested.

I didn't know he's currently crewing on a 546, and thus eligible to direct a doc the upcoming semester. And I had no idea he'd be interested. He is. We agree to meet.

He shows up in La Cañada on Sunday, and we go for a drive up the Angeles Crest. He's smitten by the project. It's a quick Vegas wedding, and we agree to codirect. That night, we rewrite a long application and get it done at 1 A.M. I deliver the application the next morning, an hour before it is due. That week, we edit a pitch tape—Brent is much faster than I am at editing, and in our first editing session, I mistakenly erase an updated version of our pitch, costing us hours of work. Ooops. At the end of the week, we make our pitch to a group of faculty judges—and an audience of forty or so students. We're questioned about safety issues, a reasonable question, considering we're doing a documentary about people who drive their motorcycles at a hundred miles per hour on a narrow, twisty, cliff-lined road.

After our pitch, I head to the gym with Manny and blow off some steam. In a hallway, I meet my documentary instructor, who is heading for a swim. The verdict is in, she says, and then she cracks a smile. We got it!

Brent and I, mere acquaintances just a few days earlier, will now spend four months codirecting a twenty-six-minute documentary while overseeing a crew of a half-dozen students. But first we need to select our crew.

Sometimes, be careful what you wish for. Brent and I are thrown into the maelstrom of choosing the students who will crew with us. Our topic is sexy, and it seems every cinematographer on campus wants to shoot our racing streetbikers. Every editor wants to cut it. Finding other crew positions is harder. Only one producer wants to work with us. And not a single student is interested in doing sound for us, a common problem with all the documentary films that year. That same weekend, I'm attempting to write my Casper term paper. Unlike my TEACHER'S PET one, this is a hasty affair. I pick LOVE ME TONIGHT, a 1932 musical by the great director Rouben Mamoulian and starring Maurice Chevalier and Jeanette MacDonald. I spend only four days buried in the Doheny Library, watching the film over and over and typing as fast as I can. I'm rushed, I've got nothing to prove, and I just want the paper done, pronto. I focus on Mamoulian's production techniques, which saves me doing a lot of research. I take breaks from writing to meet Brent and interview prospective crew members for the doc. I've also got a final due for my cinematography class—I need to shoot several minutes of sixteen-millimeter film that must show some exceptional cinematography—no other rules. And my CRAZY-HOUSE script is supposed to be done. It's not. In fact, it's much shorter than when I started my screenwriting semester.

I'm trying to remember that this was supposed to be my mellow semester. I'm running from Doheny to the film school and back again, over and over, and I'm lining up the cinematography shoot with the help of Manny. Luckily, I'm fast at writing, and luckily I've helped Manny a couple of times during the semester for his cinematography class, and now I'm calling in my chits. He's extremely knowledgeable about shooting, and we're going to build a rear-projection display in one of the USC soundstages, and we'll use his car as a prop. It's an ambitious project, and I'd never be able to do it without Manny's help. We're going to make it look as if an actor in a car is driving it through the streets of Los Angeles, even though the car is parked in the soundstage. Rene is the actor, and I in turn help Manny and Rene shoot their cinematography finals. In Rene's filming, I play a prisoner in a dimly lit cell. We all help each other build sets, set up lighting, move props. In one day, in one soundstage, all three of us, working together, shoot three cinematography finals. It's an important lesson about film school. Many hands make the work go faster. Many of the other cinematography students are spending days alone shooting their final projects. Working together, we get ours done in one day. Our pace is so much faster than my Vagabond shoot in 507 it makes me smile, and the entire time the three of us are laughing like hell, having the time of our lives.

I run, run, run. This is what film school is—running. In between bursts of racing around, I see how far I've come in just one school year. It's late April, and I've established myself. I'm going to be codirecting one of USC's premier films. I've established myself as a leader. My grades since coming back are all As (with one A-minus). I've got friends to help me out in tight spots. And as a cherry on the top, Rob K. loves my cinematography final. I don't want to spill the beans that the technical expertise for the shoot came courtesy of Manny, so I just nod modestly when Rob K. tells the class: "FOX spends twenty grand a day to shoot a driving scene that doesn't look any better than that!"

I've learned how to play the game and enjoy the process. The more I give, the more I receive. I've got no chip on my shoulder. I'm just enjoying myself and trying to get every ounce I can out of my experience at USC. And mainly, I'm happy to be alive.

11

Right Time, Right Place

The sun is dropping toward the smoggy horizon when I walk toward the film school. On this late April night, in the Spielberg conference room, I'll be doing my final pitch in front of the panel Callaway has gathered. A few weeks before, he gave out the names of who would be coming. They were indeed big shots. One is actress Amy Brenneman of JUDGING AMY and NYPD BLUE fame. Another is Ted Gold, formerly the head of FOX's drama division. Another is Kary Kirkpatrick, writer of many films, including OVER THE HEDGE, THE HITCHHIKER'S GUIDE TO THE GALAXY, and CHICKEN RUN. The others are producers and writers and executives, eight in total, and we'll be pitching four of them at a time over two weeks. Our class is splitting up pitching duties. Half will go the first night with the first group of Hollywood judges. Half will go the second week with a different group of judges. I'm in the first group, and I feel lucky because Ted Gold will be listening. I know a lot about him already, because another of Callaway's lessons is: know thy audience. He wants us to find out as much as we can about our panelists. During the past semester, every time we have a guest speaker, Callaway has gone around the room asking each of us to give a bit of interesting trivia about the speaker. So I research all eight of the panelists, but I focus on Gold. I feel a bit like a stalker as I delve into my research, but I'm impressed by what I learn about. Gold, a former high-ranking executive with Aaron Spelling's production company, headed up FOX's drama division for several years before leaving just a year ago. Exactly what Gold is doing now is something of a mystery. But all I care about is that he's a real-deal TV executive, a guy who ran one of the best drama divisions in television.

Outside of the conference room I see Caraballo. "Are you ready?" he asks. He's nervous. Those of us about to pitch are milling about in the hallway, while the others in the class and the panelists are in the room. Caraballo and I are pitching back to back. I'm fourth on the list, Caraballo is fifth. I'm disappointed he can't hear my pitch because he's someone who helps put energy into a room. I'm getting a drink from a fountain when Caraballo approaches me. "Hey, Steve, I think you should do CRAZYHOUSE ON SKIS!"

"You serious?" I'm wiping my mouth off.

"Yeah," he says. "That's a great pitch. They'll love it."

Caraballo gets me to thinking. Maybe I *should* pitch CRAZY-HOUSE. Maybe I am squandering my chance with my TV show. I look at the ceiling and think. "Chris, that's like changing your answer on an SAT question at the last second. I'm gonna do the TV show. One of the dudes on the panel was the head of FOX's drama division for cripes sake."

Caraballo frowns. "Okay," he says, putting a finger into my chest. "But don't blame me later."

Out in the hallway, we're timing the first pitchers. They're taking much longer than twenty minutes. That means the panelists are giving plenty of feedback. Those of us waiting in the hallway wonder if that's a good thing or a bad. One student stays close to the door, his ear inches from the crack. He whispers periodic reports on audience responses.

For nearly two hours, I'm pacing up and down the hallway, rehearsing my pitch, when the door to the conference room finally opens for my turn. I'm wearing my good-luck outfit: a pair of faded Levis, my lucky and now very worn two-toned cowboy boots, a short-sleeved blue button-down work shirt. My daily fitness regime has made me as fit as I've been in years. My hair is long now, and I've slicked it back with some cheap gel from Walgreens. In my boots, I'm a bit over six-foot-one, a tanned 190-pound cowboy ready for action. I look like a Wyoming ranch hand dressing up for a job interview at the local Walmart. And that's just the way I want it.

The panel is three men and a woman, plus Callaway in the middle. They are arranged behind a large wooden table, AMER-ICAN IDOL-style. Behind me sit my classmates . . . minus the four still in the hallway. I walk in, my legs like springs. There is a chair I am apparently to sit in, but I pace instead. I don't want to let my energy lag.

Hi. My name is Steve Boman, and thanks for taking the time to come here tonight. As you can see, my "sell-by" date is a bit different from the rest of the students here.

A chuckle rises from the panel members, who aren't expecting a fortysomething cowboy to come striding into the room. I see Callaway crack a small smile. I'm giving a different ramp into the pitch than I had practiced in class, which is intentional, and I have *much* more energy than I ever displayed in class. In front of the panel, I'm amped up and animated, and I pace like Tony Robbins giving a motivational speech. I continue to ignore the chair I'm supposed to use. I've just cracked open a forty-ounce can of whup-ass, and I'm riding my adrenaline.

I'll be honest. I'm nervous. I'm not used to being the one talking. For a long time, I used to be a newspaper reporter, so I spent a lot of time listening to other people talk. But I'm thrilled to be here . . .

When I was a reporter, I covered a lot of stories. Buildings that burned down. Planes that crashed. People who fell into wells. But there is one story I never reported on . . . although it was very interesting. There was a young man who worked at the University of Chicago back in the '90s. He was a transplant coordinator, which means he harvested human organs from dead people. Livers, mostly. But sometimes hearts or kidneys or even lungs. Now, what made this guy interesting is that he was only twenty-five years old, and he had absolutely no medical training to do his job.

I pause. The panel is eating it up.

Now, this guy, this twenty-five-year-old, was actually assisting in surgeries. In fact, on one occasion, on a Christmas Eve, because the hospital was short on medical staff, he scrubbed in and assisted on an experimental liver transplant surgery. At the University of Chicago, one of the most prestigious hospitals in the world. And remember, this guy had no medical training whatsoever. The guy was a freakin' English major.

I take a drink of water. I give Callaway a knowing glance. The panel members are leaning forward. The room is dead silent.

Now, here's the reason I never wrote about this guy. He was me. I was the twenty-five-year-old helping take organs out of dead people.

The panel members are impressed. I've saved my good stuff for when it matters.

You see, I was hired by the University of Chicago to harvest human organs when I was twenty-five years old. I had been a radio news reporter before that and accepted the job on a lark. My girlfriend knew the wife of the guy who was hiring. What the hell, I thought. I was ready for a change. Compared to being a reporter, it paid great. I flew all over the country in private jets. And I assisted in the removal of organs from dozens and dozens of brain-dead people. It was a great adventure. It was also where I got the material for the show I'm about to pitch you called HEART & SOUL.

I pause again. One panel member seems particularly impressed: Ted Gold.

What I saw as a transplant coordinator, what I saw in operating rooms and in emergency rooms and all the places in between, I've never seen represented well on television. My show, HEART & SOUL, will change that. It's a one-hour drama that focuses on transplantations and the doctors who perform them. I know something about doctors. I'm married to one. Both my brothers are physicians. My uncle was a doctor. And so was my grandfather. And let me tell you, transplant surgeons are a different breed of doc. They're cowboys. Real gunslingers. There's a saying in medicine: if you want to save the world, you become a pediatrician—my wife is a pediatrician, by the way. If you want to make your tee-time at four every day, you become a plastic surgeon. And if you're an adrenaline junkie and you don't want a family life, you become a transplant surgeon. This series will follow a handful of these transplant surgeons—these ass-kickin' cowboys—and every episode will focus on a donor, and a recipient.

I take another drink.

The structure of this show is based around a single transplant operation. The through-line of every episode is from donor to recipient. We'll meet the donor, the donor's story. We'll meet the recipient and the recipient's story. And in the middle is the transplant team, who will react to and become involved in each of these different stories.

For the next fifteen minutes, I describe the television show I had spent several months developing. I talk about the main characters, the show's tone, and I walk them through a pilot episode.

The pilot opens in a small Louisiana harbor town. Aerial wide shot. The camera tracks from a shrimp boat approaching the docks to a delivery truck driving down the town's main street. The truck stops near the town's small hospital. The camera is punched in now. The deliveryman exits. He's carrying a good-sized box, carefully. He enters a small clinic. A psychologist's office. There's a receptionist, a box of Kleenex on the counter, a couple sitting in the waiting area. From behind a closed door, we hear a terrible argument. It's a man and a woman, shouting at each other. The deliveryman walks past a surprised receptionist and pushes open the psychologist's door. We see the layout: it's a counseling session. A crying man on the right, his angry wife on the left. In the middle is their counselor, a professionally dressed black woman, midfifties.

The argument stops in mid-yell. All eyes are on the deliveryman. He reaches into the box he's holding and takes out a big honkin' Molotov cocktail. As he lights the rag, he says to the psychologist: "Thanks for the great advice, bitch."

We pull back to an exterior wide-shot and see the windows of the clinic blow out in a fireball . . .

When I get done, the students and panelists break into applause. I'm so excited! I feel like I'd nailed a gymnast's perfect ten. Ted Gold is the first panelist to speak.

"Do you feel there are a hundred episodes here?" Gold asks.

"Oh, absolutely," I answer. "The format of the show allows for great flexibility. You could focus primarily on a donor, or primarily on a recipient, on success or failure, or solely on a surgical team member. The sky is the limit." Gold nods, looking pleased.

The woman on the panel, an executive, speaks up. She looks peeved. "I have to say this: I didn't like how you stood over us. During a pitch, you always need to sit down. Otherwise, it gives your pitch a bad vibe."

The man next to her shakes his head. "Oh, I don't know," he says. "I liked it. It had a lot of energy."

The woman doesn't back down. "You always need to sit during a pitch," she lectures. "I felt you were towering over me. Executives like to feel they are in control."

I speak up. "I understand. I was planning on sitting, but I was pretty nervous and just felt much better pacing."

"Still," she says through pursed lips, "you need to sit."

Gold is smiling through the entire exchange. That's a good sign. My time is up, and I walk to the back of the room. Next up is Caraballo, and I know he'll be good, and he is. His comedy pitch about street-corner Hispanic day laborers is very funny. During Caraballo's talk, I catch Ted Gold looking at me and smiling. I'm elated.

When the evening wraps up, I walk out into the night air. It is past 1 A.M. back in Minnesota. I leave a message on Julie's cell phone. I tell her I've nailed my pitch and I know, I just know in my heart, that in a week or two I'd be able to call this television executive named Ted Gold and at least introduce myself again.

The next day, Friday, is just another day at film school. In the afternoon, I'm moving lighting equipment. It's hot. I'm sweating.

I'm hoping to have an early dinner with my brother and his wife, who are visiting Los Angeles to see Mikey. A little before 5 P.M., the moving complete, I debate blowing off the rest of my work, including checking my emails. It is times like this when I envy my fellow students with their BlackBerry and iPhone smartphones. Sweating, I walk to my favorite computer lab where I can log on and check my messages. There on my screen is an hours-old message from Callaway. He asks if I would mind him passing my info on to Ted Gold. My heart jumps into my throat. Would I mind?!

My heart is still beating fast when a new message pops on my screen a few minutes later. It's from Ted Gold's assistant. *Could you meet Ted at Paramount/CBS Studios?* I shoot back an immediate yes. She answers a few seconds later: *How does 9 A.M. Monday work?*

On Monday morning, I'm parked on a side street by the Paramount/CBS studios. I'm an hour early. I've got my pitch down stone cold solid. I wonder if I'll be pitching in front of other executives. I didn't sleep much the night before.

At a few minutes before 9 A.M., I walk into Gold's bungalow. It's next to the soundstages for CSI: NY, and it's so dang Hollywood I wanna pinch myself.

Gold's assistant offers me water. I, of course, accept a nice square bottle of Fiji. She shows me into Gold's office, and it's just him and me. We shake hands and he tells me to sit. I'm expecting to do my pitch over again in front of an audience, but Gold is interested in talking more about my background. He's friendly and warm. I'm not expecting this, and it seems like we're just talking over a backyard fence. Then he shifts gears, and he's all business. He asks me to take notes. He wants me to create a list of obstacles the characters could face—everything under the sun. He wants story obstacles. Medical obstacles. Weather obstacles. Logistics obstacles. He wants to see my list of story ideas—as many as possible. He says he wants to see if it is indeed possible to create a hundred episodes or about five years of episodes. "It's not that hard in the big picture to get a television show on the air," he says. "What's really hard in this business is to get a television show that will last for five years. *That's* hard."

I scribble down notes. Then we talk some more. After an hour, Gold wraps up our meeting. We shake hands again, and I exit.

I drive to USC feeling stunned. Julie wants to know how my first "meeting" went. "Good, I think," is my understated response.

When I get back to USC, I go straight to my favorite computer lab—a place where film students rarely venture—and start writing. I write page after page. I take a break and go for a run and eat and type some more. I do it again the next day and email my stuff to Gold. I email another big hunk of information the day after that. I've sent Gold more than four thousand words about obstacles and twenty story ideas and my vision of the world these transplant surgeons operate in.

I'm thankful I've stayed ahead of my class work at this point because I'm ignoring everything related to USC. Only when I go to screenwriting class do I speak up about my adventure. My classmates are stoked. My instructor is wide-eyed. One of my classmates asks if I'm worried about my ideas being "stolen." It's a fair question. I answer that I've registered everything I wrote with the Writers Guild of America through its electronic registration service. But I also say, "How do you get your ideas out if you're not willing to push them and take a risk that someone is going do something nefarious?" Besides, I say, Gold is clearly a friend of Callaway's. Callaway has been a straight shooter, and so far, I explain, Gold has been the same. And so far, I say, it's been a great experience. I look around the room. It's an overheated classroom with a half-dozen badly dressed graduate students, all in debt, and one adjunct professor. We're hardly in a position to dictate terms.

On Friday morning, I get a call from Gold's assistant while I'm writing again in the computer lab. "Ted would like to talk, Mr. Boman," she says. "Can you hold?" I scamper from the room into the hallway to get some privacy. I am standing right in front of the computer lab's bathrooms. I hope Gold can't hear the sound of flushing toilets. Gold comes on the phone. He sounds happy. He asks me what I'm doing. I tell him I'm writing more.

"I think you've proven there's a lot here," he says, with a chuckle. "I tell you what: I'd like to option this idea. I think it's really good, and I think you've done a great job with this."

Gold adds that he's working with Curtis Hanson, the movie director. Curtis Hanson? The director of L.A. CONFIDENTIAL? Yes, Gold says. "I hope you'll be able to meet him soon."

I stand frozen in the hallway. Ted Gold wants to option my idea. He's dropping the name of Curtis Hanson, one of the most admired writer/directors in Hollywood. The only thing I say is: "Okay. That sounds great."

Less than two months earlier, this idea didn't exist. Then I was being pushed into yet another CAT scan, a middle-aged man pursing the somewhat outlandish idea of going to graduate school in film production two thousand miles from his home.

Now a TV executive wants to option my idea. I lean against the hallway wall and close my eyes to let the moment sink in. Time slows down. I hear a toilet flush. It sounds a million miles away.

From far away, I hear Ted Gold's voice again. "But we have one issue to clear up. I've never dealt with anyone who's unrepped," he says, then sounding like he can sense a bit of ignorance on my end, he goes on. "By that I mean everyone I deal with has an agent. You'll need an agent, too, at this point for me to keep talking to you. I've got some names of good agents that you could talk to.

Or if you want to find your own, that's fine, too. The rules of this game, though, are such that I really can't do anything more with this project until you've got an agent."

I hadn't thought of this. Getting an agent at USC is considered the Holy Grail. Thompson in my screenwriting class is the only one on campus I know who has an agent, and he got it due to his success at Sundance. Now I've got Ted Gold explaining that he's got several names he could give me, and getting one sounds like it will be as easy as buying my cheap hair gel at Walgreens. He wants to meet me again when I have one.

I hang up the phone. What does one do with news like this? I jump around the hallway next to the bathroom, trying not to hyperventilate. I stop jumping whenever an engineering student walks by to use the bathroom. I'm so excited. I call Julie. She's at work. She's busy with patients. She asks, "What's an option?"

I go back in the computer room and email my good news to a few pals and my family. I shoot Gold an email, too, saying my wife is so far removed from Hollywood that she doesn't know what an option is. I neglect to write that I do know what it is. He writes back a long, generous email explaining what an option is (it's a contract that allows Gold's production company to have exclusive rights to develop my idea).

Julie also asks how much money it's worth. Ummm, good question. I don't know. I ask Gold. I'm expecting he'll say, "That's why you need an agent." But he's right up front: this is a zero-down option, he says. My heart sinks. I am already thinking of a big over-sized check I can tout to Julie. *Here, honey, go buy yourself a pretty dress. We're going dancing tonight.* The fact that it's a zero-down option tempers my enthusiasm but only a bit.

When my friends hear the news, they invariably ask the same question as Julie: *How much is it worth?* They're disappointed to learn the truth. But I explain to them: "That's just the option. If the project gets developed, then I see money." *How much?* "I don't know. I have to find an agent who will negotiate that."

It's nice to have Krause on my speed dial. I call him pronto. I get his answering machine. He's on set. "Say, Pete, it's Steve. Hey, I got a television executive named Ted Gold who wants to option a television series I pitched him. I need an agent now. Know anyone?"

He calls during a break. He's got a good match, he tells me. We agree to meet for dinner the next night.

A fter I give Pete the same pitch I gave Gold, he leans back in his chair at the Italian place where we're eating. "That's good," he says. "That's really good."

Pete puts me in touch with an agent who reps his friend. He's a partner at Endeavor, one of the blue-chip talent agencies in Hollywood. Sunday, The Agent calls. Sure, he'll do the deal, he says. Yes, The Agent says, he knows Ted very well. He calls him *Ted*. It feels like I've been admitted to a very exclusive high school.

Monday morning, I'm back at USC and the world has changed. I've got an agent repping my idea to Ted Gold, who once ran FOX's drama wing, and who now has a bungalow on a TV studio lot, and is in partnership with Curtis Hanson, the Academy Award–winning director. The semester is done. I've only told a handful of friends on campus the news, and almost everyone has left for the summer.

I stick around L.A. for a few days, delaying my trip home because I think The Agent will do my deal in the snap of a finger. How naïve I am! At the end of the week, I ask Ted (I'm calling him *Ted* now, too) how long it might take, and that I'm delaying my trip to Minneapolis so I can meet Hanson and his producing partner, Carol Fenelon. With what sounds like a touch of pity in his voice, Ted tells me not to wait. "These things can take time," he says.

So I load up my Suburban and point it east but not before strapping a twenty-foot-long sea kayak on my roof. The kayak belongs to my brother, and Mikey had used it, but now I'm bringing it back to Minnesota. Unfortunately, it's May. I hit freezing rain and a near-blizzard in New Mexico and wild side winds in the Great Plains. With the kayak on my roof, I'm pushed around the road like I've got a sail on the truck. I'm waiting for it to disappear into the wind like Dorothy's house in the Kansas tornado, but it doesn't. I arrive home on a sunny, intensely windy spring day. I get home in time to meet Maria and Sophia walking back from elementary school. It feels so great to feel their hugs.

The Agent does indeed take his time. Weeks go by. More weeks. He says he's pushing CBS for a deal. It goes on long enough that I start to fret. I worry he's gonna lose the deal. The Agent doesn't ask me what I think I should get, he just tells me that CBS' offer was way too low. "Whatever they offered, I doubled it," he says. "Don't worry, Steve; it will be a good deal for you."

Ted calls me one day and says, "Whatever [Your Agent] is doing, he's making some people at CBS a little mad."

I'm both heartened and nervous. Maybe he really is going to lose the deal. My Agent assures me that everything is going to be fine. He's treating this like a sport, it seems, and he's pushing the network just because he can.

Finally, at the end of June, there's an agreement. The money up front is indeed nonexistent. However, if CBS decides to extend the option—by just keeping it on the table—then they'll pay me $5,000. If they exercise the option, they owe me $15,000. If it goes to a pilot, they owe me another $20,000. And if it goes to series, I'll get about a quarter million. If it stays on all season, it's closer to $400,000. I also get additional pay for any writing I do for the show. And I own 3 percent of the show.

I fly back to Los Angeles. I'm meeting Ted, Curtis Hanson, and Carol Fenelon. I couldn't be more pleased. Ted is glad to see me, and we spend the morning talking over issues. We've spent a lot of time emailing and talking on the phone, and he's made one thing clear to me: I can demand to hold total power over this idea or I can share it. If I hold it to myself, there's little chance of it going forward, he says. "You can do whatever you want, but that's just how the world works. The chance of it going anywhere with only you and me pushing it is very slim," he says. I'd faced the same issue with *GeezerJock*. Investors wanted in, but my partner Callahan and I had to give up power to get the money. It's not ideal, but it got the magazine published. I tell Ted I'm happy to bring in the best people we can. They, of course, will get the lion's share of the wealth if it goes forward. I'm reminded of that old saw: *better to have a small piece of something than all of nothing.*

Ted and I walk to lunch by the studio and eat at a nice little white tablecloth restaurant. A hamburger is $24. When we sit down, a well-dressed guy comes over and shakes Ted's hand. It's all smiles and warmth. Everyone seems to know Ted. When the other guy leaves, Ted turns to me and says quietly he's an agent who's been a real jerk in the past.

As we walk back to the studio, Ted says he almost never works with anyone new to the industry. He explains the setup: CBS would like to get Curtis Hanson involved with television production, and Curtis Hanson would like the same. Ted is the matchmaker and the talent scout. If Curtis and Carol like my idea, the three of them will continue to push it forward. Today, I'm pitching my idea to Curtis and Carol.

We talk money. Ted knows my deal. For a first-timer, he says it's pretty impressive. He says my agent is a good one. He says the real money comes only after a few years of success, and it comes to those who own a percentage of the show. He cites a successful show, LOST, and estimates it is worth in the neighborhood of $400 million to $800 million to those who own the show. I do the math. If this class project blooms into a hit, my contract is potentially worth more than $25 million.

I roll the figure around in my head. *Twenty-five million dollars.* It beats working as a reporter in gritty urban areas for $35,000 a year. I try to appear cool and collected, like I'm used to contemplating multimillion-dollar payoffs. Ted, however, points out the extreme rarity of success. "Most shows fail. That's just the way it is, so get used to it," he says. Besides, he says, we're still many hurdles away from even getting my idea onto the air.

But Ted is clearly having fun. At FOX, he was the guy listening to pitches, green-lighting the good ones, killing the duds. Now he's on the other side of the fence. He's an owner of my idea now, too, and its chief cheerleader. We walk back from lunch, talking like old college friends.

We spend so much time talking in Ted's office, we lose track of time. Ted calls ahead and warns them we're going to be late, and he tells me to follow him. I'm driving a low-budget rental car, and we're driving from Studio City in the San Fernando Valley down to Curtis Hanson's office south of Hollywood. We face a ten-mile drive through heavy traffic on the expressway. Ted is in his black BMW, and he's driving fast. I'm thrashing my little Kia to stay on his bumper. When we hit Hollywood, there are black BMWs everywhere. I'm careful not to lose him. We're racing through traffic, running yellow lights, and I'm thankful I've driven for years in congested cities. When we arrive at our destination, Ted is smiling. "That wasn't a problem staying with me, was it?"

"Naw," I answer. "You didn't have to slow down just for me."

This is way too much fun for work.

This is the first time I've had to repitch my material formally. My first meeting is with Carol Fenelon. She's a tall, elegant woman. Today, however, her hand is painful. She's suffering from gout apparently, and she's waiting for a doctor to call her back.

Ted tells me the floor is mine. I start into my pitch. It's going well and I'm right at a climactic moment when I rise out of my seat to talk about *life or death events* and . . . Carol's assistant rings. The doctor is on the phone. Carol excuses herself.

I sit back down. Ted looks at me and smiles. "Sorry about this. But this is how the real world works," he says. Together, we make small talk for ten minutes, sitting alone in Carol's office.

Carol reenters. I spring back to my feet to restart my pitch at my high emotional moment . . . and she waves me off. She seems irritated. "I get it, just keep going," she says. I do.

When I'm done with my material, it's hard to know if she likes it or not. Then Curtis Hanson enters. He, too, wants to hear my series idea. He's a thin, surprisingly tall man. His hair is wild. He's wearing old jeans and an old shirt.

In Hollywood, everyone wears a uniform. Agents and studio executives wear suits. The creative side goes for bohemian. Hanson is very bohemian.

Hanson shakes my hand. Then I go into my pitch again. It's a shortened version, just the high points of the series, how I see it structured, obstacles, story ideas, the potential for a long life on the network.

It's surreal. The meeting is very serious. I've got one of the greatest American filmmakers and his producing partner gathered in a room listening to me with attentive expressions. Ted sits back and lets me talk. He keeps smiling though.

After an hour, the pitch meeting is done. We all stand up, shake hands, and I'm walked to the door by a young assistant, probably a recent film school graduate. The word must be out that I'm *That*

Lucky Bastard in Film School because the assistant shoots me a dirty look as I leave.

A few hours later, Ted calls me. "They both loved you. Really. They *love* the idea."

Really, I ask, even Carol? She didn't seem to like me at all. "Oh, Carol thought you were the greatest. They're both on board with this. Very excited."

The next step is to find a show-runner. That's the person who will, literally, run the show. In television, they're the big dog in charge of day-to-day production. They're almost always writers who oversee story development and shape the series.

And here's where the rubber meets the road about my decision to give up power for the potential of greater success. Ted has explained that if I write the pilot episode, or share in the writing of it, the top tier of show-runners will likely pass. This decision gives me great pause. It's very difficult. I know I can write one hell of a pilot—I've already got one sketched out, but it's the hard reality of television. There is no easy answer or right answer. I really want to push for writing the pilot. (And at the time I'm naïve about writing credits—the person who writes the pilot gets the *Created by* credit, with a corresponding financial windfall if the series becomes a success.) But I keep thinking of my family. What would be the best for them? Going to graduate school is an exceptionally high-risk financial decision already. Who am I to hold out for even higher risks?

I tell Ted I'm willing to pass on writing the pilot script. When Ted and Curtis and Carol go fishing for show-runners, they'll be able to dangle a great piece of bait: a developed show idea, with the pilot script a blank slate. The handoff makes me feel a bit queasy, but I think I understand the odds. And I'm still completely ignorant in the ways of television, for good and for bad. Only later do I realize the full value of writing the pilot script. It's huge. It means money and power and prestige and control. But at this point, I'm a newbie in TV land, and I don't realize the importance of my actions until I look back at them. The experience in the real world of Hollywood is like graduate school: the learning curve is steep, and I seem to discover important information only after the fact.

Back in Minnesota, it's life as usual. The kids are off from school, and there are a handful of house projects that have been deferred over the past year . . . and I'm officially a producer under contract to CBS/Paramount Network Television. I buy a DVR so I can record television shows and watch them. I watch as much network television as possible after the kids are in bed.

Not long after I'm back, I get a call from Ted. Great news, he says, there's a show-runner who wants in. "It all happened very quickly. She was our top pick. We heard she was interested and we had a meeting and she liked the idea a lot," he says. She's Carol Barbee, under contract with CBS and, until very recently, the show-runner for JERICHO. Ted says she's leaving almost immediately for a monthlong vacation and said *yes* almost instantly. He's thrilled. Barbee is extremely well regarded at the network, he says, and it gives our show a huge push forward.

From that moment onward, I swallow my pride about writing the pilot and move forward. The month of August I become a producer. I'm going to give Barbee the best possible introduction to the world that I pitched. I call dozens of people involved with transplantation. Within a few days, I have the top heart doctor at the famous Cleveland Clinic offering to open the doors to Barbee when she comes back from vacation. The surgeon, Dr. Gonzalez-Stawinski, aka "Dr. Gonzo," is surfing in Puerto Rico when I contact him. He's the perfect person to show Barbee the cowboy side of transplantation. He's one of the world's best transplant surgeons by night, a surfer by (vacation) day.

I line up tours for Barbee at the Southern California organ donor organization. I get a UCLA transplant surgeon on board. And I write a background briefing book about the real world of transplantation.

One day, Julie asks me if it's worth the time and energy I'm putting into this. I'm still not being paid a cent for all my efforts. I won't be paid anything until CBS orders a script, and it's a script that I won't be writing. She doesn't understand any of this Hollywood stuff—it's so foreign and mysterious compared to the very clear-eyed world of medicine. It appears to her as if I'm working on some secret brew. I'm on the phone constantly and typing up material. Is it worth it?

To keep my wife happy, I'm also landscaping the front yard between calls. One day I'm dirty from yard work, my shirt off, and I'm in the process of moving several tons of decorative stones with a shovel. During breaks, I'm tapping out emails on my BlackBerry, my first acquisition since I got back from California. A neighbor walks over, asks me how school is going. I say, "Great." He asks me what kind of school projects I'm working on. I lean on my shovel. "Well, I'm producing a show for CBS. We hope to get it on the air next year," I say. I know I sound like a crazy man. It's all rather fun.

With all the excitement and demands of the television show and my usual summertime duties at home, I'm giving short shrift to my duties as a codirector of a documentary. We're supposed to start shooting as soon as fall semester starts. I'm hoping Brent can jump-start us, but he's got other work going on the side.

I know this: I'm planning on continuing in film school. I intend to get my MFA, no matter what. If distance and having kids and a stroke and pancreatitis didn't stop me, neither will a television show.

When Barbee returns from vacation, she goes right into meetings with the people I've set her up with. I'm due back in L.A. about the same time. This time Julie's using the Suburban, and I've got her Pontiac—a teal-blue V8-powered rocket with leather seats, XM radio, and big, fat tires.

Another drive out to Los Angeles and thanks to my touchy pancreas I've sworn off caffeine, chocolate, and all liquor, beer, and wine, which makes me a dull boy. I drive through Wyoming, and it's gorgeous as I fly down the empty roads. The car is fast, and because I stop every hour or so to get the blood pumping in my legs (no more strokes on this drive), I'm constantly repassing a small handful of cars for much of the trip.

When I'm finally back in L.A., I get together with Carol Barbee. We meet at her office. She's very polite, very interested in the series, very smart. It's a little awkward for me—Barbee is doing the job I'd like to have. But her résumé is a bit longer than mine: in addition to JERICHO, she's been an executive producer on JUDGING AMY and SWING-TOWN, and she wrote for PROVIDENCE. I'm in graduate school.

She's very interested in my experiences inside the world of transplantation. I tell her a few stories. She is intrigued at the very fact I was hired as a coordinator. I tell her about my first night on the job, when a disgruntled surgeon from another transplant center called me a "radio disc jockey" in the OR. I also tell her how less than a year later, I saved the bacon of another large transplant center when I carried a heart back to Chicago when their surgical team was too timid to fly through severe weather.

We have a good meeting, and I cross my fingers. Carol is going to be the one writing the pilot. As I drive away, I realize my baby is now in her hands.

Luckily, we seem to be blessed. CBS does indeed like Carol Barbee, and our whole team. The network orders the pilot script in what Ted says is record time. First network hurdle crossed.

During the next four months, I'm working constantly. The documentary shoots every weekend. We struggle. Being a two-headed director means we move slowly because so many decisions have to be discussed beforehand, and every mutual decision takes time. And our timing is terrible. The same month we start filming, the California Highway Patrol decides to clamp down on speeding on the road. The word spreads quickly. Bikers avoid the Angeles Crest, but the additional police presence means we're watched constantly by the authorities. The police keep tabs on us and stop us repeatedly, asking for our permits, checking our driver's licenses, inquiring about my Minnesota license plates. To add to our woes, the Angeles Crest Highway travels across land overseen by the National Forest Service, and the local ranger station apparently decides it doesn't want us filming the dirty little secret of racing motorcyclists on the Crest. The station does everything it can to shut us down, to the point of asking the Highway Patrol to arrest us on sight, which they don't do, because we're not breaking any laws.

With all the attention focused on us, the size of our crew is a serious hindrance. We have Scott the cameraman and two producers and Brent and me and someone with the sound-boom. Instead of a stealth project, we clank into battle like Redcoats. And our footage suffers. We can't shoot from the side of the road for fear of getting arrested. We fail to get decent footage from riders' helmet cams. All we have is talking heads and some nice footage of the majestic mountains. Our street bike documentary footage has all the visual drama of MY DINNER WITH ANDRE. We keep hearing from instructors and classmates that they're not getting a sense of the excitement and danger the bikers keep talking about.

Many weeks into filming, and exasperated by our failures, I ask Scott the cameraman to ride on the back of one of the bikes to get a point-of-view shot during a group ride by some hard-core bikers. Scott is game. He likes shooting high-octane sports footage of skiers and boarders. I gear him up with a full-face helmet and my Red Wing boots and heavy jacket. I attach a short rope to the camera and secure it to Scott's waist so he can't drop the USC-owned equipment. I explain to the crew of bikers that I don't want any shenanigans, just mellow riding. As the bikers rev their engines and prepare to give Scott a taste of the Crest, Scott gives me the thumbs-up. I'm not overly worried. I spent my teen years riding passenger on my brother's motorcycles.

The police see us, as usual, and ignore the cameraman riding on a passenger seat. The biker he's with is excellent, and a commercial truck driver as well.

Later that morning, Scott returns. He didn't fall off or drop the camera, and no one crashed. We watch the footage. It's fantastic. We see bikes in formation, riders flitting between shadows, through the canyons, past blurry trees. We show it in class, and our instructors love it. *That's what we're talking about!* they say. Everyone in class is excited. But a few days later, the head of the USC cinematography department picks up gossip of the shoot and she blows a gasket. She says we broke school rules about camera operator safety. She wants my head on a platter. Then she ups the ante. She wants to kick me out of school. She wants to kick Brent out of school. She wants to kick Scott out of school. For long weeks, I spend time in discussions with Brent and Scott, both of whom are also caught in the web. The head of the cinematography department never meets with us, never finds out the details; she just hands down her edict. It's a big pile of academic manure. I plead guilty and apologize and explain exactly what we did but to no avail.

My antagonist has a reputation on campus as a bitter tyrant, as a man hater. She spent several years on a Marxist collaborative in her younger days, something she's proud of, and she apparently has a temperament well suited to be a commissar of . . . *something*.

Luckily, the drama ends when my documentary instructors, loyal to a one, wait her out. When she leaves for a trip to Africa, they vote to end the matter. The three of us will receive a lower grade, and we'll lecture incoming students about the importance of following the USC safety guidelines. And for the record, I will state clearly here: *Follow the USC Safety Guidelines! Do Not Do Stupid Things Like Asking a Cameraman to Shoot as a Passenger on a Motorcycle!* (I later had the honor of speaking to all new USC film students and explaining how I got into hot water and warned them to, yes, *Follow the USC Safety Guidelines!*)

In the midst of this little drama, I ask an old salt at USC who had worked in the industry for years (and who shall go nameless) if I would be facing the same results if I'd been a student twenty or thirty years earlier. "Probably not," he says, shrugging. "A few decades ago, there were some students who took a vial of nitroglycerine out to the desert and blew up a car for a film. Really spectacular results! But so stupid. They coulda blown themselves up! Then there was the case of some guys who trucked in the remains of a small plane in the middle of the night and put the fuselage right in the middle of campus. They planned to film it in the morning, with smoke coming from it, but the TV news found out about it and reported that a plane had crashed into USC."

I hear stories like this repeatedly from some of the other long-term faculty. My case brings out a lot of official headshaking and tut-tutting from the department, but several of the older faculty members privately pull me aside and tell me about *their* stupid exploits. In the end, I understand. USC has no interest in becoming party to a lawsuit or finding its name in the media. And the school has a very low tolerance for risk. When I worked as journalist, there was an understanding there'd sometimes be risks. I got sent to cover a refinery explosion that was still sickening dozens even as I drove onto the site; I climbed the exterior ladder of a construction crane 175 feet in the dead of winter without safety gear; I covered stories in high-crime areas. As a transplant coordinator, I flew in planes in awful wind-storms and rainstorms. It was just what was expected. *Git 'er done* was the watchword. At USC, git 'er done got me in deep doo-doo.

Meanwhile, my new dual life emerges. Gold and Barbee and others involved with the transplant series are happy as clams with me. Throughout the semester, I feed information to them. Barbee visits Cleveland and spends several days under the leadership of Dr. Gonzo. They each call me afterward and they're effusive in their praise. Dr. Gonzo says he worried a Hollywood type would be an arrogant jerk, but he says Barbee was a joy to work with. Barbee, for her part, says the trip was amazing. She watched an open heart surgery in the OR, and she says Dr. Gonzo will help her shape the characters in the script. She also went to Pittsburgh, where Dr. Thomas Starzl is a transplanting legend.

Meanwhile, the word is spreading around USC that I'm working on a television show for CBS. It makes life very interesting. Suddenly, fellow students I hardly know meet me on the sidewalks and want to talk. The gym, once a place where I rarely saw a film student, becomes a veritable film school hot spot. I could complain and say my privacy was intruded upon, but in reality, it's a great deal of fun. Like money, popularity is more fun to have than not have.

Like every other semester, I'm swamped with work. I'm planning to graduate after five semesters, so I'm overloading, again. I'm codirecting the doc, and I'm enrolled in a television production class in which we write and shoot a pilot episode (double-rich irony) and a film analysis class, and I'm sitting in on Casper's Hitchcock class. Because Brent and I never could find anyone to do sound for our doc, we're doing it, which means we go to sound classes, too. Our saving grace is that Brent and I had spent our 508 learning sound under Frank the drill sergeant, and we're both leaps ahead of the other sound students.

Busy or not, the time seems to fly by. CBS extends the length of the option, which gives me my first dab of money. I take the call while I'm in my television class. At the time, I'm wearing gloves and moving lights when The Agent calls. I duck out of class early, telling my instructor I've got to take a call from My Agent. It sounds so smarmy, so sweet, and so damn exciting. It's as if I'm a walking parody of the Hollywood name-dropper now. There's been a regular group of us lunching at the Jocketeria—it's Manny and Rene and an ebb and flow of others. When I join them late after taking the call, I tell them, "Sorry, boys, I was talking to *My Agent!*"

The semester flies by. Barbee is working on the script, and buried in it. She's got less than four months to get up to speed on the topic and write an hour-long pilot and develop characters and a plausible season arc. It's a lot to do. I feel her pain as I race to finish class work. Film school is like Hollywood, or so it appears to me, in that there are periods of nothingness and then long stretches where you work your tail off. I'm so busy I don't have time to fly back to Minnesota for Thanksgiving, so Krause invites me to his house. I eat, I drink, I sleep, I play Monopoly with his son. Then I go back to USC and start working again the Sunday after Thanksgiving.

After a marathon of long nights tweaking the soundtrack, Brent and I finish the doc and we screen it on a bitingly cold and rainy night to a crowd in Norris that is smaller than expected. I'm so tired I want to sleep during the performance. The turmoil and politicking over our shooting from the motorcycle has taken its toll. The doc is good—dark and unexpectedly moody—and some bikers love it, and some hate it. I'm told that night my grade has been lowered from an A to a C+ to appease the safety gods. It's my worst grade by far in grad school. When it's done, I hardly want to celebrate, I just want to go to bed. Julie has flown out again, and the fatigue of the semester catches both of us by surprise. She's been a single mom in Minnesota for three full semesters now, and it's getting old. I'm working hard, and the fate of the transplant show is now in the hands of a woman I don't know well, and she's doing final rewrites on the script. In early December, there's a period of radio silence from CBS. I don't know how to interpret the quiet. Is it good news? Or bad news? There's a lot on the table.

I'm supposed to fly back to Minnesota the day after Julie flies back. As I drive her to LAX, we simultaneously bring up the notion of me driving back instead of flying. We have only one car back home, and the break is a month. Plus, I'm absolutely exhausted. I've been directing a documentary crew, shooting a television show for USC, feeding information to Barbee and Gold. I've been constantly surrounded by people for four straight months. Every single day I'm surrounded. I need a break.

I cancel my air ticket and load a suitcase of dirty clothes into the Pontiac. There's a major winter storm bearing down from the Pacific Northwest when I leave Carl and Irene's house. It's supposed to rain that night, and snow in the mountains. Carl and Irene don't like me driving; they cluck like parents, but I need some space.

The drive is wonderful. The roads are empty. It's mid-December, and no one is out. I haul ass, knowing the storm is coming in fast behind me. The sun sets and I'm just hitting Arizona. I drive through the night on roads lined with snow banks with light flurries falling. Every hour I stop and do jumping jacks, then get back in the Pontiac and let it rip. I make it nearly to Texas before I pull over to rest at a cheap motel. The next day I do it again. The silence, the empty highways, the feeling of being away from Los Angeles all recharge me. I'm staying just a few hundred miles ahead of a snowstorm that seems to be chasing me across the country. At one point in West Texas, flurries fall again. I push the gas pedal down to stay ahead of the storm. I'm cruising at 100 miles per hour, then 110. I get ahead of the flurries. On empty stretches, I push it to 120 and faster. The Pontiac rumbles along the highway with plenty in reserve. The road is flat and straight and empty. All the while, I'm just listening to music, relaxing, watching for police and mule deer, and monitoring the oil pressure gauge on my dashboard. I've survived another semester.

The last four hundred miles is through a hard snow. The roads are covered with ice. I can hardly see a thing. I arrive at our home forty-seven hours after leaving Los Angeles. The Pontiac is covered with so much ice and road salt it's hard to know what color it is.

On the kitchen table, there's a check waiting from CBS. It's for the option extension. I deposit half and take half out in cash. I carry a thick wad of fifties in my pocket, and every cent we spend over Christmas comes from CBS.

12

It Keeps Getting Better

When I drive back to Los Angeles in early January, I'm feeling absolutely recharged. Film school is intense, not because you learn a lot (you do), but in part because it's such a social environment. Filming is always a group activity. I'm an extrovert, and it says a lot that I got tired of the constant contact with other people. After spending nearly a month with just my kids and Julie, I'm ready for one more round.

And this time, the weather driving to Los Angeles is simply spectacular. It's unseasonably warm, and I drive in bright sunshine the entire way. Not a cloud in the sky from Minneapolis to Los Angeles via Oklahoma City.

As I'm driving through Arizona, Ted calls. Good news: CBS is talking about casting some roles for our television show. Nothing is set yet, but it's a good sign, he says.

Over the break, I've read Carol Barbee's script and it's fantastic. It's tight and emotional. I understand why Gold and Hanson and Fenelon wanted Barbee aboard. I'm humbled, too. The script is so darn true to the vision I pitched it gives me goose bumps. Julie reads it and she's also excited.

Barbee has added a character not in my pitch: he's a radio reporter turned transplant coordinator. He's a young, geeky, Midwestern hayseed who, it turns out, is smarter than he seems. During the call, Ted tells me they're looking at an actor to play the role. "How cool is that? They're looking at a guy to play *you!*" When he says that, I almost veer into a ditch.

Barbee has changed the name to THREE RIVERS. It's set in Pittsburgh, not Chicago as I had pitched it. I like the name—it's meaningful, in that every transplant is an interweaving of three different stories: the donor, the recipient, and the doctors. But . . . I do like more on-the-nose titles. I named this book *Film School*. As a pup, I loved Bruce Springsteen and the E Street Band. I am named Steve. I like simple names and simple titles. ER. GILLIGAN'S ISLAND. SEINFELD.

Leave it to the French to name their films LE CHARME DIS-CRET DE LA BOURGEOISIE. Americans like GUNSMOKE. But the title THREE RIVERS? It's less direct than I'd like. It's not my first choice . . . but I can live with it.

Yet the one thing I simply don't like is the location. I love Chicago as a character, and it's a big, dynamic, massively corrupt city that people recognize. I've never spent any time in Pittsburgh and, Steelers aside, I don't know much about it.

This is a minor quibble, though. In real life, Pittsburgh is home to the largest transplant center in the United States, and Ted tells me Curtis loves the city. Besides, he says diplomatically, Chicago has been home to enough big medical dramas already with ER and CHICAGO HOPE. I see his point, and I cross my fingers.

This semester is simple. Just three classes. A scene-writing class. A really outstanding class on understanding visual relations in film. A film history class. Only six credits. When I finish, I'm done. I'll get my degree.

The word around campus has accelerated about my role with CBS. Classmates start asking me if I can get them a job on the show if it becomes a reality.

I gently explain that that's a long way from happening. Our next hurdle is to be approved for a pilot. Ted, my personal tour guide to all things in network television, explains it's a matter of constant winnowing down by the network. The network will hear thousands of pitches every year. The network might then order a hundred or so scripts. Of those scripts, they'll approve maybe ten pilots in a good year. And of those pilots, all shot for millions of dollars each, they'll maybe order three or four or five series. Of those series, maybe one or two will last several years. Of those, a very rare one will be a hit, making the owners of the show rich and famous. We have a lot of hurdles left.

We're at the level where a script has been written. We're one of a hundred.

But we know we're in the top tier. We have a sought-after show-runner in Barbee. Executive producers Hanson and Fenelon and Gold are all top players. Krause calls to tell me he hears lots of good gossip about the show. I'm hoping we'll be in the running to get a pilot shot. If CBS orders it, I'll have achieved something remarkable. I'll have taken a grad school class project all the way to the pilot level. It's unheard of at USC.

As the semester moves forward, I'm locked into the gossip on Nikki Finke's Deadline Hollywood website. She's the ultimate insider in TV land, and I constantly log onto her site, looking for news about the upcoming pilot orders.

Then I hear bad news: Jerry Bruckheimer also has a medical show in development at CBS. Jerry Bruckheimer is to television what Arnold Schwarzenegger is to bodybuilding. He's a legend.

330 ■ FILM SCHOOL

He's already got megahits like the CSI franchises at CBS and WITHOUT A TRACE and COLD CASE, and he's a producer of a bazillion big-budget movies. He's arguably the most powerful producer in television. CBS doesn't need two medical shows, just one. The gossip seems to be it's a horse race between THREE RIVERS and Bruckheimer's show, an action-filled drama about trauma surgeons based in Miami called MIAMI MEDICAL (speaking of naming it on the nose!).

When I hear this, my heart sinks. Suddenly, our crew seems like a little engine compared to the massive freight train that is Bruckheimer. I tell Gold we'll just have to be the Little Engine that Could. Suddenly, the platinum-plated names on our team don't look so luminous.

The pilot season comes closer. The week when we're supposed to hear is a cold and rainy one. It's midwinter in L.A., and I never cease to be amazed how much it actually rains in Los Angeles. It rains every single day. I can't focus on my class work at all. I can tell Ted and Carol Barbee are also on pins and needles. It's agonizing to wait. The decision is made by the networks, and it seems like we're waiting for white smoke to rise from a Vatican chimney.

On Monday, Tuesday, Wednesday, and Thursday, the other networks announce their pilot orders. I watch the announcements via my BlackBerry. CBS is going to be the last. On Friday of Hollywood's informal "let's announce the pilots" week, I can't stand it. I've hardly slept.

I go to USC and find myself unable to do anything but pace. Today, we'll find out if we make it to the next step. If my idea becomes a reality on film, I'll get enough to pay a semester of tuition. This entire semester I'm working as an assistant for a professor for ten measly bucks an hour, plus a thousand bucks off my tuition bill. Now I'm waiting to hear if I'll get a nice fat check that will make that assistantship seem like chump change. To relieve my nervousness, I finally take shelter in the film school library. It's Friday afternoon, and no word yet. I check out THE WAGES OF FEAR, the classic 1953 French film about a group of men on a suicide mission who drive trucks filled with nitroglycerine up a treacherous mountain road. The tension and bleakness of the film help calm my nerves.

At 5 P.M., the library closes. I walk through the rain, not wanting to check my BlackBerry. Finally, at 6 P.M., I can't help myself. I have to know. I look up Nikki Finke online and . . . there it is: Bruckheimer's MIAMI MEDICAL, our competition, has been picked to shoot a pilot. We've lost.

I feel so bummed out I can't describe it. I just feel the energy drain from my body. For an hour I sit on a couch, not moving. I call Julie and tell her the bad news. She only says, "Oh, I'm sorry." I know she's bummed, too. She's cut back on her hours this semester to be home more with the kids, and money is tight. We could use the cash.

Finally, I walk toward my car. It's pouring outside. I get in and start the slow slog toward Carl and Irene's house. The seventeen miles will take more than an hour in the rain. Traffic is a mess.

My parents call, and I hardly have the energy to tell them the transplant show is dead. I hang up and drive, watching my windshield wipers go back and forth.

Now what will I do? I'm just a regular old grad student again. The ride is over all too quickly.

I'm working my way up Highway 2 in stop-and-go traffic when I notice the message light blinking on my BlackBerry. I pick it up and look at the text message. It's from Ted.

IT'S A GO!!!

I call Ted. He's freaked. CBS announced very late in the day they're ordering a pilot of THREE RIVERS. I start screaming in the car. Truly screaming. I call Julie. I'm screaming. She can't hear me.

She finally understands. I start to cry. I call my parents. I scream to them. It's been a complete and total reversal in two short hours. I've never experienced such a swing of emotions.

When I get to La Cañada, it's still pouring. I park in a lot by my favorite bar and leave messages for my brothers and some close friends. I'm still screaming. I walk into the bar—it's a classy steak joint, less than a mile from Carl and Irene's—and climb onto a stool. I tell the bartender to give me a drink of single malt scotch. I order the biggest steak they have. I order drinks for the guy on my right and the couple on my left. When they ask me what the reason is, I tell them: "I just sold a television show to CBS."

In March, I'm checking into a room at the grandest hotel in Pittsburgh. THREE RIVERS is starting its pilot shoot. We're the biggest story in town. It's late—my plane through Philadelphia was delayed by bad weather—so everyone else is already asleep. Shooting begins in the morning. I try to sleep, but it doesn't come.

In the morning, I meet with Carol Barbee and Curtis Hanson and Carol Fenelon and Ted Gold. More than 120 cast and crew members are on the set. The excitement in the air is tremendous. I spend the day sitting in those nice director's chairs reserved for big shots. I'm an executive here, and I'm a little weirded out by how deferential some of the crew are. They treat me like royalty. I can't get over the contrast. At USC, I'm still coiling my own cables, doing dirty work, and here I'm being asked if I would like another cup of coffee while I sit and watch the monitors in the director's video village.

Sometimes I feel the same lightheadedness I felt after I was released from the UCLA hospital. I know I'm fine this time. I can't believe my luck. I'm sitting shoulder to shoulder with Curtis Hanson. I tell him I very much appreciate the scene in L.A.

CONFIDENTIAL where a stunned Det. Jack Vincennes is shot in the chest by his boss, Capt. Dudley Smith.

Carol Fenelon is warm and gracious to me. She explains the good luck Curtis Hanson (her ex-husband) has had with USC. "His first big film was THE HAND THAT ROCKS THE CRADLE, and that was written by a USC grad student! Isn't it fitting that his first foray into television is also from USC?" I nod my head like an idiot. "Yes," I blather, "it's a very good thing."

The money being spent is incredible. We have a forty-eight-foot semitruck holding electric gear. Another semi holding grip equipment. A five-ton prop truck. A semi carrying cameras and sound equipment. A sound effects truck. A set decorating truck. A twenty-two-foot construction truck. A twenty-four-foot construction truck. A fuel truck. A generator truck. A forty-eight-foot wardrobe truck. Five trailers for talent. A freight truck. Four shuttle buses. And one *honey wagon*—Hollywood talk for a rolling toilet.

A comparatively small amount of money is going to me, but I'll be making more than I made in my entire first year working for Minnesota Public Radio. I'm beginning to like television very much.

Visiting the pilot shoot is a gas, pure and simple. I meet our lead, Alex O'Loughlin, and another lead, Kate Moennig. I tell both of them my kids' college funds are depending upon their acting. O'Loughlin is a teaser, always quick with a joke. Both of them came from previous shows that had zealous fans (O'Loughlin from MOONLIGHT, Moennig from THE L WORD). They're simultaneously intense and fun.

I go out for drinks with Ted, eat with the director and Carol Barbee, and talk with CBS and Paramount executives who are being sent by headquarters to see how the shoot is progressing.

Parts of the pilot shoot go well, but others do not. The problem is not cast or crew, but locations. The sites we're shooting at are simply not very high tech. The hospital is a small, now closed community hospital a short drive from Pittsburgh. The interior scenes simply don't look very cutting edge. It's clear that the local crew, however eager to help, sometimes slows things down.

One scene involves an exterior shot at an airport at night. We have a rainmaker—a fire truck with two big wind machines. We're going to duplicate a hurricane. The problem is, it's already raining hard. It's March in Pittsburgh, and it's cold. One of the local wind machines, which we need for the shot, won't start. No wind, no hurricane. Time after time, the crew tries to start the thing. It nearly catches, and then dies. It's a giant fan the size of a truck, and everyone on set is paying attention to its troubles. I can smell the starter fluid they're spraying into the carburetor of the machine's old engine. Finally, after dozens of tries, the old engine kicks into life. The whole set erupts in a cheer. It's nice, but we're two hours behind schedule. I calculate the cost in my head, just like an accountant is doing back in Hollywood. More than a hundred crew, paid overtime, for a couple of extra hours. It's a $10,000 delay, and it's because some old engine wouldn't start.

I fly back to USC, tired and thrilled. In a mere six weeks, I'll be graduating. My goal is simply to get a passing grade in each class. I've missed some school, but I've got a heck of an excuse. David Howard, my writing instructor in the scene-crafting class and the author of several bestselling books on screenwriting, chides me for missing class: "Are you saying a pilot shoot is more important than here?" He's kidding, of course. Howard tells me the scribe of THE HAND THAT ROCKS THE CRADLE, Amanda Silver, was one of his first writing students. I tell him a few tales about the pilot. Jack Epps, the guy who first heard my pitch, is also interested in finding out more about my adventures. When the pilot was announced, Jack was one of the first to write me a very nice email congratulating me on the good news. I'm now part of the inner circle on campus. I sit in Epps' office, and he gives me advice on navigating

Hollywood. Callaway, who is thrilled with the status of THREE RIVERS, is just a phone call away. Howard, the screenwriting guru, is happy to spend time talking scriptwriting.

It's a happy time and a relaxed time. It's the first time in film school that I have time to shoot the breeze for an hour and not worry about it.

Meanwhile, Barbee is editing THREE RIVERS. We'll find out in May if we get chosen to be developed into a series. For whatever reason, and I can't explain it, I'm less nervous and worried about going to series than I was about getting a pilot made. My hope originally was just to get a pilot. Once that happened, I'm in uncharted water. A series? With my name in the credits? It's just too difficult to comprehend.

Graduation is approaching, and the networks are announcing the new fall schedules at the same time. Like having a stroke and have plumbing pipes burst on the same day, the timing is too clever by half. I'll get my MFA and find out whether my television show goes on the air all within the same week.

The events become a bit overwhelming. As a result, I relax. My mom and dad and Julie and Lara and Maria and Sophia all fly out for graduation. Carl and Irene host us all. I rent a big SUV that can carry nine passengers. We drive to USC for the graduation ceremony at the Shrine. It's hot and crowded and my kids are bored. They listen to speeches by screenwriter and GREY'S ANATOMY creator Shonda Rhimes (the very woman I dissed in my first TV pitch when Jack Epps was filling in for Callaway, a fact I feel bad about as I listen to her very compelling speech) and Laura Ziskin, the big-shot film producer. My kids have no idea who these people are. Then the students get to march across the stage. The announcer is an administrator at the film school with whom I've become friends. He's an opera singer by night, a college administrator by day, and he's got a deep, resonant voice. As I walk onstage, I tell him to say my name really slowly. He does it. "Steve Boooooooooooooooman!" He sounds like a professional wrestling announcer. The crowd laughs. My kids think it's very funny. I get a big hug from several faculty, and afterward we take pictures in a sweaty mass and hug classmates and mill in the hot sunlight until my kids can't take another minute of it. So we go.

That night, Carl and Irene, even after putting me up in their house for two-and-a-half years, take us all out to dinner. We go to Cal Tech, where Carl has faculty privileges. The campus has a gorgeous private dining room, exceptionally formal. We have a huge dinner, course after course. It's very expensive. When we finish, I slip out and talk to the manager. I want to pick up the tab, but the manager says, "That's not possible. Only members of the club can sign for meals." When I come back to the table, Carl is smiling triumphantly. He's paid the bill already. He knows what I was trying to do. I tried to outsmart the rocket scientist and failed.

During this time, I'm waiting for a call from Ted. We could get early word any minute about the fate of THREE RIVERS. It's Friday. Network announcements are in New York during the coming week, but early word leaks out before that. Shows that are picked get the green light to hire staff, setting off a mad dash of musical chairs among writers looking for a gig.

Saturday morning, I'm up at six to shuttle my family back to LAX. I need to clean my belongings out from Carl and Irene's house. Whatever happens in the future, it won't be the same arrangement I've been enjoying. At midafternoon, my old pal Tom is flying in. I need to move my stuff back to Minnesota and wait for word on the future of THREE RIVERS. I figure being on the road will be helpful. Anything is better than just sitting around in L.A. being nervous. Tom has agreed to join me for a road trip, just like old times. Movement is good. I won't be in New York; that's for the network brass.

Tom entertains Carl and Irene while I pack. Carl and Irene look sad. They've enjoyed my constant stories, my late-night comings, and my early-morning goings. Since I arrived on their doorstep, they've clucked over me and fed me. Now I'm packing up the Pontiac. Film school is done.

At 6 P.M., I'm ready. Tom and I are heading to Vegas for the night. After that, we're planning to travel through the high country of Colorado on our way home. I give Carl and Irene a big hug, and tell them I'll see them again soon. Tom takes some pictures of us to record the moment. Then Tom and I get in my car and drive away.

We don't talk much on the drive to Vegas, just listen to some tunes from his iPod. The sun is setting behind us as we cruise down the highway. The future will be very different for me, whatever happens. That's the only thing I know.

We drive into Vegas in the dark. It's always beautiful at night. It's a cliché, I know, but coming across the desert in the dark and seeing the brightness of Las Vegas is simply beautiful.

The recession of 2009 is in full bloom, so the hotels are pretty quiet. Tom and I pull onto the strip. We're going to stay at the Monte Carlo. It's a discount hotel on the strip, big and cheap, and I have a hunch no real high-rollers stay there. Years earlier on a cross-country road trip, Tom and I had stayed there and checked in behind a huge woman with a cigarette burning in her mouth who demanded to stay on the thirty-first floor. It became one of our inside jokes. After that, we'd adopt a low smoker's growl and say, "When you want to stay in a real classy place, make sure it's the thirty-first floor of the Monte Carlo."

Now we're going to get a room. It's going to have to be an upper floor, of course. I pull into the parking lot. It's hot in the dark night. Tom and I get out and stretch. My phone rings. It's Ted. He's short and sweet: CBS is going to order thirteen episodes of THREE RIVERS.

I don't know what to do, in all honesty. Tom and I get our bags and walk toward the entrance of the Monte Carlo. It's about 11 P.M. I'd graduated from USC the day before. Tonight I've learned news that will put a lot of money into my bank account, more than enough to cover the costs of going to film school. I've just done what no other student at USC has ever done while in film school.

When we stand at the check-in counter, Tom tells the woman that we'd like to stay on the thirty-first floor or higher. She nods blankly. "I should tell you, my friend here just sold a TV show," he says. "To CBS. It's going to be on your television. You can watch it." She nods again. Her blank expression doesn't change. She gives us a room on the fourteenth floor.

Afterword

Film is a funny thing. It's all based on tricking the mind to think that a series of static images, if they are shown at twenty-four frames per second, are actually moving. They are not. They are just still pictures, frozen in time. Only when they are put in motion do the pictures come to life.

A few days after the network's pickup of THREE RIVERS was announced at a big splashy event for the media in New York and lots of stories were being written about it, I took Lara out of school for a day and we drove to a nice dog breeder far outside Minneapolis. I had promised the kids we'd get a dog when I finished film school. Lara picked a cuddly and oh-so-cute brown puppy that slept in her arms like a baby. We bought the pup, and it slept in her arms for the entire two-hour drive back home.

THREE RIVERS premiered in October 2009. It was scheduled on Sunday nights, 9 P.M. Eastern, 8 P.M. Central, following 60 MINUTES and THE AMAZING RACE. It was a hugely high-profile spot. Before THREE RIVERS hit the air, the critics' reviews were mixed. Some liked the show a lot; some were dismissive. The good news is that more than nine million people tuned in for the premiere. The bad news is that CBS expects its shows to have more than nine million viewers. On another network, those numbers might mean success. But CBS is the No. 1 network and, like playing for the Yankees, it's put up or shut up.

Those of us with our names on the show endured a roller-coaster ride. The slim ratings dropped more in the second week but then held steady and even crept up a bit. There was the hope, however little, that the ratings would climb more. They didn't. To be fair, our competition was brutal. We were against DESPERATE HOUSE-WIVES on ABC and NFL SUNDAY NIGHT FOOTBALL on NBC, two highly rated shows. Overruns from Sunday-afternoon CBS football games meant we were often airing late in major markets. In addition, the network wanted the lead surgeons all to be heroic. I had originally pitched the show to be darker. I felt it would have been stronger with more conflict between the transplant surgeons, but that's Monday-morning quarterbacking. Whatever the reason, we were consistently at the bottom of the rankings.

The week after Thanksgiving, CBS announced it was pulling THREE RIVERS off the air. For two sweet months, I'd had my name on the front of a show on television. Then it was over, mostly. The news sucked, but because the entire journey up to that point had been such an unexpected gift, I didn't cry any tears. And with our ratings it wasn't a shock. Thankfully, CBS kept shooting the entire slate of episodes, which they then ran in the summer of 2010, when fewer people watch TV. The good news is I got paid very well, and I got to put on my résumé the fact I had a show on the air from 2009 to 2010. It's right there on IMDb.com. Looking back, the amount of toil and effort that went into creating this show was astounding. Many very talented people worked extremely hard on THREE RIVERS. The set itself was huge. Paramount knocked out the walls of two adjoining soundstages and built a connecting hallway between them to give us extra space. The whole enterprise was breathtaking in its scale. It was like building a warship, which then sails out of the harbor all proud and sparkling clean . . . and is promptly sunk in battle, to the dismay of everyone onshore.

The transplant community loved the show, and the money was very nice indeed. Julie and I paid professionals to landscape our backyard that summer and I didn't have to lift a shovel. Julie bought some furniture. We paid off debts. I acted like a Hollywood knucklehead and bought a shiny new sedan with a 415 hp V8 and a stick shift that was, fittingly, one of the last Pontiacs ever made before GM killed it off, too.

The experience was worth more than the money, by far. I met and worked with some exceptionally talented people. I learned a whole lot about how television networks really work. I have great contacts and good friends. The entire experience was also remarkable for what it did to my time in graduate school. For a year, I was the belle of the ball at USC, and it opened doors and helped me meet people I never would have met had I not gotten so lucky.

THREE RIVERS is now history, forgotten by most people like yesterday's newspaper. But I'm occasionally reminded of the reach of one short-lived television show. I've heard many secondhand stories of people being receptive to organ donation because of THREE RIVERS. After the series aired, the organization Donate Life America and pharmaceutical maker Astellas conducted a nationwide survey and found a 6 percent jump in adults' willingness to register as organ donors, something they attributed to THREE RIVERS.

And I just got an email from a friend in Japan who is watching rebroadcasts of the show there, a year after it went off the air in the United States. Meanwhile, the star of our show, Alex O'Loughlin, became the leading man in CBS' very popular remake of HAWAII FIVE-O.

For me, life has only gotten better. I'm developing a new television show, and writing more stories, and I'm doing them with people I once only dreamed of working with, so keep your eyes peeled for more details. My family is doing terrifically, and my health is good, as is Julie's, thank you very much. My brain functions fine. I've had zero stroke-related issues, knock on wood. I take my blood thinners every day and I'm on a first-name basis with the nurses in the blood-draw lab. But I haven't slowed down. I still shave with a razor blade, I still use a firm toothbrush, I haven't given away my sharp tools, and I still water-ski often and hard; when I recently crashed and cartwheeled across the water going in the neighborhood of fifty miles per hour, I surfaced, made certain my limbs were still attached and my ribs weren't broken, and I took another run. Other than a nice big black-and-blue bruise on my rump, it was all good. So not much has changed in my life.

Only the dog has changed. The cute little puppy I bought the girls is now a ninety-pound Labrador with long legs and a barrel chest, and he's sleeping on my feet as I write this. Jett is a beautiful hound, with a breathtakingly lustrous coat and soft brown eyes. Our big Lab is loving and gentle and endlessly energetic, but he's not without an occasional fault, and when he chews on a sock or something else he shouldn't, the kids will upbraid him sternly using his full and proper name: "Jett CBS Boman, you drop that right now!"